We the Elites

Why the US Constitution Serves the Few

Robert Ovetz

PLUTO  PRESS

First published 2022 by Pluto Press
New Wing, Somerset House, Strand, London WC2R 1LA

www.plutobooks.com

Copyright © Robert Ovetz 2022

The right of Robert Ovetz to be identified as the author of this work has been
asserted in accordance with the Copyright, Designs and Patents Act 1988.

British Library Cataloguing in Publication Data
A catalogue record for this book is available from the British Library

ISBN 978 0 7453 4473 7   Hardback
ISBN 978 0 7453 4472 0   Paperback
ISBN 978 0 7453 4476 8   PDF
ISBN 978 0 7453 4474 4   EPUB

Typeset by Stanford DTP Services, Northampton, England

Simultaneously printed in the United Kingdom and United States of America

Contents

Preface

This book has been a project many years in the making. Ever since I read Michael Parenti's *Democracy for the Few* and William Domhoff's *Who Rules America* (which I just learned is still in print) as an undergraduate, and later Charles Beard's *An Economic Interpretation of the Constitution* of the United States several decades ago, I looked far and wide for a class analysis of the Constitution and found precious little. I am eternally grateful for what they taught me and have sought to pass it along to my thousands of undergraduate students in my Introduction to US and California Government and Politics students at four community colleges and three universities where I have taught as an untenured professor, sometimes at three or even four at the same time. I am forever grateful for their patience and passion for learning.

This book would not have been possible without the loving guidance of my editor, David Shulman, at Pluto Press who first unexpectedly asked me what book I would like to write when we met four years ago in London. He immediately embraced this book and has continued to do so despite my frustrating behavior. Your support, patience, and firmness helped make this a much better book. This book would not have been possible without the help of others at Pluto including Patrick, James, Kieran, Emily, Robert, and Dan. I am also eternally grateful to Manny for all his years of support for my work.

Writing this book totally absorbed my attention when Darshana and I joined families. Thank you for always being there when I emerge from the "groove." This book is for my daughter Nisa. May it help clear a way for the fight you have just begun and can win.

West Marin County, CA, USA
April 1, 2022

Introduction: The United States, Democracy or Republic?

At the beginning of my "Introduction to US Government" class, I always ask my students the same question: What type of system of government do we have?

The overwhelming majority consistently give the same answer: they have no idea. Is it a republic? A democracy? A representative democracy? A democratic republic? An oligarchy? A plutocracy? The one no one ever picks is a monarchy. Those of us who grew up in the USA have learned since childhood that the USA rebelled against a king.

My students are not as confused as they think they are. We cannot agree on what to call the US system—almost unchanged since 1787—because it clearly does not actually function the way we are told to believe it does.

The Framers of the Constitution, like their fellow wealthy elites, abhorred democracy as impossibly both anarchic and despotic. Democracy meant rule by the "people out of doors," a term used for the common people who literally worked outside, who held not merely the vote but also the power to make laws about property—property belonging to the elite.

The aim of the Framers was to form a republic. A republic is a representative system that lacks a king and aristocracy.[1] It allows only the propertied elites to vote for their own who rule the entire population. They are under no obligation to make decisions by majority rule and most often make decisions according to influence, power, rank, and status. Any system with representatives, including authoritarian systems, are republics because they have representatives even if they are not elected.

The Framers designed a republic because they tossed out the monarchy and aristocracy and left all power in the hands of the propertied elites. In our system, only white men with a certain amount of property could originally vote and even their vote was limited to electing some of their representatives, while lacking the power to remove the rest and having no authority to make law or change the Constitution. As our system of voting has expanded it could now better be called a democratic republic or representative democracy. The USA is not a direct democracy because the people cannot directly make the law, decide policy, or vote on issues of taxes, war, and peace themselves without an intermediary.

The Framers' genius was in designing a virtually unchangeable system that provides the people with a semblance of participation and allows a few to select some representatives while the rest of us relinquish the power to self-govern. How and why they did that, why it still functions in that same way, and why we need to move past it is the focus of this book.

It's no accident that mavericks, outsiders, and independents run for office promising to go around and above the Constitution. Despite learning that our constitutional system works according to majority rule, that elections matter, and that pluralist coalitions of interest groups can become the majority and put power into the hands of the common people, in reality the Constitution makes majority rule the exception and not the rule. More often than not— in fact, throughout the country's entire history, with just a handful of exceptions—the system has thwarted the will of both the economic and political majority.

The electoral college, our bicameral Congress, supremacy power, executive veto, the Inter-state commerce clause, the President, treaty making, and the high threshold to amend the Constitution, among many other features, are all part of the reason why the Constitution impedes political democracy and prevents economic democracy. The 39 Framers who signed the Constitution in September 1787 were intent upon using separation of powers and checks and balances to compartmentalize the powers of the federal government, making it nearly impossible for the majority to rule each branch of the national government at the same time. Just to be sure, in the event that the majority should rule any one branch, the other two branches would be able to check and thwart them.

In this way, the Framers designed the Constitution using what journalist Daniel Lazare called the "miracle of complexity" that constrains, muffles, and absorbs all efforts by the vast majority of people to change the system. As a result, we have an undemocratic system that serves the interests of the elite few.[2] The Framers were quite aware of the complexity of the system they designed. In the Constitutional Convention debate about whether states should have an equal vote in the Senate, James Wilson warned that "will not our Constituents say we sent you to form an efficient Govt and you have given us one more complex indeed."[3]

The Constitution impedes democratic control of government at the same time as it prevents democratic control of the economy. By concentrating government powers over the economy in Congress and then placing numerous minority checks on that power, it is extremely difficult, if not impossible, for any political party, president, or Congress to carry out their initiatives to constrain or even gradually transition away from a capitalist economy.

Contrary to claims that we are governed by a "living Constitution" that can be adapted according to the changing norms, interests, and values of society, the Constitution was designed and continues to operate to accomplish the exact opposite. That the Constitution has been changed a meager 27 times in about 230 years—with not a single change in the past three decades.

It might be difficult for some to understand that the Framers designed a "democratic" constitution that functions undemocratically. We are treated to countless books, movies, documentaries, websites, and speeches about the genius of the Framers, but the reality is that they were men of the late eighteenth century who shared a single overriding nationalist interest, whether they owned slaves or not. They wanted a strong national government that would help them defend and expand the border, promote foreign trade, raise taxes to repay outstanding Revolutionary War debts, set up and fund a military, and establish a powerful national market economy.[4] Their genius was in setting up a system that allows the elites to accomplish their objectives.

From childhood, Americans learn the catchphrases of "separation of powers," "checks and balances," "power of the pen," "majority rule," and "the Bill of Rights." Political scientists and historians remind us that because the Constitution is still in operation after more than two centuries we can count ourselves among the fortunate few to have never departed from peaceful transfers of power every four or eight years. We learn to celebrate our constitutional system as "exceptionally" stable and peaceful without understanding that such stability is made possible by thwarting true democratic change.

Because the system is perceived to be so stable, when efforts to make change are thwarted we see the cause of our failure everywhere but where it belongs. We blame contemporary elites, the quality of our "leaders," abuse of the rules, corruption, complacency, or our lack of ability to organize for change, rather than the insidious design of the Constitution itself to impede and prevent change. All of the myriad problems and crises we face—a long list indeed—are explained as existing *despite* the Constitution, not caused by it.[5]

To take just one example, James Madison warned that when each state has the same number of votes in the Senate regardless of population, "1. the minority could negative the will of the majority. 2. they could extort measures by making them a condition of their assent to other necessary measures."[6] Despite this coercive potential, it is the very system that Madison played a leading role in designing.

If the Framers were visionaries who designed the Constitution to last, its longevity has come at the expense of the majority interests that it purports to serve. Their vision is not what we are told it is. The Framers distrusted democracy and majority rule, what James Madison called the "oppressive combinations of a majority," and sought to prevent it. Alexander Hamilton denounced democracy as the "amazing violence and turbulence of the democratic spirit." John Adams warned that democracy "wastes exhausts and murders itself" and even felt "terror" when he thought of elections, which were "productive of Horrors."[7] The "fathers of the country" were not fathers of a democracy.

Their belief that human nature brings conflict, disorder, and danger led them to design a constitution aimed at preventing all change desired by the majority. Writing to John Jay in mid-1786, George Washington lamented, "[w]e have probably had too good an opinion of human nature." Humanity was incapable of governing itself, he thought: "Experience has taught us, that men will not adopt & carry into execution, measures the best calculated for their own good without the intervention of a coercive power."[8] Because humanity was governed by a flawed human nature, Washington believed that there was a need for superior coercive force to control the people.

Lacking trust in democracy, Madison, Hamilton, Washington, and the other Framers designed the system so that change could only occur if it was supported by the minority of the elites who control government and own the economy.

To be clear, while the Constitution would certainly be used this way to counter a president like Bernie Sanders, it is also used against a president like Donald Trump when his policies do not have the support of the elite minority. Whether the issue be immigration, climate change, or corporate taxes, candidates of both the Democratic and Republican parties, who between them win nearly 99 percent of all elections, once elected must obtain the consent of the minority to make law.

At every step in our constitutional system the vast majority of people are forced to obtain the consent of the elite to their demands, or see their concerns go unheeded and their interests unmet. Whether it be the electoral college, or the need for every bill to pass through two houses, avoid presidential veto, and survive being struck down as unconstitutional in the courts, the majority never has the final say. The elite minority need only win once to prevent change, while the majority must pass every minority check, often by compromising more and more in order to move past it.

The irony is that we cling to the idea that the system works in the interests of the majority. But the system was designed by a small group of men who took seriously philosopher David Hume's idea that "as private men receive greater security, in the possession of their trade and riches, from the power of the public, so the public becomes powerful in proportion to the opulence and extensive commerce of private men."[9] Even today we are told that the system works for all of us when it works first for those at the top, after which wealth "trickles down" to benefit all. The Framers' legacy today is that we continue to confuse the interests of the elites with the interests of the rest of us.

We mistakenly see the reason why government does not serve the interests of the majority as having the wrong people in office. If only we could elect someone else or could change the party in leadership, we are told repeatedly, we could finally get what we want. This idea has its origins in President Washington's 1796 farewell speech, in which he warned about whose hands lay on the reins of government. Such "combinations or associations" may at first appear to serve majority interests, he warned us honestly, but are run by "cunning, ambitious, and unprincipled men" who "will be enabled to subvert the power of the people and to usurp for themselves the reins of government, destroying afterwards the very engines which have lifted them to unjust dominion."[10]

Coming out of the Trump era it's easy to blame our problems on one or another unsavory leader. However, nothing should alarm us more than the fact that this warning was coming from Washington, the man who was there from the start and was now heading out the door. The reins have since only been passed back and forth between different factions, parties, and combinations or associations of the elite, as one or the other proved to be most effective at wielding the powers of the Constitution.

Without the consent of the elite minority, the only remaining way to make change is to force it on them. Forcing them to accept change is the cause of the greatest periods of reform in US history. Universal white male suffrage, the abolition of slavery, Reconstruction, Populist and Progressive Era reforms, women's suffrage, rights for workers, the civil rights movement, ending the Vietnam War, environmental protections, and rights for LGBT people were not benevolently given but were won by force.

Law professor Jeffrey Toobin calls explanations for the disfunction in the system the "customary absolution of the founders: the virtues of the system are all due to them; the defects are all due to us."[11] The ineffective, paralyzed, unresponsive, and bloated system of government we have today cannot be attributable merely to partisan bickering and division or righted by elections and lawsuits. The cause can be traced to the Constitution itself, the very rule book for how the system is supposed to work. The US government is not "broken," it is working just as the Framers designed it to work. The reason for this is that, as Yale President Arthur Hadley once explained, "the rights of private property are more formally established in the Constitution itself," so that voters could elect whomever they wished and "could make what laws [they] pleased, as long as those laws did not trench upon property right."[12] Claims of constitutional neutrality hides that it protects property against efforts of economic democracy.[13]

The rules of the Constitution work to diffuse, delay, and dampen change by rendering the system for making change, one of the "inconveniences of democracy" that Madison wanted to avoid, inefficient.[14] Our system of government is mined with countless roadblocks and obstructions that make significant change impossible. The rule of property is protected against economic democracy.

This book examines how the Constitution was intentionally designed—and continues to effectively function—just as the Framers intended: to impede political democracy and prevent economic democracy. The documentary evidence lays bare the purposefully inefficient design of the US Constitution to protect both government and the capitalist economy from democratic control, and how change can only be made by tearing up the rule book and starting over again from the bottom up.

Time for Political Science to Catch Up with History

This is not a book of history but one of political analysis. That said, it is impossible to understand the Constitution without understanding it as a struggle over who would rule. Over the last 110 years, progressive and social history scholarship has recovered the history of the Revolution from the perspective of the "many-headed hydra," or a common eighteenth-century term for the tumultuous common people. However, my own field of political science continues to be

rooted in an ahistorical perspective, as if none of the critics and opponents of the Constitution—even those who left the Convention early
and voted against it, native peoples, slaves, insurgent leaders, and
foreign observers—mattered. It's as if the entire discipline has yet
to acknowledge what historian Carl Becker called the two questions
of the Revolutions: "[The first was] the question of home rule; the
second was the question ... who should rule at home."[15]

By shutting out these critical voices, the field of political science is
unable to explain why the Constitution is not up to the task of solving
the problems of today. We have yet to grapple with the emerging
consensus that it was designed to solve the pressing problems facing
elites in the 1780s: by suppressing demands for economic and political democracy from below and preventing them from resurfacing.

It is startling how few political scientists have acknowledged
the Framers' overt efforts to construct the Constitution to protect
property, despite more than a century of work by historians docu-
menting this. There are a few exceptions, such as Robert Dahl, the
eminent originator of the concept of pluralism and former president
of the American Political Science Association, who wrote late in life
that "a substantial number of the Framers believed that they must
erect constitutional barriers to popular rule because the people would
prove to be an unruly mob, a standing danger to law, to orderly
government, and to property rights."[16] Today, Dahl's Cold War-era
pluralist theory has become enshrined in the public vernacular of
contemporary representative democracy. This is ironic considering
its author highlighted the Constitution's built-in anti-democratic
and pro-capitalist features.

To solve the problem of threats from below, the Constitution was
designed as the set of ground rules by which everyone else must
engage in politics. It is long past time for political science to analyze
why our system works or does not work, and for whom it works
and for whom it does not. As historian Herbert Aptheker insightfully pointed out, "when one moves away from factual chronicling to
analysis and evaluation, he enters at once into the area of debate and
controversy."[17]

In his analysis of the Constitution's design, Lazare shows that we prefer to "blame anyone and everyone except the founders" when the system refuses to change, even while we celebrate the Constitution as unchanging.[18] The greatest design feature in the Constitution—that it is nearly impossible to change by amendment—becomes its greatest virtue. That fundamental unalterability is the very root, not just of the lack of political and economic democracy, but of the system's inability to address even the most basic problem or crisis: what I call the "constitutional pothole problem." While all local governments are expected to pave potholes and keep the lights on, the federal government can't even do that. The reason is not due to failure, corruption, or lack of will. "Government in America doesn't work because it's not supposed to work," Lazare observed.[19]

Ordinary people therefore either seek to bypass government or protest against it, while the elites continue on their way unmolested and unconcerned about accountability for their crimes and neglect. As Ira Katznelson, Mark Kesselman, and Alan Draper insightfully observe, "[w]hen public power is unable to rule because it is gripped by deadlock, private power rules in its place."[20] The design of the Constitution is the cause of ever-creeping authoritarian rule by elites in the "private sphere" who simultaneously exploit the rules of a system from which they continue to be exempted. We live not merely under what Lazare called a "dictatorship of the past" but of the present, in which the elites are essentially outside of and above the state—which, as philosopher Hannah Arendt described, is the basic feature of totalitarian systems.[21] While our system is not the Nazi and Stalinist Soviet systems Arendt was concerned with, we nevertheless live under a class dictatorship in which the right of property is above the state, protected as the supreme law that trumps all else—even the very survival of the planet, as rapidly worsening climate catastrophe is ignored to protect the property rights of the owners of fossil fuels.

The historical record is clear: the Constitution was designed by elites with differing property interests but a shared class interest to give themselves a minority veto over any efforts to change the system. The Framers believed that property should rule, and if property was to share power with the people (democracy), property should have the final say. Gouverneur Morris made the elite interest in government clear at the Convention, writing that "property was the main object of society. ... If property then was the main object of Govt. certainly it ought to be one measure of the influence due to those who were to be affected by the Government."[22]

The Framers were of one mind when it came to serving their shared elite economic interests. Their letters, debates, pamphlets, and speeches all contained fascinating discussions of political economy or how government related to the economy. While considered as propaganda for the service of the ratification campaign, historian Charles Beard called the *Federalist Papers* a "remarkable work as a study in political economy." It described how the new system contains the powers "to break the force of majority rule and prevent invasions of the property rights of minorities" and "restrictions on the state legislatures which had been so vigorous in their attacks on capital."[23]

What is illuminating about reading James Madison's notes, revised later in life, and those of William Jackson, Secretary of the Convention, as well as other incomplete notes smuggled out of the Convention by dissident delegates John Lansing and Robert Yates, was that unlike letters, journal entries, and pamphlets, the Framers felt secure enough to speak honestly and were plainly assured that the order of secrecy would prevail. Luckily for us, there were cracks in that secrecy giving us a record, filtered nonetheless, of their closed-door debates and deliberations.

The need for a new national government that would be empowered to constrain the democratic impulses of the "people out of doors" runs through many of their private letters, records of the revolutionary and Confederation Congress, drafts and reports on the Articles of Confederation, notes from the Constitutional Convention, debates of the state ratifying conventions, published articles such as the *Federalist Papers*, and the observations of some who attended them. This book relies heavily on all of these documents.

The design of the Constitution was the outcome of the war between democracy and property at the end of the eighteenth century, a war overwhelmingly won by property.[24] Today we commonly believe that any preference given to property is a result of favoritism, conflict of interest, "big money," or some other misalignment of the Constitution. But we have it entirely wrong. In the late 1920s, historian Vernon Louis Parrington explained that the apparent plutocratic character of the system was not a departure but a realization of the Constitution. Rather than creating a democracy, "it had been conceived in a spirit designedly hostile to democracy ... erected as a defense against the democratic spirit that had got out of hand during the Revolution."[25] It was, after all, Thomas Jefferson who insisted that "an *elective despotism* was not the government we fought for."[26]

The notion that the Framers strove to design a Constitution that served the "general will," "public interest," and "the people" without distinction of economic interests is simply untrue. In their letters, pamphlets, speeches, and notes, nearly all the Framers speak explicitly about "the many" and "the few" and other like categories that denoted their awareness and concern about the existing and growing class divide and the tensions it caused. We now know that they and their Anti-Federalist opponents knew this intuitively. It was reflected in the growing class divide in income, wealth, property, and political power. Jackson Turner Main concluded from his study of these issues at the time of the Revolution that "the great distinctions between rich and poor, and the concentration of property, are decisive evidence of the presence of an economic class structure."[27]

We have not merely taken for granted the relationship of democracy to the Constitution.[28] The true meaning of the law lies behind the words and is found, says Blackstone, in "the *reason* and *spirit* of it; or the cause which moved the legislator to enact it."[29] For Beard, we can only understand the unspoken purposes of the Constitution "by a study of the conditions and events which led to its formation and adoption."[30] Those conditions, he reminds us, were those which demanded order, good credit, and economic development. The Framers, he wrote, "were not philosophers, but men of business and property ... they had no quarrel with the system of class rule and the strong centralization of government which existed in England."[31]

It was no less than President Woodrow Wilson, one of the few chief executives to have taught either law or political science, who urged us to separate the reality from the myth of the Constitution more than a century ago. Wilson said that ratification was followed with the end of criticism and an "undiscriminating and almost blind worship of its principles." For Wilson, the concentration of power in the legislative and executive branches at the time "have broadened the sphere and altered the functions of the government without perceptibly affecting the vocabulary of our constitutional language." Wilson was quite blunt in pointing out that "we are really living under a constitution essentially different than that which we have been worshipping as our own peculiar and incompatible possession."[32]

Understanding the "reason and spirit" of the Constitution is the project of this book: to synthesize what we know about why the Framers said they designed the Constitution the way they did, and in order to understand why the Constitution works for the elites and not for the rest of us. In short, the first three words of the Constitution, "We the People," could more accurately read, "We the *Elites*."

A Note about Terms and Sources

Words matter and because they matter more than they sometimes should, I have attempted to use recognizable, commonly used words that can stimulate mutual understanding rather than division.

Economic democracy is my preferred term for any post-capitalist economic system which is run democratically by the people who are affected by the functioning of that system. The terms democracy and economy as commonly used are heavily loaded with meaning and often thought of as referring to representative democracy and the capitalist economy respectively. This is contrary to my intended meaning.

Elites is my substitute for the ruling class or bourgeoisie. They were often also called "the few," "aristocrats," "junto," "aristocratic junto," "natural aristocracy," "well-born," or the "better kind of people" by their opponents. The elites had few words they used to describe themselves because they were mostly talking with one another and didn't need to speak to what was already evident.

I use the terms economic majority, small farmers, subsistence farmers, laborers, mechanics, and slaves to refer to the components of the working class, and working class when the discussion turns explicitly to capitalism and the class system. I also reference the wide variety of terms used by elites at the time of ratification, including "the many," "sorts of people," "meaner sort," "people out of doors," "rabble," "tyranny of the majority," "anarchy," "mob," "democratic spirit," and the "hydra" who sought "disunion," "breakdown," and other "catastrophes". If you want to see a long list of derogatory terms for the working class you'll find them in the 1786 book-length poem *The Anarchiad*. Historian Roger Brown insightfully examines these different terms and the framing used, concluding that they represented "limited popular risings against specific unpopular or unwanted policies, not a generalized breakdown of law and order."[33] I would venture to go further: that these risings reflect a different idea of a political and economic system, one controlled by the vast super-majority of the common people and which serves their interests.

The word majority is also distorted in meaning because, while we are told that our system operates on majority will, it most often actually runs according to the will of the minority (another term that requires explanation). Here I use majority to imply the economic majority of people who have little or no power in the workplace other than to withhold the sale of their labor. In this book, majority simply implies the outcome if the vast proportion of the people were actually allowed to genuinely meet, debate, and decide what they wanted, rather than have it decided for them by appointed and elected representatives.

Likewise, minority today is closely associated with the idea of a segment of the population distinguished by their racial, gender, sexual, or other identity. As used in this book, minority does not in any way mean demographic minority but rather the elites: the small proportion of the population that hold political power and own the economy.

The reader will frequently come across the word property, and rarely the words capital or capitalism. Many people who do not own property aspire to, although the vast supermajority of those who do own only a tiny sliver of the total property. But this is beside the point. Property is not meant here to refer to the tangible property of buildings, factories, houses, financial securities, etc. Rather, it refers to the economic *system* of capitalism, which places the highest priority on the exploitation of human labor and nature for profits and social control, and on the acquisition, growth, and protection of property.

Our version of a republic could be described as a *representative democracy*, a hybrid arrangement in which members of Congress are now elected directly, two are indirectly elected by the electoral college, and the rest are appointed. Our representative democracy is only a democracy for those representatives who have the exclusive power to make the decisions. Of course, our capitalist economy is entirely undemocratic, even tyrannical, and has only those who own the economy as self-appointed representatives. A more apt term might be *res plutocratica* or for the plutocrats, the word drawn from the Roman god Pluto, the god of miners, wealth, and the underworld. Plutocrats are, after all, the ruling class elites who wrote the Constitution to serve their interests for "our Posterity" as they promised in the Preamble.

I use a class analysis of the Constitution to understand how the Framers themselves saw politics through the lens of their own elite class. Reading the memoirs, letters, notes, journals, speeches, pamphlets, articles, and plans of the Framers and other elites of the time demonstrates that they already had a class analysis of their own—from above as elites.[34] One hardly need to go looking for a class-conscious ruling class, it was already there.

Finally, I attempt to keep all the primary texts as they appear in the original. Don't be alarmed if you see many of the Framers' texts filled with excessive unnecessary capitalization, run on sentences, or other grammatical issues. That's how they wrote, or at least as it was transcribed into print.

While there is no bibliography, full references are given the first time a source appears in a chapter. All letters, notes, and reports written by the Framers that can be publicly found online do not include a full reference but only the title and date. In the footnotes, some of the transcripts of the Constitutional Convention are referenced as appearing in M. Farrand (ed.) (1966 [1911]). *The Records of the Federal Convention of 1787*. New Haven: Yale University Press,

Vols. 1–3 are referenced as the name of the Framer, the date, in M. Farrand, *RFC*, 1911, volume number, and page numbers.

Lastly, I use shorthand references to the Constitution in the text. Since I refer to the Constitution many times through the book I use the following shorthand for references to the Articles: Article number in Roman numerals, and section and clause numbers in Arabic. For the amendments I use: Amendment and section numbers, if they exist, in Arabic numerals. For example, Article I, Section 1, Clause 1 would appear as I.1.1 and Amendment 26, Section 1 would appear as 26.1.

1

The Framers' Vision

Those who stormed the US Capitol on January 6, 2021 held signs, posted memes to social media, waved the US and revolutionary-era flags, and chanted slogans that gave the impression that they were defenders of the US Constitution. The paradox is obvious—their assault on a branch of our constitutional system of government to restore the President to an office for which he had not won re-election was, in fact, an assault on the Constitution.

Which constitution did they think they were rising up to defend?

One of the greatest sources of confusion in the USA is over which constitution we were given, which one we have, and which one governs us. That there are multiple answers to these questions has more to do with ideology than with the fact that few have actually read the terse document, let alone studied its meaning.

Far-right seditionists mistakenly think the Constitution grants them the right to overthrow the government by force. They apparently have not read that "[t]he Congress shall have Power ... To provide for calling forth the Militia to execute the Laws of the Union, suppress Insurrections and repel Invasions" (I.8.15). Also possibly overlooked is the "guarantee to every State in this Union a Republican Form of Government, and shall protect each of them against Invasion; and on Application of the Legislature, or of the Executive (when the Legislature cannot be convened) against domestic Violence" (IV.4). Those engaged in an insurrection to overthrow the Congress believe they were authorized to do so by the same Constitution that prohibits threats of domestic violence against our "republican form of government."

Those assembled on the steps of the Capitol who sought to defend the government while attempting to overthrow it turned the Constitution into the exact opposite of what it says and means.

The document enshrined an unlimited liberty to do whatever one wants with their private property, while also preventing anyone from changing it. What the January 6th insurrectionists overlooked is that the people out of doors, the common people, do not have the right "to alter or to abolish it, and to institute new Government," a right once offered in the Declaration of Independence and a couple of revolutionary state constitutions but denied to us since 1787.

Their mistake is not unusual. Most people have little understanding of what the Constitution says, what it means, and why it was written the way it was. We say the Framers had a "vision" but few understand what it was.

Waiting for Change

The Capitol insurrectionists are not alone. Liberals commonly think the Constitution was designed to *give* us rights, even *unlimited* rights. Liberals are less interested in altering or abolishing the government than in holding it accountable. Liberals insist on receiving the promise of a government that serves everyone equally. They seek to use one part of the government to make the other follow the rules. Liberals think of the Constitution as "living"; as changeable whenever the times necessitate change.

For my entire lifetime, liberals have seen themselves as the guardians of a woman's right to choose an abortion. Failing to secure that right in either federal law or by most state legislatures, they turned futilely to the Supreme Court. The right to privacy, found nowhere in the text, was found to be implied in the 1973 case of *Roe v. Wade*. Today, when Supreme Court ruling after ruling have whittled away access to safe and legal abortions, liberals still hold on tightly to the hem of the justices' robes waiting for that right, now all but dissolved under the bright lights of judicial review, to be restored to women.

Every four years brings a rush of excitement about the prospects of change. Those on the left of the Democratic Party, frustrated with dashed hopes and unfulfilled promises, field a candidate who will change the party and bring deeply rooted change to the country. Like clockwork, those too timid to work outside the system see their insider candidate derailed and sidelined, the system restored, and the possibility of change evaporate as they mark their ballots while holding their nose for the "least worst" option. And when change does not come we turn on ourselves and one another. Somehow we never seem to get it right. We had the wrong message. We weren't organized well enough. We were divided. They turned confrontational and violent. In the face of failure many turn away in frustration, disgust, or distrust. Left behind are those that believe in the Constitution, trust it to allow change, and restore its legitimacy.

And when change does come, it is almost always a watered down version of what was demanded, diluted in the course of dragging it around and over the innumerable roadblocks and impediments of the system. An amendment that supposedly abolishes slavery but leaves slavery intact in the case of prisoners, is held up to reaffirm the faith that the system can be changed by using the Constitution.

Admirers of the Constitution rarely grasp that the Constitution we have is an eighteenth-century rule book written in secret by 55 white men, of whom only 39 signed, 13 left, and 3 refused to consent to. These 55 achieved what previous plans to control their states and the previous confederation had failed to achieve through elections.[1] These Framers needed a new system that would let those like them write the rules for how we are governed. Divided among themselves along varying competing interests, the Framers unified around the need to leave government to those like them with property and wealth.[2] Of the 70 delegates, about a third could be considered rich, nine of moderate wealth, and the remaining well off.

The Constitution is a rule book written in 1787 that still dictates how we govern ourselves in the twenty-first century. Our world has changed dramatically since 1787, but the Constitution is virtually the same. It is a rule book written by those who distrusted democracy and the people who would wield it, if they were allowed to rule. Madison distinctly warned against the people governing themselves, something proposed by "those who contend for a simple Democracy, or a pure republic, actuated by the sense of the majority."[3] These "people out of doors" (or the common people) were denigrated and feared as the mob, rabble, and Jack Tar (a derogatory terms for sailors). Power was only for those who could pass through the entrance reserved for the people "in doors." Political scientist Michael Parenti observed that "democracy is a social order with a social class content" the Framers feared could be used by the economic majority.[4] The best security against such risk is to ensure that the vast majority of the population have little power to use the Constitution to make change in their economic interests.

In their straightforward case against the Constitution, law professors John Manley and Kenneth Dolbeare show that it was designed and still functions "to *permit political participation* but *prevent democracy* in the United States" and is the cause of the innumerable political failures and crises we face today.[5] Although this could have easily been written today, it was written in 1987. Since then nothing has changed and perhaps the situation is now even worse.

"Partisanship," conflicts between the two dominant parties over factional interests that impede "compromise," is the great phantom menace of American politics today. Whenever the winning party fails to deliver on its promises the cause given, without fail, is partisanship. A passage from the popular and profitable musical *Hamilton: An American Musical* gives us a glimpse into the first partisan divide of the new Washington administration over credit, banking, and taxation. There is a telling debate between Secretary of the Treasury Alexander Hamilton and Secretary of State Thomas Jefferson and Senator Aaron Burr. Hamilton mocks Jefferson "Doin' whatever the hell it is you do in Monticello?" Burr then comes to Jefferson's defense by mocking Hamilton because "Wall Street thinks you're great | You'll always be adored by the things you create." Thus is captured the partisan divide among elites: slave-based agricultural v. financial capitalism.

Dividing Power, Preventing Democracy

To avoid the mortal threat to compromise we are taught that the Framers established a system of "limited government" armed with "checks and balances" that would prevent any one class, faction, party, or power-hungry despot from dominating, thereby protecting the "liberty" of the "majority." George Washington, James Madison, Alexander Hamilton, Gouverneur Morris, Robert Morris, Elbridge

Gerry, John Jay, and other Framers repeatedly expressed the need to check the ambition and tumult of struggle over power by factions.[6]

These partisan elite factions drew on the system of separated powers between king, aristocracy, and "democracy" described by the Roman Cicero in *De Republica*[7] to replace the decentralized Articles of Confederation which lacked sufficient minority checks and allowed the people to have too much influence over the states.[8] The Articles decentralized power in such a way as to allow the common people too much influence. Such power was a fatal flaw to James Madison, who found it running through the confederacies of the past leading to dissolution and defeat by stronger, more centralized powers.[9] The only solution, Madison would repeat time and again for the next several years, would be to replace the Articles with a Constitution that *constrains* political democracy and *prevents* economic democracy.

They also drew from Montesquieu's idea in *The Spirit of the Laws* that dividing power allows elites to successfully suppress any rebellion and remain in power.[10] John Adam had earlier realized this model, based on what was called the Whig theory of separation of powers, in Massachusetts' revolutionary state constitution designed to protect the "natural aristocracy among mankind."[11] From them we have our "mixed system of government" driven by their distrust for the people out of doors to govern themselves and for the Constitution to prevent them from doing so.[12]

Anti-Federalists opposed the system of mixed government. The pseudonymous Brutus warned his readers that the Constitution will establish what "will literally be a government in the hands of the few to oppress and plunder the many."[13]

A coalition of convenience among the different competing factions of property-owning elites—slave owners, merchants, bankers, traders, creditors, and large landowners—wrote the rules of our constitutional system in order to protect property; the same rules by which everyone else has to operate to this day. According to J. Allen Smith, the Constitution was designed to "establish the supremacy of the so-called upper class."[14] As Smith put it so well so long ago, "[i]n the United States at the present time we are trying to make an undemocratic Constitution the vehicle of democratic rule. ... It was framed for one purpose while we are trying to use it for another."[15]

Capital's Constitution

On January 30, 2013, in his last speech to the Senate before taking up the position of President Obama's Secretary of State, long-time Senator John Kerry fired a shot across the bow of deep-pocketed interest groups. These groups, he warned, use their power "to set the agenda, change the agenda, block the agenda, define the agenda of Washington"[16] by which all who enter the political arena must agree to struggle over interests and power.

This reality of economic power being translated into political power is not an aberration, distortion, or tarnishing of the Constitution. The rules of Senator Kerry's Constitution not only make this awesome power of big money possible but expected and protected, particularly by Article I, the 1st, 4th, 5th, and 14th amendments.

Take the 1st amendment, for instance, which protects lobbying as a constitutionally protected right to "petition the Government for a redress of grievances." As the Supreme Court is increasingly fond of reminding us in cases stretching from 1976 *Buckley v. Valeo* to the more recent 2010 *Citizens United v. FEC* cases, using money to buy elections is similarly protected "speech." This was made possible by the 1819 *Trustees of Dartmouth College v. Woodward* case which protected its 1769 corporate charter as inviolable property thereby granting an early constitutional right to property.

Money is the symptom, not the cause, of the fatal problems our constitutional system of government faces today. The overwhelming power of those with money is the expected outcome of the Constitution's extension of rights to property. Those rights are numerous and well shielded. Creditors, landowners, merchants, ship owners, and slave owners all have their own clauses in the Constitution. These particular interests are enveloped in the larger protection for property itself, written by the bosses, for the bosses in 1787 and today. The Constitution is the wellspring of the big-money threat, not its target. Rather than a shield against the power of deep-pocketed elites, the

Constitution was designed as armor to protect them for "posterity" as the Preamble promises.

Most people have been miseducated to believe that the Framers created a democratic system of majority rule in which the majority of the people actually do rule. Fearing the outcome of the Revolution, Gouverneur Morris spoke for his fellow elites when he feared "we shall be under the worst of all possible dominions; we shall be under the domination of a riotous mob."[17]

This myth of democracy sits paradoxically with the fact that the Constitution established a capitalist economic system that is not even remotely governed by the will of the majority, nor does it serve the majority's interests. The economic system, owned by the few and serving the interests of the few, is a sort of inverted mirror to the myth of political democracy.

The Constitution's numerous minority checks assure the elites that democracy will never get in the way of capitalism. Because the Framers understood that the greatest threat to property was too much democracy, the solution was to design a system with little democratic control. The formal system of representation instead provides limited access to power while installing the means to continuously check, divide, isolate, and override the majority will.

A Shared Interest

A little more than a century ago, Columbia University historian Charles Beard's much debated 1913 book, *An Economic Interpretation of the Constitution*, argued that the Framers designed the Constitution to favor their own class interests. Beard's thesis survived an onslaught of attacks for decades after it was published and continues to prove hard to dismiss more than a century later. Beard's research, based on incomplete records, showed that some of the Framers stood to profit personally from the new Constitution when their outstanding debts were repaid, a point his critics have used to deflect from his more important observation that their design of the Constitution served their shared class interests. Beard didn't do himself any favors by focusing on the immediate personal interests of a number of the Framers.[18]

Beard's insight was that the Framers set aside their different and at times competing, contradictory, and varying interests to recognize their shared interests as members of the elite.[19] The elites unified around the recognition that they were stronger if their factions cooperated in an alliance of "class-conscious leaders."[20] Doing so allowed them to establish a new federal system of government that would set up, manage, and protect property. As a result, they designed an economic document that integrated their diverse economic interests into one set of rules protecting *all forms of property* from the ravages of economic democracy.[21]

Take Framer Robert Morris, for example. Now nearly forgotten due to his scandalous term in office during the Revolution, bankruptcy, and stint in debtor's prison before dying nearly penniless, Morris was more influential than Washington, Madison, and Hamilton at the convention despite saying very little. About a quarter of the delegates had done their banking with Morris, who had also hosted George Washington and his slaves in one of his houses in Philadelphia.[22] One of his closest business associates, James Wilson, was among the handful of the most influential and active delegates. The delegates represented a slender slice of the upper elite of the country with all its varying and competing concerns.[23]

In *Federalist #10*, Madison urges his fellow elites to set aside their competing interests (e.g., "faculties") and unify around the shared "uniformity of interests" of property. "The protection of these faculties is the first object of government. From the protection of different and unequal faculties of acquiring property, the possession of different degrees and kinds of property immediately results."

The Framers' recognition of their shared class, rather than personal, interest, is portrayed in how public debt was addressed 30 days before the Convention ended on August 18th at the urging of the Committee of Detail. Here the Framers did not line up according to their personal interests, some not even holding any securities still supporting debt repayment. By one estimate only four who had a personal stake as creditors supported adding this to the Constitution.[24]

The Framers were quite explicit in their efforts to construct a new Constitution to serve their class interests.[25] They demonstrated that the victor doesn't just write the rules, they write the constitution by which the rules can be made.[26]

Depredations of the Democratic Spirit on Property

By the end of the tumultuous American Revolution, the elites were on the ropes in many of the states. Rather than the "domestic tranquility" celebrated in the Preamble, conflict and struggle was widespread. Organized small farmers and their allies managed to revise most of the state constitutions to make them more democratic, pushed through laws that allowed paper money to be used to repay debts taken out in coins made of valuable metals, established land banks, reduced property requirements to vote or hold office, put controls on prices, and began to phase out slavery. Particularly in the New England states, farmers organized into local town and county conventions that frequently sent instructions and "memorials" (what they called petitions) to their state legislatures outlining their demands. When ignored they quickly formed militias, marched into towns and state capitols, confronted elites, surrounded courthouses and legislative buildings, and even carried out armed attacks. The end of the Revolution did not mean the end of the rising of the ordinary people, the "people out of doors."

Some states were in such turmoil that it sparked an existential crisis for local elites. Volunteer militias carried out armed protests against a couple of state governments and Congress, armed farmers protested against foreclosures of their farms for outstanding debts and taxes that would force them to repay debt speculators, Native Americans mounted organized resistance to violent white squatters, and slaves rose up on numerous occasions, even joining up with the British. The shortage of workers kept wages high and cheap land kept the supply tight. In the midst of these conflicts, few elites were willing to invest and looked overseas for investment opportunities.

The Revolution had turned the world upside down and the elites were unsure how to get it back upright. Several failed attempts to amend the Articles of Confederation, the first constitution, left the states empowered and Congress weak. Some wanted to give Congress the power to tax, pay its debt, and set up an army to use against farmers, native peoples, and slaves. Having failed, when they arrived in Philadelphia in May 1787 the Framers almost immediately threw out the entire Articles and replaced it with the Constitution. In doing so they shifted power upwards to the new national government, giving it concentrated powers stripped from the states.

The Constitution became the conservative reaction to the radicalism of the Revolution. As historian Staughton Lynd observed, "the Constitution was a settlement of a revolution. What was at stake ... was more than speculative windfalls in securities: it was the question, what kind of society would emerge from revolution when the dust settled, and on which class the political center of gravity would come to rest."[27]

The Constitution brought relief to many but none more so than Hamilton, whose political power would be fueled by the economic powers of the Constitution. He understood its promise, writing in unpublished notes to himself that the "commercial interest" will recognize that the Constitution will protect and extend trade, providing

> the good will of most men of property in the several states who wish a government of the union able to protect them against domestic violence and the depredations which the democratic spirit is apt to make on property; and ... the hopes of the Creditors of the United States that a general government possessing the means of doing it will pay the debt of the Union.[28]

The fear of the unwashed majority with their hands on the reins of power instilled fears of "leveling," a reference to an early principle of socialism in which the property of the rich is expropriated and redistributed to the poor, and other obstructions on property and the erosion of elite power resulting in "anarchy" and "despotism" of majority rule.[29]

The End of Government

The Constitution protected all forms of property, even those not yet imagined. It contained numerous protections for slavery, federal assumption of state and Confederation debt, setting state boundaries, and regulating shipping, trade, and tariffs. Most of all, the enumerated and implied powers of the Constitution were backed up by the hammer of Article VI that made the Constitution and the national "federal" government it established the "supreme law of the land." The design of the Constitution was intended to both govern the population by constraining the vast majority's capacity to self-govern and protect all forms of property, whether it be financial, land, or slaves.[30]

The Framers, particularly Hamilton and Madison, took their inspiration from British doctor and philosopher John Locke very seriously. Locke saw property as the purpose of government, even going so far as to argue for the right to alter, change, or abolish a government that violates property. "Government has no other end but the preservation of property," he wrote. This is "the end of government."[31]

The one form of property that fared best of all—without ever being explicitly mentioned—was the owning of human beings as chattel slaves. Slavery was central not merely to the political but also the economic system. The word "slavery" may not appear in the Constitution—what historian David Waldstreicher called "a consensus to be silent"—but it is woven into every facet of how the system was designed and still governs today. Every issue over voting, taxation, the electoral college, the relationship of the states to one another, and national security were all rooted in how to govern slavery.[32]

The Constitution was designed not merely to protect slavery as a separate economic model but as integral to the basic right of what Waldstreicher called the "power over other people and property (including people who were property)."[33] As a result, divisions between the elites of Northern and Southern states were not about size but about how many slaves resided in each of them. Even Madison admitted as much:

> [T]he States were divided into different interests not by their difference of size ... but principally from the effects of their having or not having slaves. These two causes concurred in forming the great division of interests in the U. States. It did not lie between the large & small States: It lay between the Northern & Southern.[34]

Despite these divisions of interest, the delegates shared an interest in protecting all forms of property—especially slaves. Responding to proposals to prohibit or tax the importation of slaves, John Rutledge and Charles Cotesworth Pinckney encouraged fellow delegates to recognize that they all had a shared interest to preserve slavery as they stood to profit from selling slave-produced goods and carrying the slaves on their ships.[35] The personal interests of the Framers was not the issue but, according to Lynd, rather "an alliance between Northern 'personalty' and the particular form of 'realty' which dominated the South."[36] The Constitution "represented not a victory of one over the other but a compromise between them." The Framers set aside all of their varying, and even conflicting, interests over not only slavery but also the impost (e.g., tariff), export and import trade, land and securities speculation, land taxes, and debt relief.[37]

Slaves were and would long remain the most valuable form of property in the country. In 1860, the total value of all the slaves was $4 billion, double the value of the South's entire farmland valued at $1.92 billion, four times the total currency in circulation at $435.4 million, and 20 times the value of all the gold and silver then in circulation at $228.3 million.[38] Slavery was a national (even global), not a sectional, asset.

The shared interest in preserving slavery can be seen in the lack of discussion of the issue until late in the Convention. Between May 14 and June 19 it was only debated when discussing the apportioning representation. The report issued by the Committee of the Whole made no mention of it and none of the 23 resolutions sent to the Committee of Detail on July 23 and 26 mentioned it. Northern delegates even removed the two-thirds supermajority requirement to pass a navigation act in exchange for delaying a ban on the importation of slavery: "The Migration or Importation of such Persons as any of the States now existing shall think proper to admit, shall not be prohibited by the Congress prior to the Year one thousand eight hundred and eight, but a Tax or duty may be imposed on such Importation, not exceeding ten dollars for each Person" (I.9.1). As with this passage, the words slave or slavery do not appear at all in the final text.[39]

The Constitution does not only protect chattel slavery as property but it protects *all* property. The Constitution does not only protect slavery as a system of labor exploitation but it protects *all* forms of labor exploitation.[40] This is the same Constitution that remains virtually unchanged today. While most of the population, excluding prisoners, has been freed from slavery by the 13th amendment, we remain in a system that forces us to work to survive, that places property supreme over human needs, and that prevents the supermajority from changing it.

A Majority United by a Common Interest or Passion

While the Framers designed the Constitution to protect property, not all property was protected in the same way. While land was cheap and relatively accessible, the country was hardly egalitarian. There existed extreme divisions of wealth, power, and property at the time of the Constitutional Convention. While many free white men owned some form of property, most commonly small plots of land on which they worked as subsistence farmers on the margins or outside the commercial market, most were cash poor. The limited tax records of the time showed that only a small percentage owned large concentrations of tangible property, including human slaves, and possessed the majority of the wealth.

Concerns about the growing number of subsistence and tenant farmers and landless men alongside the immense wealth of the merchant and landed elite, many of whom owned huge tracts of unused western land often in several states, were on the rise. Elites were increasingly denounced as a "junto" of "aristocrats" by Anti-Federalist small farmers who battled against great economic wealth being further translated into vast political power.[41] Cato's 1723 letters, which may well have been written by insurgent small farmers in the late 1790s, warned that concentrated wealth is dangerous because it creates an inequality of power and dependency while threatening to "destroy, amongst the Commons, that balance of property and power, which is necessary to a democracy, or the democratic part of any government."[42]

While the call to constrain the concentration of economic power before it swamps political power was there even *before* the Constitution, it re-emerged in the early and late 1800s, during the great depression, and in the 1960s, and is still widespread today.

The country was born with two classes: elites and workers. The vast majority of the population during the Critical Era of the period between the end of the Revolution and the Convention were the so-called "freeholders," the small farmers who owned their small plots and mostly produced for the subsistence needs of their families and local communities, using barter and cashless reciprocity at a distance from regional markets. As farmers they were also workers, with the unique characteristic that they worked for themselves, keeping and consuming most of what they produced. These small subsistence farmers were the largest segment of the working class which also included unskilled rural and urban laborers, skilled artisans and mechanics of the towns, indentured servants, and especially slaves who worked without pay.

The propertied elites included slave owners, merchants, bankers, creditors, absentee landowners, and large farmers who produced for distant markets in port cities and Europe, and comprised a much smaller class. It was by and for them that the Constitution would be designed and they alone that it served.

Neither Hamilton or Madison hesitated to explicitly identify the class structure of the country and both feared the outcome of unconstrained class conflict. Madison believed that the class divide of the country was uncontrollable without a strong centralized national government that could restrain yearnings for political democracy and prevent further efforts at economic democracy. He spent years working out his own class analysis from an elite perspective.[43] In April 1787, just before the Convention began, Madison made explicit the class hierarchy: "All civilized societies are divided into different interests and factions, as they happen to be creditors or debtors—Rich or poor—husbandmen, merchants or manufacturers—members of different religious sects—followers of different political leaders—inhabitants of different districts—owners of different kinds of property &c &c."[44]

Madison would carry his analysis into *Federalist #10*, warning that "the most common and durable source of factions has been the various and unequal distribution of property. Those who hold and those who are without property have ever formed distinct interests in society." The danger, he warned, was the lack of minority checks on the economic majority: "In republican Government the majority however composed, ultimately give the law. Whenever therefore an apparent interest or common passion unites a majority what is to restrain them from unjust violations of the rights and interests of the minority, or of individuals?"[45]

As voting became universal the majority would flex its power. "An increase of population will of necessity increase the proportion of those who labour under all the hardships of life, & secretly sigh for a more equal distribution of its blessings." As a result, Madison focused on how to prevent or restrain the powers of the economic majority.[46]

These concerns were responses to the ongoing struggles over inequalities of wealth and power expressed by demands for land banks, paper money, and regulation of prices and wages.[47] As the 1786–7 Shays' Rebellion of insurrectionary farmers in Pennsylvania brewed, Henry Knox warned Washington:

> In some of the counties, one fifth part of the people of little or no property are dissatisfied, more with their pecuniary than their political circumstances, and appeal to arms. Their first acts are to annihilate their courts of Justice, that is private debts—The Second, to abolish the public debt and the third is to have a division of property by means of the darling object of most of the States paper money. A Government without any existing means of coercion, are at a loss how to combat, or avert a danger so new & so pressing.[48]

Lacking the "means of coercion," the elites desired a new system of government that could not merely suppress but prevent such dangers.

Early in the Convention, Edmund Randolph described the Framers as meeting on "the eve of war," a reference to the recent Shays' Rebellion of "regulators" in Massachusetts. Fearing that rule of the people "swallows up" the other branches, he urged "sufficient checks against the democracy."[49] Democracy was on the minds of the Framers but they held the economy close to their hearts. We cannot understand the undemocratic Constitution without understanding the capitalist Constitution.

Randolph pointed out that "[t]he chief danger arises from the democratic parts of our constitutions," a reference to the state governments. Praising two of the states that contained more restraints on democracy, he added that they are "yet a stronger barrier against democracy, but they all seem insufficient."[50] For the Framers the corrupting influence of power only worked in one direction: from the bottom up.

Distrust of democracy led Madison to want to replace the Articles of Confederation and majority rule as "evil." In designing a new system, democracy was to be prevented at all costs. The ease by which laws could be repealed, changed, or replaced was a threat to be avoided by limiting who could rule.[51]

Those Who Own the Country Shall Govern It

In *Federalist #10*, Madison endorsed the Constitution as the best means for regulating class conflicts in favor of elites. "The regulation of these various and interfering interests forms the principal task of modern legislation, and involves the spirit of party and faction in the necessary and ordinary operations of the government."[52]

Madison proposed making the system impervious to change in order to indefinitely protect the privileges and power of the "opulent" minority "to last for ages." While the landed elite were predominant now, he pointed out, "when the number of landholders shall be comparatively small, through the various means of trade and manufactures, will not the landed interest be overbalanced in future elections, and unless wisely provided against, what will become of your government?"[53] This was a warning that "demography is destiny." Minority checks were essential because future population growth would make the propertied elite a smaller and smaller fraction of the population, causing it to be outvoted by larger and larger margins in perpetuity. If that happens it would be powerless to prevent the propertyless majority from voting for and implementing forms of economic democracy that would put their property and power at risk.[54] For

Madison, the Constitution should control "the conflicting feelings of the Class with, and the Class without property."[55]

Hamilton shared Madison's concern with the dangers of class conflict. In his notes for a speech at the Convention, Hamilton observed that:

> Society naturally divides itself into two political divisions—the *few* and the *many*, who have distinct interests. If government in the hands of the *few*, they will tyrannize over the many. If (in) the hands of the many, they will tyrannize over the few. It ought to be in the hands of both; and they should be separated. This separation must be permanent. Representation alone will not do. Demagogues will generally prevail. And if separated, they will need a mutual check. This check is a monarch.[56]

What makes Madison's *Federalist #10* so illuminating is that it was a tacit admission that the balance of power was not then in the elites' favor. It is a classic treatise on the role of class conflict over both government and economy from an elite perspective. Because he has his own theory of class conflict, it is hardly surprising the Madison has been called the "Marx of the ruling class." Madison is quite forthright about how class structure informs the Constitution.

Propertied elites had seen their powers constrained in most of the states and were similarly checked in the Confederation Congress. Calling first for a convention to fix the Articles of Confederation they then almost immediately threw them out and wrote an entirely new constitution that placed the people further from the reins of power without entirely being excluded.[57] The Framers co-opted the tactics of their adversaries, "adopting the methods of the revolutionary leaders who had used extra-legal and extra-constitutional bodies to achieve independence."[58] While supporters of the Articles agreed that some adaptations were needed, they opposed the elites' effort to either transform it into a national government with coercive powers over the states or replace it altogether.

Madison and the other Framers implicitly drew from Adam Smith's observation that "[c]ivil government, so far as it is instituted for the security of property, is in reality instituted for the defence of the rich against the poor, or of those who have some property against those who have none at all."[59] The Framers didn't design the Constitution according to abstract principles of "liberty" or "limited government," let alone "democracy," as we are told. Rather, they designed it as a two-pronged strategy of survival for elites in a time of bitter and turbulent class conflict.[60] First, it would give the elites an indefinite and unchangeable weapon in their battle with well-organized and powerful small farmers to impede democratic control of the state in order to prevent "agrarian law."

Secondly, the powerful national government they set up would protect and promote a national capitalist economy. The economy would be placed outside the reach of the majority and even beyond the limited and uneven democratic impulses of some of the states.

In effect, the Constitution was designed to *impede* political democracy and *prevent* economic democracy. John Jay provided the logic for such as system: "Those who own the country are the most fit persons to participate in the government of it."[61]

If the Framers could be said to have a "vision," a claim repeated ad nauseam, it is was the vision of the need to protect the shared economic interests as the property-owning elites from democracy. Recognition of their shared *class* interests compelled them to restrain the demands from below with a new federalist system that could check organized movements from democratically controlling the states while blocking the democratization of the economy.[62] They were correcting an oversight—protection for all forms of property— lost during the Revolution.[63]

To ensure the interests and security of property the Constitution was designed to *impede* democratic self-governance by the economic majority by setting up a national capitalist economy that would function according to a single set of nearly unalterable rules enforced by a powerful national government. In doing so, the Constitution *prevents* the democratic control of the capitalist economy.

Rather than setting up a system of the economic majority to govern, the Framers established a system protecting the *liberty* of the economic minority to do what they will with their own property and wealth. By limiting political power exclusively to the elites it set up a "negative, do-nothing system" that cannot function unless elites will it so.[64] It is this system that still governs us more than two centuries later with very little alternation.

Minority Checks on the Majority

The Framers' strategy of *impeding* political democracy and *preventing* economic democracy was woven into the Constitution in order to achieve two primary objectives. First, majority control increasingly asserted, demanded, conceded, or exercised in the state governments was transferred to the exclusive domain of the national, or "federal," government. With these powers now residing in the national government, the "federalist" rules of the system granted the federal government the power to "negative" or "veto" on the states' and the peoples' remaining powers, rights, and liberties as the "Supreme Law of the Land" (VI.2). This gave "supremacy" power not merely to the federal government in VI.2 but to the elites as the ruling class.

While there were some substantial differences between the three main competing plans presented by New Jersey, Virginia, and Hamilton at the Convention, they had more in common in principle than they had differences in practice.[65] None allowed for direct rule or direct votes on laws and the Constitution, and all three contained numerous minority checks. In other words, they differed not on whether but how many minority vetoes to include. Hamilton went the furthest by proposing a monarch for life as the final minority check.[66]

When facing their Anti-Federalist adversaries, the Framers did not advertise that they wanted the Articles entirely overthrown and a new powerful national government installed in its place to "explicitly constrain the redistributive tendencies of the more populist state governments."[67]

Like "liberty," conservatives are keen to claim the Framers established a "limited government." The Framers drew upon the ideas of Aristotle, Montesquieu, John Locke, and later British Whig theory. According to Whig theory, the most effective means for protecting property is to divide the powers of government among the people, elites (aristocracy), and executive (king).[68] For the Framers, this translated into a system riddled with numerous minority checks of one branch on the other while constraining the people from ever exercising power. Limited government meant preventing the economic majority from democratic self-rule while also limiting the elites from the rule of a single dictator or king.

But limited government was coded language for leaving the liberty of property owners unmolested with regard to their own property, whether that be human chattel slaves, capital, land, or vast outstanding unpaid credit. Without exception, the Framers subscribed to Locke's claim that a government can never take "the whole, or any part of the subjects' property, without their consent."[69] The government enshrined by the Constitution is *limited* for the supermajority of everyday people, and *unlimited* government for the minority of the property-owning elite.

Minority checks were installed throughout the Constitution to use the state to protect capitalism while preventing the majority from ruling and changing the economic system.[70] Such minority checks, today commonly know as "separation of powers" and "checks and balances," provided the requirement of elite consent before any action can be taken, thereby assuring the economic elite that their property would be secure.

Late in life, Madison breathed a sign of relief that "power was less likely to be abused by majorities in representative Govts. than in democracies." This was accomplished "by dividing the powers of Govt. and thereby enlarging the practicable sphere of government" to make it hard for majorities to form that could pass what Hamilton called "bad laws" for the propertied elites.[71]

This book attempts to examine some of the most potent minority checks littered throughout the Constitution, especially in the first three Articles and the Amendments. It is worthwhile to take a preliminary peek at some of those that were explicitly debated by the Framers.

The supremacy of the federal (e.g., national) government over the states is perhaps the most potent check of all. Calling the new system "federal" was a masterful rebranding of the nationalist central government with the term that then had the complete opposite meaning—a decentralized, state-dominated system that cooperated in a weak Confederate Congress. This reframing was intended to redirect attention away from the supreme central powers over the states which threatened to tank the ratification of the new Constitution—and nearly did. The belief that states have "rights" today is not merely a myth concocted to retroactively resurrect the "lost cause" of the Civil War Confederacy. It is the propaganda of the faction that usurped the principle of their adversaries as its own moniker—one that bore no resemblance to their own actual commitment to centralized national power.

Echoing Hamilton's 1775 proposal, Madison called for supremacy, what he called a veto, over state laws as "the only defense against the inconveniences of democracy."[72]

The design of the Constitution allowed the Framers to realize their second objective to so dilute, fragment, and impede the organized majority from unifying that it would be prevented from controlling or changing the economic system.[73]

The Framers' Love Letter to Future Elites

The Framers sent a love letter from the eighteenth century to elites of the future by creating a set of rules that favor those who do not want meaningful change and who profit from things remaining as they are. "Today's Constitution is biased toward control of the heirs of the ruling class of 1787—those who hold the greatest assets of power."[74]

This bias lies in privileging the rules in favor of those who oppose change. Political scientists Katznelson, Kesselman, and Draper explain how:

> The legislative process puts innumerable roadblocks in the way of those who seek to use the government to bring about change. … Opponents … need to win only once at any level to defeat the bill. A legislative process that creates so many opportunities for obstruction, that promotes failure rather than success, makes it difficult for the disadvantaged to enlist public power against corporate private power.[75]

The Framers designed the Constitution to create a perpetual power of the elite minority to check the will of the majority, a minority check invulnerable to every legal, judicial, and constitutional reform short of a complete constitutional overhaul.

These are not "defects" or "failings" as much as the consequences of an intentional design logic. This was celebrated by Hamilton and Madison, who wished to divide the population so sufficiently that they couldn't effectively join forces with one another across differing secondary interests.[76]

Today, "limited" government continues to serve as code for the *unlimited* privilege to do whatever a property owner wishes to do with their property. We should not be surprised, then, that the entire organizational structure of the Constitution serves to enshrine rights for property before rights for people, other than *habeas corpus* and privileges and immunities, were even enumerated in the Constitution. The Constitution was designed this way to protect against the very real threats against the economy presented by the popular movements of the time, ranging from efforts to abolish slavery without compensation for the slave owners' losses, redistribute land, engage in debt relief or default, tax the wealthy, overthrow the government by force, and change the economy.

In the twenty-first century we continue to be governed with a system of government designed in the eighteenth century. Although there have been some reforms of the way we are governed, such as with voting and civil rights vis-à-vis the state, the ungovernability of property is still firmly in place and virtually unchanged. Property has been placed beyond the pale of democratic control.

Divide and Conquer

In *Federalist #51*, Madison proposed how the axiom of divide and conquer would work in the federal system: "whilst all authority in it will be derived from and dependent on the society, the society itself will be broken into so many parts, interests, and classes of citizens, that the rights of individuals, or of the minority, will be in little danger from interested combinations of the majority." Divide and conquer was already being used against native peoples. In 1784,

Jefferson instructed US Indian Commissioners to negotiate separate treaties at different times and places with Native American tribes to thwart their efforts to form a united front under Shawnee leadership against western expansion.[77] The Washington administration used the same strategy a decade later by officially promising peace while escalating its military offensive against native forces.[78]

This counter-insurgency strategy was enshrined in the design of the Constitution so as to amplify these divisions. "Divide et impera, the reprobated axiom of tyranny, is under certain qualifications, the only policy, by which a republic can be administered on just principles," Madison wrote.[79] In *Federalist #43*, Madison warned that in a large country it would be difficult for the majority to unify because "the people are broken into so many interests and parties, that a common sentiment is less likely to be felt, and the requisite concert less likely to be formed, by a majority of the whole."

In *Federalist Paper #10*, Madison celebrated the divisions as necessary to protect property.[80] The economy could be best protected by removing economic powers to the national government and then separating and checking the states:

> A rage for paper money, for an abolition of debts, for an equal division of property, or for any other improper or wicked project, will be less apt to pervade the whole body of the Union than a particular member of it; in the same proportion as such a malady is more likely to taint a particular county or district, than an entire State.

Madison was continually working out the need for a system of checks and balances that would function automatically in order to neutralize change. He wrote to Jefferson that it was necessary "to controul one part from invading the rights of another, and at the same time sufficiently controuled itself, from setting up an interest adverse *to* that of the entire Society."[81]

In this way, the design of Constitution is an expression of class conflict in the form of law.[82] It emerged at a time in which society was immersed in ubiquitous class conflict which the elites had lacked the political tools to suppress.

While Madison and Hamilton certainly had a class analysis, their opponents also had theirs. While the theme of the "few and the many" runs throughout the Anti-Federalists letters, pamphlets, and papers, one of the sharpest analyses of the role of class came from William Manning. In his proposal to form the first national labor union, Manning observed that "labor is the sole parent of all property".[83]

Manning proposed unifying the working class because of "a conceived difference of interest between those that labor for a living and those that get a living without bodily labor."[84] He accurately perceived, just a decade after the Constitution went into effect, that the concentration of power in the hands of the elites was deadly to a system supposedly based on self-rule, writing that "free governments are commonly destroyed by the combinations of the judicial and executive powers in favor of the interests of the Few." They "so raise themselves above the legislative power and take the whole administration into their own hands and manage it according to their own wills and the interests of the Few."[85] The elite, according to Manning, become a class above the state, to borrow Hannah Arendt's term.

We should not make the mistake of confusing the absence of political and economic democracy for the lack of struggle to achieve it. The demands and accomplishments of the people out of doors such as Manning went far beyond anything elites were willing to entertain, but not far enough before they were defeated. While certainly some of the struggles recounted in this book undermined and disrupted elite control, domination, and exploitation, they were flawed and contradictory at best. These struggles demanded economic and political systems in which the vast majority didn't just get to vote but had control. They resisted efforts to strip them of their access to land, subsistence way of life, and cashless system of mutual aid.

If the Anti-Federalists failed to stop the Constitution from being ratified they managed to delay it and change some of its substance but not its logic.[86] But there are lessons to be learned from their efforts, not merely for daydreams about how the USA might have turned out differently, but to understand how the constitutional system and capitalist economy we have today was constructed in 1787 to counter the threat of something radically different taking its place.

2

Preamble: "Intoxicating Draughts of Liberty Run Mad"

No part of the Constitution is more misunderstood, misquoted, and over-valued than the Preamble.[1] The courts have mostly shied away from attempting to interpret the short, vague paragraph and apply precedent, Congress and the executive have ignored it almost altogether, and historians and political scientists mostly neglect it. This neglect is in stark contrast with the importance given to it by "We the People," who use it to understand what the Constitution does and should be doing. The Preamble is distinctively written as a philosophical aspiration rather than in the dry, legalistic style that characterizes the rest of the Constitution. Perhaps this is why the Preamble has grabbed the attention of ordinary people: it expressed what we would *like* the Constitution to be and do, even though in reality it does something very different.

We can mistake the text's generalities as timeless, universal, and adaptable to the changing norms and values of the time. But the Preamble expresses the material relations of the late eighteenth century as a rationale for the rest of the document. If we examine the meaning of the eight key principles found in the Preamble we find a preface to a set of golden handcuffs constraining political and preventing economic democracy.

We the People

We the People of the United States, in Order to form a more perfect Union, establish Justice, insure domestic Tranquility, provide for the common defence, promote the general Welfare, and secure the

Blessings of Liberty to ourselves and our Posterity, do ordain and establish this Constitution for the United States of America.

While we have come to see ourselves as the "People" the Framers designed the Constitution to serve, nothing could be further from the truth. The Framers, the 55 of the 70 state-accredited delegates who showed up, were a group nearly indistinguishable among themselves as wealthy white men of whom only a handful were not rich (but still affluent). They saw themselves as the "People" who would be afforded not merely rights under the Constitution but the power to run the government. They intended the document to serve men like themselves.

The elites faced not merely the Shays' Rebellion and armed land squatters in Maine but an ongoing triple threat of insurrection from poor whites, Native Americans, and slaves. Their fear of these threats compelled them to hesitantly embrace the cause of independence and continued unabated under the Articles.[2] Under the Articles of Confederation, state after state had succumbed to the organized protests and even armed insurrections of the "lower sort": small farmers, debtors, laborers, mechanics, and sailors who challenged their exclusion from the state governments and suffered under onerous tax and debt collection policies, and insisted that they be changed.

These insurgencies were used by the elites as a "shock" to strengthen their case for a strong national government that would prevent the overthrow or break-up of the Confederation.[3] The elites felt under siege by the people out of doors taking up arms, beginning to abolish slavery, voting themselves into office, and threatening to seize control of their property. It was, in their eyes, economic and political democracy run amok. It was "leveling," the realization of economic democracy by the tyrannical majority. Fear of a nationwide Shays' Rebellion is what motivated the Framers to meet in the Convention.[4]

The elites also saw states as being too weak to defend themselves from unified Native American armed resistance to violent settler encroachments on their lands west of the Appalachians and in Georgia, Virginia, and Pennsylvania, and aligning themselves with the British and Spanish to repel westward expansion. They were similarly gripped by the fear that they were unable to prevent or suppress slave uprisings that were becoming ever more frequent, especially after thousands went over to the Loyalist side during the Revolution. The totality of the people out of doors, native peoples, and slaves rising up in rebellion instilled an existential dread in the elites, who wanted a strong government for protection.[5]

The Framers did not mean the same "We the People" as we do today: the wide variety of ethnic, racial, gender, and sexual identities, and differences in income and wealth. That the phrase means something different today is the result of more than two centuries of peaceful and even violent struggle to expand and stretch its meaning.

A More Perfect Union

For the Framers, the Articles established a flawed system that subjected the elite to pressure from below. Formed as a confederation of sovereign nations, each state voluntarily assented to participate in the Congress. In the last paragraph of the Declaration of Independence, the "UNITED STATES OF AMERICA" is referred to twice as composed of "FREE AND INDEPENDENT STATES" and once as "INDEPENDENT STATES" with the power to do all that sovereign nations are assumed to have the authority to do because they "have full Power to levy War, conclude Peace, contract Alliances, establish Commerce, and to do all other Acts and Things which Independent States may of right do."

Each state issued its own currency, took on its own debt, made its own laws, negotiated its own agreements with foreign nations that often conflicted with Congress' enumerated treaty making power, taxed imports and exports to and from other states and countries, banned or regulated slavery, raised their own sources of revenue not shared with Congress, extended civil rights and liberties, and even went to war against Native Americans who were considered separate, hostile nations.

The Confederation was described as being on the verge of collapse due to the difficulty of amending the Articles by consensus. Dire warnings that states were engaged in tax policies and foreign relations hostile to other states instilled anxiety among elites who feared a loss of independence. Most dire was the continued unjust treatment of the "better sort" of people on whom a future empire would be built: the very people who were at the mercy of the majoritarian-controlled states and who refused to do business until things changed in their favor.

The Framers didn't want to improve the Articles but replace it with a "more perfect Union" for elites, a *national* system empowered to set up and run a single national economy, military and foreign policy, and the necessary revenues to fund them.

Establish Justice

Justice is an inspirational concept that undergirds nearly every social movement. Justice has come to popularly mean the achievement of a preconceived outcome that will reset the imbalance of power, change the law or policy, end harm, compensate the grieved, and mete out sanctions against the perpetrator. But in a representative democracy, justice means that government is expected to apply the law fairly and consistently to everyone, regardless of one's position in society or the outcome.

That is exactly what was on the minds of the Framers when they inserted the phrase "establish justice" in the Preamble. The phrase specifically points to the Framers' intent to tip the balance of power back in favor of the elites. Doing so would reverse the damage done by states that had conceded to the demands of organized small farmers at the expense of the landed and merchant elite. In 1783, Madison had already made clear what justice meant writing that "the establishment of permanent & adequate funds to operate generally throughout the U. States is indispensibly necessary for doing complete justice to the Creditors of the U. S., for restoring public credit, & for providing for the future exigencies of the war."[6] To Madison, to "establish justice" meant doing what some of the states were unable or unwilling to do—pay our debts and protect property, whether it be slave, financial, or land.[7]

Justice for creditors meant being paid at par (the original face value) with interest in *specie* (the term for a standard of value based on actual valuable coin literally minted in gold or silver). To do this the states were expected to impose taxes to obtain the revenues for Congress and their creditors. Both domestic and foreign creditors were demanding payment after Congress stopped paying interest with paper money in 1780 and Superintendent of Finance Robert Morris stopped paying interest on bills of credit in 1782.[8] The problem worsened when the fighting stopped and the Treaty of Paris was signed in 1783 and ratified in 1784 by Congress. By that time the USA had defaulted on some of its loans to France in 1785, only to begin repaying interest and the principal in 1788, and stopped paying its debts to Spain.[9]

The Confederation's poor credit record drove the demand for elites to demand a new constitution.[10] While few doubted the debts were a serious issue, farmers and merchants differed on how to repay them.[11]

Small subsistence farmers, the majority of the white population, insisted that if they were to be taxed to repay the debts then they should be able to pay in paper money or in kind with crops. If they must pay in specie then they demanded the right to renegotiate the terms of repayment, delay payment, or change the law.[12] They also insisted on progressive forms of taxation that placed the heaviest burden on the elites and repaid debt speculators only the value of what they had already paid for now much-devalued certificates, not at par.

Nothing was more objectionable to the planter, merchant, and landed elite who invested in debt expecting a hefty profit than to have their debts discounted or delayed. Many of them were both creditors and debtors, having borrowed heavily to raise the capital to invest.

Neither beacons of democracy nor reliable protectors of elite property, the states were under attack from above and below. From below, some states were attacked by small farmers for imposing taxes to produce revenues intended primarily to pay off creditors and then taking their property when they couldn't pay. The elites were upset that the states were hesitant to enforce tax collection for the payment of their debts to creditors, thereby lowering the perceived value of their investments which they were uncertain of recouping.[13]

The farmers had a reason to be upset. In Massachusetts, taxes were four to five times higher in 1786 than during British rule when the pro-creditor legislature raised taxes to pay their debts, sparking the Shays' Regulator Rebellion.[14] The Framers took the side of the creditors because their fellow elites had been treated unjustly by the state governments. By shifting control of government and the economy to themselves, creditors and property owners would be treated with the deference they deserved.

Insure Domestic Tranquility

Born in the blood and fire of gunshots, guerrilla warfare, and insurrection, the Constitution was designed as a strategy for containing and suppressing struggles from below to allow the elites to rule unmolested in "domestic Tranquility." The concern of the elites for their dominance due to the organized power of the people out of doors can be found in the warnings about "Convulsions within" and "exciting domestic Insurrections amongst us" in the Declaration of Independence, during a time of native resistance and the emergence of organized small farmers and mechanics writing new state constitutions and policies during the Revolution. The Constitution was the product of the aftermath of the Revolution and decades of continued class conflict.[15] Tranquility means the ability to prevent and suppress conflict and turmoil that threatened the established order and rule of the elites. To accomplish that, power first needed to be shifted to the new national government established by the Constitution.

The Framers feared the challenge to elite rule would continue after the Revolution as it did during it, because the people out of doors were increasingly flexing their political muscle by using a range of legal and extra-legal tactics.[16]

The ongoing "domestic insurrection" decried in the Declaration of Independence referred to the intensifying interconnected rural insurrections, slave rebellions, and native resistance protected against in IV.4 to "guarantee to every state" protection against "domestic violence." Those engaged in revolt had other ideas about how to organize society and government and were willing to impose them by force if necessary.[17]

The issue was not merely whether Congress or a new national government would be empowered to tax in order the repay the long unpaid war debt. This struggle over the power of taxation runs through most of the canons and mythologies of American history, mostly as a celebration of the resistance to taxation as a spark for revolution. Even today the rallying cry of "no taxation without representation" continues to define the Revolution, no matter how disconnected it is from the historical facts. Considering the repeatedly failed effort of Robert Morris and others to impose a range of taxes during the Revolution, a more accurate motto would have been "no national government without taxation." Instead, elites framed the power to tax as the central plank of their nationalist project.[18]

Since local and state governments had failed to suppress the insurrections, the authority to protect property, tax, repay the debt, enforce contracts, make bankruptcy laws, enforce federal law by court rulings, and use military force to put down insurrections were critical to preventing the continued spread of the struggle for economic democracy. In Massachusetts, Connecticut, New Hampshire, and Vermont, small farmers were elected to office and used the existing legislative process to organize into assemblies, town meetings, and county conventions that issued a stream of complaints, memorials, and petitions proposing forms of economic democracy including paper money, delaying debt collections, and allowing goods and labor to be used to pay debts. Their power demonstrated the necessity for preventing insurrection from being translated into reform through voting and the legislative process.

What troubled the elites[19] was that insurrectionists wanted to use paper money to address the debt issue. In the past paper money was issued to increase trade and set up a land bank. Now paper money was intended to serve the interests of the majority of the state's population, particularly subsistence farmers, to reduce the value of their debts rather than inflate the profits of speculation and trading. To prevent such economic democracy, John Adams and James Bowdoin rewrote the Massachusetts state constitution by raising the property requirements to run for and hold office. Revolutionary leader Samuel Adams literally wrote the 1786 Massachusetts Riot Act to counter the

Regulators. Whereas many states became more democratic, Massachusetts, along with New Hampshire, became less so.[20]

Rather than reform the states, the Framers designed the Constitution with war powers, a standing army, and authority to use military force internally and externally—a complete realization of the nationalists's objectives. Gouverneur Morris was responsible for some of the language in I.8.12, that Congress has the power "To raise and support Armies," during the final days of the Convention while chair of the Committee on Style.[21] By centralizing military force in the Constitution under the national government the elites got their own protection force against the majority's "popular despotism" alongside militias established by Congress in I.8.16 and called up by it to "suppress Insurrections and repel Invasions" in I.8.15. The Shays' Rebellion and native resistance provided the justification for forming and then expanding the army, even as much as tripling its cost and increasing the number of soldiers fivefold by 1791.[22]

Congress's new power of taxation would fund the necessary forces to protect the national economy it set up, manages, and protects under I.8 to I.10 from democratic control. The power to tax and borrow and the supremacy power to enforce contracts, protect property, and repay the debt was critical to establishing a trustworthy public credit system that stimulated the creation of an integrated national economy. Empowering the national government to make and enforce uniform laws, policies, and regulation governing the economy, all of which were supreme over all the states, ingeniously wove the competing elite factions of creditor and debtor, merchant and banker, trader and slave owner into a unified class invested in the new national system of government and the newly emerging national economy.

While they were lukewarm allies of the elites during the Critical Period, mechanics were a small but well-organized threat to its coalition partners. One might wonder why mechanics, the term for skilled laborers, were part of a coalition with elites backing the nationalist project and the Constitution. The mechanics had moved from radicalism during the Revolution, when they pushed non-importation of British goods, to nationalism with the peace, and now called for protections for domestic manufacturers. They expected the new Constitution, which included the power to regulate trade and impose tariffs on imported manufactured goods, would generate more demand for their own products and raising prices and profits. The mechanics had hitched their fortunes to their class adversary.[23]

These features of the Constitution unified the fractious elites and anchored their fortunes to the government, providing the very stability needed to restore order and govern by subduing the motley crew that sought to democratize government and economy, part of a movement that was spreading throughout the Atlantic hemisphere in the eighteenth century.[24]

As historian J. Franklin Jameson observed, the outcomes of revolutions are not determined by those who start them but by those who control and then end them.[25] If the Revolution could not have been fought without the multitude of common people, the new country could not be managed with them. The Constitution was designed to settle the struggle over who would rule at home. The American Revolution turned the world upside down with the elites ending up on the bottom. The Constitution was the strategy for turning the system right side up again so they would return to the top, bringing with them the rule of capitalism.

Provide for the Common Defense

The Framers directed their attention to the range of threats from within as well as without. In addition to the domestic threats from small farmers, native peoples, and slaves, North African "Barbary states" were attacking and seizing US merchant ships in the Mediterranean, the British maintained nine forts along its border, and Spain occupied Florida and parts of Mississippi and Alabama and closed the Mississippi to boat traffic, seizing a US vessel for violating it. Foreign creditors' insistence that they be repaid risked a possible military invasion and occupation.[26] The US government's ability to defend its borders, protect trade, and pay its debts were in doubt.

Foreign nations, especially the UK, were attempting to lock US ships out of the Atlantic. Although the 1783 Treaty of Paris and the 1794–5 Jay Treaty granted US ships access to British Caribbean colonies and Europe, it was by no means assured they would reach them. Soon after ratification, vessels sailed to China, the Indian Ocean, Africa, and elsewhere but lacked the protection of a navy. Funding for a national "common defense" benefited both the Northern merchant and Southern big slave states.[27]

The power to establish and fund the army, navy, and militias, declare war, negotiate treaties, and protect the country from invasion provided the desired combined strength that the Framers found lacking in the Confederation and the states. Once the Constitution allowed a stable system of public finance to be created, and national taxes collected, the war debts could be repaid, allowing the country to obtain the security necessary for property.

Promote the General Welfare

The Framers' preference for Rome and hostility to Athens was not merely about controlling who had the reins of government—the elites as in the Roman Senate, or all free men as in the Athenian assembly. They were terrified about what the people out of doors could do with the reins of power when it came to setting up a market economy. Since the elites owned most of the property in the states they would exclusively decide how to use it for the "general Welfare" of the population.[28]

The long history of Rome and short history of Athens were extremely tumultuous. Madison warned late in life, perhaps with the plotting of his former ally Hamilton in mind, that crisis becomes the pretext for extending the executive powers of war. Madison likely also had the use of executive powers in the economy on his mind as well. Decades earlier, Madison warned in *Federalist #10* about the immediate consequences of not only the Shays' Rebellion but the damage to property that might be inflicted by the organized economic majority should they gain control of state power.

The elites denounced the use of paper money by seven states, requirements that the money be accepted as legal tender by a smaller number, and the use of loan offices and land banks by a few to expand credit to small farmers.[29] In fact, none of these were new and had been used by colonial elites for decades before the Revolution, and they would be used again after ratification. It is often overlooked that Congress first asked the states to recognize its Continentals as currency that can be used as legal tender.[30] Paper money certainly had the effect of reducing the value of debts and was widely renounced by creditors and speculators alike, especially in states where it could be legally be used to pay off debts. Yet, as long as land values remained low and paper money lost value, land speculators also profited from its use as legal tender to buy vast tracts of land on the cheap. Many creditors were simultaneously debtors who had gotten rich by buying low and selling high.

The problem was not paper money, but who used it and who benefited. For example, New York funded its debt repayment and even became a creditor of Congress owning $2.9 million in federal securities in 1790. It did this by using a state tariff, selling Loyalist and unsettled western lands, and taxing real estate and personal property. This revenue and paper money was used to pay interest and principal on all the kinds of state and two kinds of federal debts which were more broadly owned than the unfunded debts owned by several hundred rich New Yorkers. As a result, Governor George Clinton's party was able to harness the creditors to the state government.[31] New York and other states' capacity to reduce or pay off their war debts, and the refusal to amend the Articles to give Congress the power to lay an impost, which New York rejected three times, put the nationalists' project for a new constitution at risk.

The elites made vast fortunes by expropriating land from the native peoples, and by exploiting the unwaged labor of slaves and indentured servants, as well as the waged labor of "free" workers. On the other side of the divide were more numerous small farmers in every state who barely eked out a subsistence after years of unpaid service in the revolutionary army and state militias. They returned only to find unpayable debts, rising taxes, and threats to foreclose on their lands, tools, livestock, and personal possessions unless they paid in scarce specie. Alongside them were the mechanics losing their livelihoods to cheaper British imports being dumped in the new country from which rich merchants profited by selling to rich farmers.

Finding themselves on the same side of the class conflict, small subsistence farmers in rural areas and mechanics in the cities were elected to local office, took over the lower house of some state legislatures, and elected friendly governors. Alongside the paper money and legal tender bills, they passed stay laws that blocked debt collections and foreclosures and set up state land banks to lend to small farmers using land as collateral. States also banned suits by British creditors whose debts went unpaid and Loyalists whose lands were expropriated during the Revolution. This would change with the 1783 Treaty of Paris which ended the war with England by allowing these creditors into state courts to recover unpaid debts paid in specie and expropriated lands. Some states also allowed the use of paper money to retire British debts and prevented taxes on people and land in favor of laying them on imports of luxury items consumed by the elites.[32] The loudest cries could now be heard from the same planters who wanted to close the courts to British creditors during the Revolution when they fell into debt as tobacco prices dropped so low that they could not repay their debts. They now recoiled in horror when small famers insisted on the same.[33] One of the most detested democratic economic policies pushed by the coalition of small farmers and mechanics was the issuing of state taxes that could be paid with paper money and war-era IOUs and other kinds of financial paper, schemes that helped some states pay off their war debts without raising taxes.

Using paper money to pay off debts was reviled by Superintendent of Finance Morris. Morris's failed plan for a Bank of North America and debt repayment proposed three days into his position as Superintendent of Finance was first used in Pennsylvania was later folded into Hamilton's financial plan.[34]

William Manning rather feared that by locking the people out of doors out of government the Framers would put into place economic measures such as Hamilton's financial plan at the expense "of the farmers and common laborers."[35] What Manning perceived so well is that the elites defined their own class "interests and influence" as the general welfare in diametrical opposition to the majority.[36]

Secure the Blessings of Liberty to Ourselves and Our Posterity

The Framers set up a national government that could singularly protect property above all other concerns indefinitely into "Posterity".

The Constitution achieves this by placing an array of roadblocks and impediments in the way of majority demands for economic democracy. These roadblocks and impediments are not designed to merely prevent a wannabe dictator from simply concentrating power into their own hands but to also prevent tyrannical majorities from democratically making policies that "despoil & enslave the minority" by infringing upon the "Blessings of Liberty" (e.g., property rights) of the elite.[37]

The ultimate security is the extreme difficulty of altering or changing it by amendment or constitutional convention. Studded with innumerable roadblocks and impediments, the elite has a plethora of opportunities to issue a minority veto of any changes by law, regulations, or court rulings that might threaten property. The Constitution, in short, was designed to last for "Posterity"—forever unchanged and unchangeable.

Do Ordain and Establish This Constitution

During the two meetings in Mount Vernon and Annapolis preceding the Convention, the emerging nationalist group of elites learned important lessons about the difficulty of replacing the Articles of Confederation. Achieving consensus proved to be an impossible task, as demonstrated by several previous failed efforts to extend the power to tax to Congress. Because there was no authority to hold a convention to revise or replace the Articles, the nationalists struggled to finally achieve authority from Congress to meet in Philadelphia to propose revisions to Articles, throwing that aside days later in favor of replacing it.

Knowing that they had explicitly exceeded, even violated, Congress's mandate for the meeting, the Framers prepared for the inevitable opposition to what would be perceived to be a "Framers' coup."[38] Because their plan would certainly fall far short of the required consensus of the states, Article VII allowed for ratification once it was approved by nine state conventions—not the popular vote of the people.[39]

The design of the Constitution is inseparable from the process of putting it into effect—the direct influence of the people on the national government would be removed and replaced by the narrowly defined "We the People." The strategy shifted authority from the states, which had exclusive authority to amend the Articles and which had frequently operated as a vehicle of power for the people out of doors, to the small slice of "the People." The states had proven dangerous because organized people had demonstrated their ability to pressure state elites in making concessions, or failing that, to take control of the legislature and change the laws in states where the executive veto was rare and judicial review non-existent.

Instead of allowing ratification by a vote of the few thousand "People" then qualified by the states to vote and hold office at the time, the Constitution was indeed "ordain[ed]" by the elites who "establish[ed]" it. The dangers of concentrating power in the new federal government didn't escape the wrath of Anti-Federalist critics such as Framer Elbridge Gerry, one of three who refused to sign the Constitution. He warned "how easy the Transition from a Republican to any other Form of Government, however despotic! & how ridiculous to exchange a British Administration, for one that would be equally tyrannical, perhaps much more so?"[40]

3

Congress: Justice to Property

The Revolution convinced the Framers that the states were incapable of resisting the demands of the people out of doors for economic and political democracy. The growing threat of economic democracy required expanding the power of Congress over property, contracts, debt, currency, and other important features to blunt the threats by the economic majority to acquire, repossess, and distribute the property of the elite.[1] Congress was designed to counter what the Massachusetts Provincial Congress called "alarming symptoms of the abatement of the sense in the minds of some people of the sacredness of private property."[2]

Protecting property from economic democracy was most apparent in the Framers' consideration of whether to remove the power to emit Bills of Credit from the draft Constitution in a close vote of six to five on August 16, 1787. In the lively debate, the differing material interests of elites who were either debtors or creditors entered the hall. Gouverneur Morris, James Madison, and Oliver Ellsworth all shared their fear that "the Monied interest" would reject the Constitution if paper money were not prohibited because it would further damage the creditworthiness of the government.[3]

Few other debates at the Convention made the Framers' objective to protect property so apparent. By empowering Congress to both constrain democratic control of government and prevent economic democracy the Constitution became the political tool intended to achieve an economic outcome that flipped the balance of class power to the elites, where it remains today.

A Just System for Property

The Framers' economic priorities necessitated the reform of the system of government. Articles I.8 to I.10 provided the power to design, set up, and protect the capitalist economy by repaying debts, protecting contracts, regulating interstate commerce, imposing taxes, establishing the currency, and funding the military to protect. It also established the supremacy of the debt in Article VI.1, stating that "All Debts contracted and Engagements entered into, before the Adoption of this Constitution, shall be as valid against the United States under this Constitution, as under the Confederation."[4]

These often overlooked economic powers housed in Article I were the Framers' response to the widespread popularity of what they called "leveling," a pejorative term referring to efforts to democratize the economy. The revolutionary passions for economic democracy continued even after peace was restored. Small farmers far from the towns, ports, and markets organized to apply sufficient pressure to implement debt and tax relief, the introduction of paper money, and laws allowing paper money to be used as legal tender to repay debts and taxes, to name a few.

Warnings about the threats to the concentration of property in the hands of the few were widespread, and even enshrined into the first Kentucky convention and Pennsylvania constitutions. When they failed in normal politics, small farmers escalated their tactics by marching with arms on local courts to stop foreclosure sales and collection of rent and evictions by landlords, squatting lands held by absentee land speculators, carrying out hit and run attacks on local targets, and engaging in armed marches and pitched battles. These post-revolutionary forms of economic democracy were efforts to defend and expand earlier wartime policies of economic democracy that included paper money, expropriation, the forced sale of Loyalist properties and estates, price controls, anti-monopoly laws, protections for debtors, and firm enforcement of non-importation.

The Revolution appeared to elites to have opened the gates of hell, unleashing the many-headed hydra of democracy. State legislatures were inundated by a range of these demands. Small farmers entered state legislatures and took up the memorials of local conventions and responded to armed Regulator rebellions in Massachusetts, New Hampshire, South Carolina, and elsewhere. As this occurred, the elites lost exclusive control over policy making, law enforcement, judicial prosecution of the violation of property rights, and economic policies that ensured their continued domination. In the face of such outright attacks on property, according to historian Jackson Turner Main, "the drive for a government which could suppress such threats to property was accelerated."[5]

Turning back this growing surge demanding economic democracy required stripping away the policy tools that allowed it from the states and the majority and relocating them in a Congress whose powers could be wielded only with the approval of elites armed with an array of minority checks. The totality of these newly federalized economic powers granted centralized power to the elites in order to set up, manage, and run a national capitalist economy and check any threats coming up from the states.

Taxation, particularly "direct" taxes on imports and land, would be essential not only for funding an army to protect property but also to establish a government-backed financial system that facilitates the acquisition of property. After taxation came the authority to enforce contracts, regulate interstate commerce, pass replevin laws ensuring repayment, establish rules for bankruptcy, repay the debt, appropriate tax revenues, dispose of federal lands, ratify commercial treaties, establish necessary courts for adjudicating property claims, and form a national army that could ensure national security against threats from without and within.

One source of revenue was the public credit system Hamilton first proposed in 1781 and established a decade later as the first Secretary of the Treasury. Hamilton was appointed by Washington and confirmed by the Senate to this position on September 11th, an attack on economic democracy. To demonstrate just how important currency, debt, and finance were to the new government, Hamilton's appointment preceded that of Jefferson as secretary of state, Jay as the chief justice of the Supreme Court, and Randolph as the first attorney general—three of the most important posts in the executive branch today—more than two weeks later on September 26, 1789.

Hamilton designed the system so that government tax revenue was recycled into government debt, as the government borrowed the money it already owned from a private bank that, by lending, made capital available for investment. In effect, Hamilton implemented what we now call monetary policy, in which cheap, publicly backed credit for the wealthy is supposed to "trickle down" into tax coffers and people's pockets, thereby supposedly avoiding the need to tax people, which he thought was unpopular and to be avoided.[6]

The financial system was created by the most potent power delegated to Congress. The so-called "elastic clause" found in I.8.18 gives Congress the power "to make all Laws which shall be necessary and proper" to implement all the powers established in the Constitution. It was actually added by the Committee of Detail late in the Convention and approved without any debate.[7]

This power has allowed Congress to stretch its vast reach over the economy to protect elite interests from all emerging threats. It is the fuel that has extended the reach of government over the economy to the immense proportions we see today. The intentionally unlimited scope of the elastic clause is admitted by Madison in *Federalist #44* as an axiom of government, "that wherever the end is required, the means are authorized; wherever a general power to do a thing is given, every particular power necessary for doing it is included." Hamilton thought that serving the "General Welfare" justified an economic system based on a public credit system run by a chartered bank that financed government-subsidized industries such as arms manufacturing, relied on immigrants and children to increase the labor supply and lower wages, protected corporations, and used protectionism to industrialize.[8] While the elastic clause was little used until the Civil War and then again at the turn of the twentieth century, the interstate commerce clause (I.8.3) was dusted off and used to make the New Deal of the 1930s.

Land, Slaves, and Labor

Congress's potent economic powers provided the necessary tools to impede and prevent efforts to democratize the economy alongside its war powers to steal and colonize native lands, expand slavery, and create a larger class of waged workers.

IV.3.1 granted Congress power to admit "New States" and the disposal and transfer of "Territory and other Property" was provided in IV.3.2, granting that "[t]he Congress shall have power to dispose of and make all needful Rules and Regulations respecting the Territory or other Property belonging to the United States." This power consolidated authority in the federal government to resolve conflicts between several states and speculative landholding companies over the distribution, division, and ownership of lands expropriated by violent force from the native peoples.

Transferring control to a Congress littered with minority checks ensured that these lands would not be available for redistribution to immigrants, landless laborers, and mechanics seeking to escape from a lifetime of tortuous work. Western lands, in fact, became the focus of decades of effort by Anti-Federalists and populist reformers who ultimately achieved the first large-scale redistribution under the 1865 Homestead Act, although much of the land ended up in the hands of the railroad companies.

Federal control also excluded landless laborers and small farmers from formal political power for decades until the expansion of white male suffrage. As property ownership was considered both a principle and a criterion for representation, voting, and serving in office in many states, these men were excluded from power because they could not be trusted to protect property.[9] Land, along with slaves, tools, housing, and farm animals, was counted toward one's property value. The propertyless or property poor had no expectation of the right of "consent of the Governed" promised by the Declaration of Independence.

By removing people from the land, or denying them access to obtain it, Congress oversaw the creation of a class of workers with nothing but their labor to sell.[10] Creating an expanded working class at once solved two long-running problems: a shortage of workers and rising cost of labor, both of which discouraged investment in commercial agricultural and industrial production.[11]

Not surprisingly, the ratification of the Constitution sparked a rise in the value and quantity of financial assets, due to the expectation of repayment at par by the new federal government, while encouraging investment by investors confident in the security of the new government-backed public credit system. As slaves and immigrant free laborers continued to flood in after the end of the war, control of the western lands provided a necessary pool of exploitable labor to lower wages, spur investment, and drive economic expansion.

Today it is argued that whites profited from stolen native lands and slavery without having to tax white farmers' land. But this is not the complete picture. While subsistence farmers' land was not violently expropriated by the genocidal settler colonialism inflicted on Native Americans, their lands were taken much more imperceptibly. They fought fiscal tax and monetary credit policies over the next century because they were an indirect form of land theft that transformed subsistence farmers into waged workers. The elites' use of racial supremacy and slavery bought the loyalty of small white farmers as part of a strategy of divide and rule that tragically worked all too well and continues today.[12] How different the outcome might have been if it were not the case that, as historian Peter Linebaugh tragically put it, "[h]uman beings were split, split from the earth, split from one another."[13]

Those Bound to Service

Many are aware of the notorious "three-fifths clause" found in I.2.3 that inflated representation for the big slave states in Congress and the electoral college. Fewer know how Congress used western lands to carve out new states into which slavery could be expanded.[14] But this is only one of several ways Congress was designed to protect slavery, including district-based elections for the House which gave power to slaveocrats who dominated their area and the granting of two senators per state regardless of population.

Designing the House of Representatives to protect slavery was as ingenious as it was insidious. States were allowed to count "those bound to Service for a Term of Years" (I.2.3), an example of what comedian George Carlin called a "weasel word" for slaves that detracted from its intent. States with a significant number of slaves received an exaggerated number of seats in the House as well as in the electoral college, where the number of seats correspond to the number of House seats in addition to the two corresponding to their senators.

The three-fifths clause originated in a 1783 proposed amendment to the Articles to count land values and three-fifths of each slave instead of the free white population when apportioning Congressional requisitions to the states. The Framers used three-fifths as a compromise over ratios of eight to two and seven to three during the contentious debate whether to assess taxes and representation by property or population.[15] Using any equivalency between slaves and free white persons was perceived as putting different groups of elites and their states, whether rich or poor in land and slaves, at a disadvantage. Delegates who came from states that had either begun to phase out slavery or had few slaves expected waged laborers to soon outnumber slaves. They proved badly mistaken as the number of slaves grew about sixfold from around 700,000 to roughly four million between 1790 and 1860.[16]

When combined with the appearance of equality between states in the Senate, the three-fifths clause, which was later removed by the 13th amendment, amplified the number of electors when picking the President and Vice President. This was to not only ensure ratification by the big slave states but to provide a minority check over any effort to pass a law or amendment regulating, phasing out, or even abolishing slavery. When we include the President's power to make appointments and their confirmation by the Senate, the Constitution gave the slave states the power to fill vacancies only with those sufficiently supportive of the supremacy of property.

Despite comprising only about a third of the delegates, the slaveocracy could rely on merchants and bankers who profited handsomely from slavery to support them. Those who owned slaves and directly profited from slavery made up perhaps a majority of the Convention. In all, slavery was indirectly protected in about 20 ways, and it was the only form of commerce exempted from being regulated in I.8.3.[17]

Supporters of slavery were likely concerned that records of the Convention, despite being behind closed doors, would eventually go public. On several occasions, a handful of delegates denounced the slave trade, although not slavery itself, eventually extracting a possible federal ban in I.9.1, with a tax not exceeding $10 per slave, that could begin no earlier than 1808. The date was set so far into the future it was made moot due to population growth and the additional time available to import more slaves.[18] The ban was not a "compromise" because nothing was conceded by the slaveocrats. The loudest "critics" of the slave trade were from Virginia which had the most slaves and stood to gain by trying to restrict imports to become the primary domestic supplier to the other states.

Over the next few decades the public's feelings toward slavery gradually took a more hostile turn. By the 1850s all the states above the 1820 Missouri Compromise line began to or had already abolished slavery. The Missouri Compromise brought a truce to Congress, stalling the secession of the big slave states. Slavery was prohibited in any state other than Missouri that entered the union North of latitude 36 degrees 30'. This allowed states north of the line to abolish slavery while allowing slavery to expand westward.

As public sentiment increasingly turned against slavery and the exorbitant power given to the big slave states by the Constitution due to the three-fifths clause, among other features, Northerners began to organize solidarity campaigns to protect runaway slaves in their states from being dragged back into slavery by slave hunters, a gruesome story told by Solomon Northup in his 1853 book *12 Years a Slave* and the 2013 film adaptation. Then came slaves Dred and Harriet Scott's unsuccessful lawsuit to claim their freedom in a state that had abolished slavery. Historians are in near agreement that the 1857 *Dred Scott v. Sandford* case was the Supreme Court at its worst.

Northern states claimed to have a reserve clause power under the Missouri Compromise to abolish all slavery within their individual state while slave states said otherwise. Not only did they point to the continued, albeit indirect, protections for slavery in the Constitution, they pointed to IV.2.3, the "fugitive slave" or "extradition clause" which reads: "No Person held to Service or Labour in one State, under the Laws thereof, escaping into another, shall, in Consequence of any Law or Regulation therein, be discharged from such Service or Labour, but shall be delivered up on Claim of the Party to whom such Service or Labour may be due."

Since the supreme law of the land was that runaway slaves should be returned to their owners, the states had no reserve clause power to refuse to cooperate. While the Northern states cried foul, the slaveocrats pointed to the intent of the Framers such as Charles Cotesworth Pinckney, who told the state convention that "we have obtained a right to recover our slaves in whatever part of America they may take refuge ... a right we had not before." He was refer- ring to the extradition clause introduced by Pierce Butler of South Carolina and approved unanimously.[19]

The protection of slave property didn't end in 1865 when the 13th amendment abolished chattel slavery, except for prisoners, or the final colonization of the American West at the end of the 1800s. Protecting slavery and granting Congress power over land became the particular form in which the principle of rights for property were established as the primary objective of government.

Cracks in public support for slavery were already showing by the 1780s when a few states began to either ban or phase out slavery. Pennsylvania abolished slavery and Vermont petitioned to enter as the 14th state having abolished slavery in its constitution.

The design of Congress to protect slavery is still with us. Dis- trict-based elections for the House, as well as state and local governments, have given us the notorious gerrymandering problem, named for Framer Elbridge Gerry. It has also resulted in the overrep- resentation of small-population states with disproportionately white populations from the middle of the country in the Senate and the electoral college. These are not merely eighteenth-century flaws to be fixed or removed. They are symptoms of the very design of the Constitution to protect property, be it slaves or other forms, from the threat of democratic control.

A War of Plunder and General Leveling

As the Revolution wound down, class conflicts flared up over who would control the economy. For nearly two decades, from the begin- ning of the revolts we call the Revolution until the ratification of the Constitution on June 21, 1788, the outcome was uncertain. During the Confederation era there were at least twelve major rural rebellions involving at least 21,000 participants and another 25,000 sympathiz- ers between 1740 to 1799, the last four occurring after 1770.[20] This turbulence led historian Carl Becker to observe two struggles: "the first was the question of home rule; the second was the question, if we may so put it, of who should rule at home."[21]

Resistance to debt was spreading rapidly and threatened the political order. In the years before the Shays' Rebellion in Massachusetts in 1786 and 1787, debtors carried out scattered assaults on courts, tax collectors, landlords, merchants, and justices of the peace who enforced contracts and carried out requests by creditors to jail debtors for failing to pay.

The term Regulator was first coined between 1764 and 1771 in North Carolina by those with unresolved grievances against government for favoring propertied elites. Such unjust policies led the people out of doors to organize for the restoration of government to the people by regulating it with petitions, resolutions, assemblies, protests, and even armed insurrection. The North Carolina insurrection spread to the states of Virginia, South Carolina, New Jersey, New York, Pennsylvania, Maryland, Georgia, and Vermont during and immediately after the Revolution.[22]

The Massachusetts Shays' Regulator Rebellion quickly seized the attention of the elites. Beginning with a proposal for fairer taxation, the ignored farmers soon ramped up the pressure. On June 13, 1786, farmers blocked a Bristol County courthouse from meeting to collect debts which were made impossible to pay due to new high state taxes, raised to meet the state's debt obligations, and the lack of specie to pay it. Perhaps a quarter of the state's population was actively involved in the rebellion and half opposed the state's attempts to suppress it by refusing to join any proposed militia, among other actions.[23] Tax collectors and creditors were also attacked, shops broken into to redistribute hoarded food, and local courts shut down for debt cases. Confederation Secretary of War Henry Knox feared that it would become "a pretty formidable rebellion." Indeed, the Regulators went beyond armed insurgency and moved toward revolutionary struggle with an abortive plan to march on an armory in preparation to take over Boston and run the state from below.[24]

George Washington sought to crush the insurrection because "mankind left to themselves are unfit for their own government."[25] If the debtors' revolt was not quickly suppressed, he feared "the combustibles in every State, which a spark may set fire to" would lead to further tyranny of democracy and leveling.[26] His fear proved to be prescient. After the Regulators were militarily defeated, allies of the insurrection took over the state legislature in Spring 1787, pardoned most of the rebels, and passed debtor-friendly legislation.[27]

The small farmers who composed the Regulators operated in a mostly barter-based cashless economy in which an estimated 90 percent of value was produced without currency, and in which even small amounts of debt produced great anxiety and political strife that led farmers and laborers to organize against those they perceived as attempting to enslave them in debt.[28]

Debtor rebellions threatened all property by demanding laws to "stay" the onerous collection of private and public debts. Several states passed laws that closed local courts, imposed stays on the collection of debts, and allowed payment in kind with agricultural products, paper money, bills of credit, and other forms of paper to be used to pay private debts and taxes. Some states issued taxes that could only be paid with the paper money they issued, which were then used to retire some or most of their debt and pay their requisition to Congress.

These policies of economic democracy were not only considered friendly to debtors but an attempt by a tyrannical majority to "level" property by evading their obligations to repay their creditors the value which they borrowed.[29] Before the word "socialism" was invented, leveling was an "anarchic" threat by the people out of doors wielding political power with petitions, memorials, clubs, and guns that put rich and poor on the same level.[30]

The Regulators symbolized a threat to all kinds of property. The big slave owners could look into the future and see that efforts to abolish or limit slavery might not be contained to only a few states. Financial speculators, among them Abigail Adams, Robert Morris, and several other prominent Framers, who owned immense fortunes in state and Congressional war debts, similarly knew that the revolt of the debtors would not end with the Regulators.[31]

Similarly, large absentee landowners hoped to expel native peoples in order to sell their property for profit. But they were also keenly aware that their lands were eyed as an inexpensive option for states to repay their war debts on the cheap while offering a release valve for rebellious laborers. By the time the Constitution was sent out for ratification, between five million and seven million acres of land had been or were in the process of being sold to just two companies in exchange for public securities.[32] Ensuring an orderly sale of public lands would drive up their price, further concentrate its ownership in the hands of the few, and ensure a larger supply of laborers no longer able to afford cheap western land.

The elites were at risk as long as states had the power to interfere with debt contracts. Debtors were often creditors whose interests lay on both sides of the ledger, none more so than Robert Morris, who both lent and borrowed money as the Superintendent of Finance. These elites set aside their own personal interests to support a strong national economy backed up by the purse and sword of government. For investors who borrowed heavily to speculate on newly expropriated lands and unpaid government war debts, the gains from a strong national government outweighed short-term gains from debtor-friendly policies issued by the states.[33] For this reason, it's impossible to claim that creditors supported the Constitution and debtors opposed it.

None better demonstrate the complexity of elite support for the Constitution than Robert Morris and James Wilson, whose wealth didn't survive to benefit from Hamilton's national credit system. Both were left broke and spent some of their last years of life in debtor prison. Because Supreme Court Justice Wilson was pursued by creditors who wanted to jail him, he was even unable to ride the circuit for fear of being arrested for unpaid debts.[34]

As long as the elites attached their interests to a particular state's financial policies, they would be divided as a class and unlikely to coalesce around the financial policies of Congress. Debt repayment served to harness the interests of all elites to the new system and provided the material basis for a new class ideology. As a result, mercantilists secured a single state-backed financial system that could provide adequate investment capital to spark an industrial expansion pursued by Hamilton in the early 1790s. Slave-owning planters found new access to foreign markets threatened by conflicting state policies that taxed exports, imports, and shipping and made it diffi-

cult to sell more cotton and buy more slaves in the foreign markets of
the Caribbean and Europe.

Congress was given the exclusive authority to pay debts in I.8.1
while prohibiting the states to "make any Thing but gold and silver
Coin a Tender in Payment of Debts" (I.10.1). This did not abolish
paper money but established a national publicly backed financial
system based on it. To understand why the states were shorn of these
powers, it is essential to understand both sides of the story. As long as
the states retained the power to make different, conflicting policies, a
single national economy would be impossible.

Regulate Interstate Commerce, Ensure Contracts, and Make Foreign Trade Policy

Policies concerning debt cannot be understood in isolation from
policies protecting slavery, regulating commerce, ensuring contracts,
protecting patents, issuing currency, imposing taxes, establishing an
army, navy, and militia, and making treaties located in Articles I and
II. State interference in the economy that constrained, restricted, or
impeded trade between the states had gone too far. As a confederation, each state had almost complete sovereignty over finance, trade,
and other types of business in their state, although under Article VI
of the Articles of Confederation, Congress could prevent states from
imposing imposts that conflicted with treaties.[35]

In 1780, Hamilton called for a new national government with
concentrated powers.[36] Over the next few years, a few states sent
representatives in an effort to draft a state compact to restrict interference in trade while unsuccessfully attempting to expand Congress's
power over shipping and tariffs.

Southern slave states were split on these two issues. Some opposed
expanding shipping, fearing that Northern merchants would set
monopolistic prices that cut profits from their slave-produced cotton.
On the other hand, Virginia's tariffs on imported slaves helped it sell
more slaves, controlled the supply of labor, avoided overproduction,
and raised the price of tobacco sold to Britain which re-exported 85
percent of it at great profit. They also preferred "home-bred" slaves to
reduce the risk of slave rebellions they blamed on imported slaves.[37]

The tariffs may have shut off the slave trade but it also raised the price of tobacco and strengthened slavery.[38]

During the Revolution, and before the Convention, states passed various temporary price controls, penalized food hoarding, banned monopolies, and restricted certain kinds of businesses. The most famous of them all was the "non-importation" ban on British goods vigorously enforced by mechanics, which brought in hesitant merchant elites who proceeded to immediately sabotage it. These forms of economic democracy were imposed from below on elites who were forced to comply in the heat and ferment of revolutionary upheaval. In the Southern slave states, the non-importation pledge included slaves, which raised the price of tobacco, reduced the influence of British creditors, and increased the share of the profits from tobacco going to the planters. This helped convince planters to support independence, from which they could profit.[39]

To stop economic democracy in its tracks, I.8.3 granted Congress the power "to regulate Commerce," and I.10.1 gave Congress, by forbidding it to the states, the exclusive power to "coin Money," "emit Bills of Credit," use anything but gold and silver coin as money, and most importantly "pass any ... Law Impairing the Obligation of Contracts."[40] That is all in a single clause—perhaps the most important clause in the entire Constitution. Slipped in at the end of the Convention without debate by Gouverneur Morris's Committee on Style, "the contracts clause had the specific purpose of abolishing debtor-relief legislation."[41]

These powers were further complimented by I.8.4, which granted Congress the power "[t]o establish ... uniform Laws on the subject of Bankruptcies," and I.8.8 that created the power of copyrights, patents, and trademarks as the "exclusive Right to their respective Writings and Discoveries." To impose a single set of foreign trade policies, I.10.1 took from the states and gave to Congress the exclusive power to make treaties, I.10.2 stripped the states of the power to tax imports or exports, and I.10.3 prohibited any tax on shipping.

Transferring these powers to the Congress while prohibiting them to the states has long served several important functions. First, it stripped from the states the very tools of economic democracy created during the Revolution, where they were being implemented in response to the pressures and coercion of the organized majority.[42] Second, it allowed for a single set of laws passed by a single legislature more insulated from public pressure and capable of serving elite interests. Third, when combined with the IV.1 "Full Faith and Credit" clause, which required each state to recognize the official records of any other state, and the IV.2 "Privileges and Immunities" clause that required all states to extend the same privileges and rights of residents and businesses from any other state in their state, it granted the federal government an implied supremacy power, specifically enumerated in VI.2, to override any innovations by an upstart state to claw back some of its lost economic powers.[43]

Relocating these powers to Congress allowed for the centralization and concentration of power to set up, manage, and protect a single national economy rather than 13 different economies (14 if you count Congress and 15 if Vermont, which was independent at the time, is included) whose different and conflicting rules impeded the formation of the "consolidated empire" envisioned by Hamilton.

Single Set of Rules, Harmonious Elite

Nationalizing economic power solved the problem of an elite class fragmented by their allegiance to their states. The I.8.3 commerce and I.10.1 contract clauses, above all, established a single set of rules for the national economy that could be used to protect the economy from democracy. This encouraged the elites to overcome their own particular competing interests to form a single capitalist class, with shared interests in acquiring and protecting all types of property.[44]

Responding to the wide-ranging efforts of states to interfere with private business, these two clauses banned local and state governments from regulating, interfering with, banning, or redistributing private property. I.10.1 was a realization of Madison's insistence on "the necessity of harmony in the commercial regulations of the states."[45] Hamilton's public credit system similarly created a single national system of finance by taking these economic powers away from the states.[46]

One issue on which elites remained divided was on bankruptcy, which was still thought of in moral, rather than financial, terms. The first federal bankruptcy law passed in 1800 only after the embarrassing imprisonment of prominent elites such as James Duane, Framer Robert Morris, and Framer and Supreme Court Justice James Wilson for unpaid debts.[47] Bankruptcy was an issue complicated by the fact that many elite creditors were simultaneously debtors who had borrowed heavily for investment capital while also lending or extending credit in turn. Robert Morris, Wilson, Gouverneur Morris, James Monroe, and Madison were just a few who bankrolled their speculative land purchases with loans, often from European creditors. The 1800 law was repealed shortly after, in 1803, as were the next two such laws passed in 1841 and 1867. States remained kinder to debtors, allowing delays or reductions in collections, abolishing jail terms, decriminalizing debt, and passing replevin laws that allowed the recovery of seized assets.[48]

If the Constitution could reopen the credit faucet, these Framers and other elites would find another way out of their financial squeeze other than debtor's prison, foreclosure, and ruin.[49] Hamilton's financial plan would be the type of solution they were looking for: a stable government-backed credit system that was attractive to foreign investors as well.

Bankruptcy complimented the need for a dependable and stable credit system and the opportunity for failed investors to start over, and enshrined the role of a new system of federal bankruptcy courts to manage financial crisis as a tool for an effective national system of credit.

4

Congress:
Designed for Inefficiency

Although given the most powers of all the branches, Congress was organized to make it extremely difficult, if not impossible, to wield its powers of the pen, sword, purse, and oversight, unless approved by the privileged minority. This inefficiency was intentionally selective. The plethora of procedural obstructions and roadblocks were designed to prevent the concentration of power in the hands of one person, group, or party that could rapidly change law and policy in dramatic ways. Congress was designed to be *inefficient* when it serves the interests of the economic majority and *efficient* when it serves the interests of the elites.

The Partisanship Fallacy

This inefficiency of Congress is often attributed to partisan squabbles between the two dominant parties. For many reasons, this oft-repeated condemnation is unsatisfactory for explaining why Congress has become the weakest of the three branches and accomplishes so little.[1]

Congress was intentionally designed to be hampered when attempting to use its multiple powers in Article I. Gouverneur Morris advocated for inefficiency to prevent "Legislative usurpations" including "paper-money, largesses to the people, a remission of debts, and similar measures" that threaten propertied interests.[2]

Because of these constraints, the most substantial changes have occurred during times of crisis such as depression and war, and temporarily during the pandemic. When the organized economic majority becomes unruly during such times they pressure the elites to make concessions. The elites set aside internal bipartisan divisions to make minor reforms tempering the fire of insurrection and channeling the rebellious leadership into the system of politics in order to control, diffuse, and manage it. Once the threat passes, the elites are free to again reorganize and tip the balance of power back in their own favor.

Consider the three 2020–1 Covid-19 Relief Acts passed by Congress and signed by a president who had already been impeached once (but not removed). To understand the rapidity by which they passed with the support of both parties, all that is necessary is to follow the money. Of the $4 trillion total spending only a fraction went to extend unemployment, paid family and sick leave, and other long-sought-after policies; more than 50 percent went to businesses, only 20 percent went to individuals, families, and workers, and 16 percent spent on the public health crisis.[3] In short, the pandemic provided a favorable policy shift for elites who stood to profit handsomely from a vast expansion of the federal government into the economy. While this massive injection of spending lowered poverty by 45 percent relative to 2018 for every age, geographical, and racial group, even as unemployment rose, it would have been impossible at a time without a crisis.[4]

Using these temporary reforms during the pandemic as a statist model for action on other long-term crises, such as the climate catastrophe, demonstrates a misunderstanding of the way Congress is designed to work.

The Covid-19 Relief Acts may have been poverty-reducing social democratic policies but they were designed to be both temporary and unfunded. President Biden's attempt to make them permanent or fund them by increasing taxes on the rich and corporations ran into an array of insurmountable minority checks. They were passed to serve elite concerns about a shortage of cheap labor and to keep the economy running as millions were infected. A crisis without a mass uprising will not lead to long term reforms.

The constitutional obligation of government to protect property ensured that these reforms would not guarantee a basic income or health care and redistribute wealth to pay for it. Responding to the pandemic by addressing its underlying causes would have threatened the supremacy of property. As Charles Beard reminded us, "none of the powers conferred by the Constitution on Congress permits a direct attack on property."[5]

Tripartite

Today, celebrating the undemocratic design of the Constitution is a matter of pride for some like Republican Senator Mike Lee, who reminded us that "[w]e're not a democracy. ... The word 'democracy' appears nowhere in the Constitution, perhaps because our form of government is not a democracy. It's a constitutional republic." Lee could have well been channeling the Framers' warning about democracy.[6]

While a hint of Athenian people's democracy would be required to sell the Constitution to the state ratifying conventions, it was the Roman tripartite system that would hold Athens in check. Despite its numerous enumerated and implied powers, Congress is constrained from using them by innumerable minority checks of the Roman tripartite system of separated power.

One essential characteristic of the Roman/Whig tripartite system is the sharing of power between the common people in the Tribune and the elites in the Senate. In the Constitution this corresponds to the direct election of the House of Representatives, which is checked by the originally unelected Senate, both forming a bicameral legislature. Just as the Roman Senate of the landed elites could veto anything passed by the popularly elected Tribunes, the US Senate was designed to be the brake on the directly elected House, what Brutus called "a f[a]int spark of democracy."[7] The bicameral structure was intended not to share representation of the elites and the majority but to check the majority from wielding power.[8]

Even Rome proved to be too democratic for the Framers. Fearing a repeat of the Senate picking populists like Gaius Marius and his nephew Julius Caesar as chief executive pro-consuls, the even less democratic electoral college and not Congress picks the President and Vice President. "Elected" without term limits, the President was originally modeled after a king. When one considers the presidential veto (eg, a "returned" bill) found in 1.7.2, our legislative system is more tricameral than bicameral with the president serving as a house of one. If we also throw in the federal courts' implied power of judicial review amplified by the Article VI "supremacy clause," we might even say we have a quadracameral legislative system.[9]

Jettisoning Athens

After the Revolution, conservative "revolutionary" leaders were caught in a bind. They attempted to overthrow the British and impose home rule for themselves while struggling to prevent its replacement by a democracy and assert their right to rule at home.[10] The answer, embracing Rome, meant jettisoning Athens. The relatively more democratic organization of the states and local governments that were a product of the Revolution had to be abandoned.

Emerging around 1774, the unicameral Provincial Congresses were pseudo parliamentary systems that combined the functions of the legislatures and executive, as they were governed by committees that enforced non-importation, oversaw militias, etc. These Congresses joined together into the Continental Association in order to coordinate the revolt. If this sounds familiar, it was basically the same structure later formalized in the Articles of Confederation. These soon transformed into the states that were much more democratic and accessible than the system that would be created by the Constitution. The effect of this multiple array of state systems made a single unified capitalist economy virtually impossible. During the Revolution, eleven states revised their constitutions, four of which became even more democratic by removing assorted checks such as a senate and executive veto. These systems included far fewer checks and balances. "The colonies were becoming democracies characterized by local sovereignty. The Whig word for this was anarchy," historian Jackson Turner Main noted.

The Framers feared that the economic majority could more easily control a unicameral legislature such as Congress, Georgia, and Pennsylvania. Unicameral legislatures were frequently denounced as a threat to property. Annual elections for unicameral legislatures were often followed by the rapid passage of new laws favoring the interests of subsistence farmers and mechanics. A unicameral system was an unchecked legislature that could change the law quickly, especially when there was rapid turnover of government due to short terms and no veto power for the governor.

Pennsylvania was the poster child of what needed to be dismantled at all costs. The Bill of Rights in its 1776 constitution included a right to "reform, alter, or abolish government." There was a plural executive of a twelve-member Supreme Executive Council whose president was elected by both the Council and Assembly and did not have a veto. The Pennsylvania legislature also held open sessions and published a record of its proceedings. The elected Council of Censors was responsible for making sure the laws conformed with the Constitution and could make amendments.

Anti-Federalist Pennsylvania Supreme Court Justice George Bryan spoke in favor of his state's unicameral legislature as the best model for a legislature because a unicameral legislature with one-year terms does not cause delays in changing the make-up of the house and passing legislation. "This tie of responsibility will obviate all the dangers apprehended from a single legislature, and will best secure the rights of the people."[11]

What Bryan trumpeted is what the Framers saw as a great danger. The quick change Bryan advocated would put the economic elite at risk of being quickly overwhelmed on every vote. They might get their laws passed in one legislative session only to be booted out of office and the law repealed or replaced the following year, which is exactly what happened in Pennsylvania.

The outcome of democratization was almost immediate. Many of the features of the revised state constitutions were the outcomes of demands made by self-organized revolutionary committees controlled by small farmers, laborers, and mechanics. The lowering or removal of property requirements meant that many small farmers and mechanics could now vote.

In New York, they used the secret ballot to elect more populist candidates such as George Clinton and support policies such as higher taxes on the rich, limits on profits, price and wage controls, prohibitions on flour exports, and confiscation and sale of Loyalist estates.[12] The last demand essentially served as a reversal of the expropriation of native lands by a few families who owned vast estates. The revolutionary state constitutions were products of the class conflicts happening during the Revolution, and the people out of doors were winning.

These constitutions exhibited an array of experiments in democratization. Virginia was the first to enumerate three distinct branches governed by the principle of "separate and distinct." Four states lowered or had no property requirements to vote, along with Vermont which had none and gave the franchise to every adult male. Nevertheless, the existing property requirements likely prevented between a quarter and a half of the adult male population from voting. Six states had secret voting by ballot.[13]

The make-up of both houses of the legislature varied along a continuum of democratization as well. Twelve states elected their lower house every year or more frequently (six months in Connecticut and Rhode Island and two-year terms in South Carolina). Three states had no senate, and six had one-year terms or were on a rotation, except for Maryland. There were proposals to abolish the senate in three of the states that had one.[14] State senates were modeled after the British House of Lords that was replicated in all the colonies except Pennsylvania as the executive council that could veto the governor and lower house.

State legislatures mostly shared power with a much weaker executive in most of the states. New Hampshire had no executive, New York was the first to have a directly elected governor, Pennsylvania had a plural executive council, and ten states appointed their governor. All but two states limited their governors to one-year terms and only three states provided the governor with a veto (New York allowed it for only one year), which could be overridden. Massachusetts gave the governor (who was popularly elected) a veto. Every state except New Hampshire and New York had an executive council to advise and constrain the governor, a responsibility transferred to the Senate in the Constitution. Some states took away the governor's appointment power and limited appointees to specific short terms, half gave them the power to impose trade embargoes, six allowed them to issue pardons, and two could issue reprieves.

There was not much of a judicial branch to contend with. New Jersey didn't set up a separate judicial branch, and nine states allowed for the election of local judges either by local voters or by the state legislatures. Judges, sheriffs, and other officials most commonly served one-year terms. New York had a "council of revision," composed of the governor, chancellor, and Supreme Court judges, which determined the constitutionality of new bills, although it could be overruled by a two-thirds majority of both houses. Seven states had a bill of rights, six had public education, and three abolished debtor's prison.[15]

Perhaps the most democratic "state" was Vermont, which was not admitted as a state until after ratification of the Constitution, followed by Georgia, whose constitution was likely written by ordinary men about whom little is known. While it still excluded slaves, native peoples, and women, Georgia briefly banned slavery in the early 1700s.

The states were hardly bastions of "agrarian democracy" after 1776. After all, local and state self-government for some white men was based on slave labor, the patriarchal enslavement of women in the home-based economy, and settler colonialism that carried out genocidal extermination of native peoples in order to seize the land that made subsistence farming possible.[16]

However more or less democratic the states were, it was a bridge too far for the elites. Those like John Adams bemoaned the removal of barriers to voting in 1776 warning that once voting is expanded:

There will be no End of it. New Claims will arise. Women will demand a Vote. Lads from 12 to 21 will think their Rights not enough attended to, and every Man, who has not a Farthing, will demand an equal Voice with any other in all Acts of State. It tends to confound and destroy all Distinctions, and prostrate all Ranks, to one common Levell. I am &c.[17]

Checks and balances, however, were weakened only during the revolutionary upheaval. Many of these revolutionary-era constitutions were overthrown after ratification and rewritten to strip out their most democratic features.[18] Ratification of the US Constitution gave momentum to the elites in nearly all the states to revise their state constitutions, reversing the trend toward democratization of either government or the economy.[19]

Pennsylvania's constitution came under intense attack by the nationalists. The 1776 constitution was replaced by the 1790 constitution written behind closed doors and supported by some co-opted Anti-Federalist leaders. It was likely not put to a popular vote because of unpopular features, including an executive veto, appointed rather than elected local judges, and replacing a unicameral with a bicameral legislature.[20]

Designed for Inefficiency

Congress was simultaneously given many powers previously reserved to the states under the Articles while constraining it from using them for any purpose other than those which served the interests of elites. To understand this apparent paradox it is necessary to explore how its organizational logic imperils democratic control of government and the economy. In other words, Congress was given the keys but never shown the door.

Consider property. Congress was given no direct power to create, abolish, or affect property in any way, slavery or otherwise. It was not given the power to set up publicly owned companies other than the post office. It was given no authority to charter new private corporations, although Hamilton made the case that it possessed implied power to do so in the 1791 bank debate.[21]

The power of Congress to tax was arranged so that the impact could only be direct and uniform, not proportional to the value of the property.[22] Organized as a bicameral legislature, Congress's power could not be exercised without the approval of the Senate and the signature or veto override of the President. The different size and term lengths of each house and the delegation of appointment and ratification powers to the Senate ensured that Congress would only act when safely in the interests of property. Engineered for inefficiency, delay, obstruction, and prevention, Congress could get very little done concerning the economy until the 1930s Depression. The

New Deal was only possible because Democrats used its near super-majority control of both houses to overcome the roadblocks and impediments to empower the President to respond to class conflict in the streets and factories.

Afraid that a unicameral legislature would act too quickly while under the spell of a charismatic president, such as a future Franklin D. Roosevelt, the Framers constrained Congress from the outside as well. They required that for all but treaties, confirming appointments, and removing an impeached official, both houses were required not only to pass bills in identical language before they could become law, but that the President would also wield the veto (or pocket veto).

After the People's Party managed to have four of its members appointed or elected to the Senate in the late nineteenth century, efforts to change the Senate gained momentum.[23] The vote on a resolution to call a new constitutional convention to change this feature failed by one vote in the Senate, leading instead to the more limited 17th amendment of 1913 which made the Senate directly elected.

The direct election of the House, in contrast, is frequently offered as evidence for the democratic intentions of the Framers. The number of members was apportioned by counting toward the total population three-fifths of each slave, thereby vastly inflating the power of the big slave states in both the House and the election of the President and Vice President until the 13th amendment abolished slavery for all but prisoners in 1865. But just as importantly, each House member serves two-year terms, while senators serve six years, with a third up for re-election every two years. Establishing the houses with staggered terms, not only with one another but also with the President and Vice President, and without term limits, serves as yet another minority check.

Each house was delegated some exclusive powers not shared by the other. The Senate was intentionally aligned with the prerogatives of the executive, as we will see in Chapter 5, by sharing some powers with the President. It exclusively confirms nominations to fill an unspecified number of executive and judicial vacancies, the candidates for which have no criteria or minimum qualification to serve other than the Article III mandate that it shall be "during good behavior." The Senate's authority to ratify treaties with a two-thirds supermajority also ensured close alignment with the President's foreign policy.[24] By contrast, the only power exclusive granted to the House is the slim responsibility that "all bills for raising revenue shall originate in the House of Representatives" (I.7.1), which still requires Senate approval and the President's signature.

To slow down and impede rapid change, all other powers have to be approved twice, some requiring the nearly impossible two-thirds supermajority threshold. Among these are the I.7.3 power to override presidential vetoes, which several Framers didn't want to allow. Even this power to override is tempered by language that grants the President a "pocket veto" in I.7.2 when the Congress is out of session. Because II.3 allows the President to adjourn Congress, it is possible to not only prevent a veto override but even rule unilaterally by fiat without Congress, as dictators are apt to do. A vetoed bill can only be overridden by passing both houses in the same session.

The complex two-step impeachment process only requires a simple majority in the House, but rises to two-thirds in the Senate to remove the President, federal judges, and other appointed and elected officers. This dual requirement has proven an effective procedural neutering of Congress's most import check on the President, as evidenced by the impeachment of only two presidents (prior to President Trump being impeached twice) in the first two centuries. In all four instances the presidents survived removal in the Senate and were not banned from elected office for life. Because it has proven nearly impossible to use, the impeachment process may have been designed less as a check on the President than on Congress.

Congressional power is further impeded by the complex requirements to amend the Constitution which is the focus of Chapter 9. Only 27 out of the more than 11,000 attempts have succeeded, most of which sought to overcome the nearly impossible hurdle of achieving two-thirds support in both houses before proceeding to the states for three-quarters approval.[25] While Congress may initiate the process, few have succeeded. After the first ten were ratified in 1791, only five more were added by 1870, nearly 80 years later.

Only twelve more amendments were added in the next 122 years, with the last in 1992, three decades ago. Article V contains the only explicitly forbidden amendment, prohibiting "no State, without its Consent, shall be deprived of its equal Suffrage in the Senate." By comparison, most countries of the world make many more amendments or even thoroughly revise or replace their constitution more frequently than the USA. The nearly insurmountable threshold to change the Constitution makes the amendment process functionally inoperable.

Most glaringly absent from the law- or amendment-making process is that the voters have been excluded from any role whatsoever. When added to the still steep property requirements to vote or run for office which were left up to the states to determine, as we will see in Chapter 9 the voters played almost no part in bringing the Constitution into effect. Rome triumphed over Athens.[26]

A Temperate and Respectable Body of Citizens

The Senate was designed as a brake on democracy in three ways. First, because all bills must pass both houses, and there are several requirements for a supermajority, the Senate serves as a check on the House.[27] Second, it gave each state two senators who were not directly elected. Third, the equal number of senators inflated the influence of small-population states with few free whites and many slaves while deflating the influence of large-population states with few or no slaves.[28] While altered by the 17th amendment, the inequality of representation has been preserved so that it continues to distort the influence of more diverse and populous states relative to overwhelmingly white small-population states.[29] For example, in the 68 years between the 65th and 99th Congress, the period between Presidents Woodrow Wilson and Ronald Reagan, there were seven instances when the party with a majority in the Senate was elected from states whose total population added up to less than a majority of the US population.[30]

Gouverneur Morris suggested that senators serve for life to preserve "stability" and "private property" again the "democratic branches." The Framers debated whether to set the term for nine years or eight years before settling on six.[31] Even the shorter six-year terms ensured the Senate would function as an instrument of Whiggism, a more powerful variation of the state senates designed in the interests of the ruling elite.[32]

In *Federalist #63*, Madison praised the role of a Senate consisting of "temperate and respectable body of citizens" that would serve "as a defense to the people against their own temporary errors and delusions" when they "call for measures which they themselves will afterwards be the most ready to lament and condemn."[33] The Senate, Madison insisted, was a minority check designed "to protect the minority of the opulent against the majority."[34]

Size Matters

While senators represented their entire state, House members serve in districts redrawn every decade depending on the number of "the People of the several States," as measured by the census (I.2.3). To dilute the influence of the directly elected House, Hamilton and Madison supported large districts for keeping the population divided into varying "factions" such as classes, parties, and interest groups.

Electing members of the House from districts within each separate state would further divide the majority, giving an advantage to the elites. The size of the country and district, Gouverneur Morris assured the Convention, would mean that "the schemes of the Rich will be favored by the extent of the Country. The people in such distant parts can not communicate & act in concert," a sentiment echoed by Hamilton and Madison.[35] The Anti-Federalist minority of the Pennsylvania state ratifying convention recognized this, warning that large districts would result in the tyranny of the few.[36]

Although we now exclusively use single-member, winner-take-all district elections for the House, some Federalists actually preferred "at-large" elections, in which the top vote-getters represent a state, and opposed district-based elections as violating the Constitution. The following phrase was originally thought to result in at-large rather than district-based elections: "The Times, Places and Manner of holding Elections for Senators and Representatives, shall be prescribed in each State by the Legislature thereof; but the Congress may at any time by Law make or alter such Regulations, except as to the Places of Chusing Senators" (I.4.1).[37]

Gouverneur Morris proposed property requirements for voting and serving in office because he thought that power over property should only be held by those who own it, otherwise the system would fall under the "savage State" of the propertyless.[38] Allowing the rules for voting and elections to be "prescribed in each State by the Legislature thereof," the Framers left this unpopular measure out of the Constitution and adopted the existing state property requirements. This cleverly continued to exclude a large portion of the adult white male population with too little property to qualify, along with nearly all of the free black male and female population, from not only voting but also holding office.[39]

Checking Change

Imagine for a moment that a new movement of the supermajority formed a new party led by a charismatic and prominent leader. The party sweeps the House in a midterm election and wins a healthy majority of about a third of the Senate seats on the ballot. However, it does not yet control the Senate so it cannot get anything passed because the two dominant parties team up to block it. There are two options available to such an upstart party. It can fight on in the next two election cycles over the next four years to win the majority of the Senate while holding onto its House majority twice. A second possibility is to heavily compromise the very principles which made it so popular by collaborating with one of the two dominant parties to "get things done."

If the upstart party chooses to fight and hold on to its principles every two years it needs to hold on to its majority in the House and pick up more than half of the third of the Senate up for re-election while also trying to win the presidency. In failing to achieve all three, it will still find its initiatives relatively easily blocked in one or the other house or by a presidential veto. If it controls the House and the presidency but not the Senate it has to start all over again at the next midterm election, by which time the President likely has lost popularity because the party cannot pass anything in the Senate. The new President must now focus on winning re-election, along with keeping the party's majority in the House and continuing to try to win a majority in the Senate. The Faustian bargain remains. Does the new party begin compromising so that it has something it can deliver to its loyal voters, or stick to its principles and appear powerless, thereby losing voters?

The party finally captures the Senate while holding on to the House but loses the presidency. Without the presidency its every move is blocked by one of the other party's President vetoing its bills knowing that the Congress does not have a two-thirds supermajority to override it.[40] And even then, there is no way to prevent one or more members of the upstart party from bolting to join one of the two main parties to deny them a majority or supermajority.

This thought experiment demonstrates that the Senate is only one of the array of minority checks that impede and prevent Congress from wielding its power.[41] Fragmenting Congress into two houses and staggering their terms with each other and the President each serve as a brake slowing down change so as to give opponents time to dilute, defeat, deflate, redirect, suppress, or co-opt the effort or movement making demands. We can also add that each house makes its own rules, sets up its own powerful committees, gives absolute power to the majority party, allows district-based winner-takes-all elections to the House, has the unequal representation in the Senate, and a single senator can "veto" a bill using the filibuster. This very design ensures that rather than wielding "All legislative Powers" (I.1), Congress is where bills go to die. Bills expressing majority demands must run the gauntlet of minority checks, and overcome their obstructions, to ever see the light of day in both houses, which few do. Those that somehow survive are so diluted by compromise until they do little of what those who first introduced the bill intended them to do or are vetoed by the President.

Attempting to use the rules of the system to bring about fundamental systemic change is a proven futile strategy unless those changes serve the interests of property.

Give Me Compromise or Give Me Death

Today we hear about Democrats and Republicans working for "bipartisan compromise" to "get things done." These promises implicitly acknowledge that Congress was designed with roadblocks and impediments to block change rather than facilitate it.[42]

The imperative to compromise is not only endemic to national politics. It is also known as the "getting to yes" strategy used in legal negotiations and "interest-based" or "non-zero-sum game" strategies unsuccessfully used by unions in collective bargaining with employers. Despite the popularity of compromise, in the preponderance of cases only one side is truly compromising—the side that wants change. Those willing to compromise are effectively bargaining with themselves.

The focus on compromise is misplaced and misleading. The numerous roadblocks and impediments woven into the Constitution already impose an obligation on those who want change to give something up in order to get something.[43] When those with the upper hand call on their weaker adversary to compromise, they are holding the process for ransom. They are saying, "give me what I want or I will use my innumerable minority vetoes to bleed your bill to death." The musical *Hamilton* got it right this once: "The art of the compromise | Hold your nose and close your eyes | We want our leaders to save the day | But we don't get a say in what they trade away | We dream of a brand new start | But we dream in the dark for the most part | Dark as a tomb where it happens."

Compromise is presented as the *antidote* to the disease of partisanship in our two-party duopoly, when really it is a *symptom* of the disease. Even this is misleading, however, because that implies that the system is sick and would work as intended if it were cured of its disorder. But the Constitution is working just as it was designed to do, and that is the problem.

5

Congress: Power of the Purse

He that hath the longest purse will certainly have the longest sword.

Simon Clement[1]

The power to tax was a critically important element of the Framers' constitutional strategy. As Alexander Hamilton pointed out in 1780, "without certain revenues, a government can have no power; that power, which holds the purse strings absolutely, must rule."[2] Taxation provided the necessary revenue to repay the debt, establish a public credit system, and issue a new currency that would provide the capital to set up, run, and protect a new national capitalist economy. For this reason Hamilton celebrated that "the proper funding of the present debt, will render it a national blessing."[3]

That Power which Holds the Purse Strings Must Rule

"No taxation without representation" is one of the most recognizable rallying cries of the Revolution. From the youngest age we are told that the Revolution was sparked by oppressive taxes.

What we are not told is that *after* the Revolution, Congress and some state governments imposed new oppressive taxes to raise the money to repay their creditors. These efforts to tax sparked both the Regulator Rebellion from below and the elite counter-revolution from above. The desire to tax brought about the Convention which created a national government newly empowered to collect the necessary taxes to fund a powerful government and economy.

The primarily self-sufficient small farming population, which mostly lived outside the cash economy, didn't expect government to do much more than made possible by the revenue collected by taxing exports or imports from other states. That all changed when Massachusetts imposed draconian taxes used to pay its requisition to Congress and repay creditors sparking the Shays' Rebellion. These taxes were immediately denounced as a betrayal of the Revolution by putting the population back under "aristocracy" and into "slavery," despite the obvious hypocrisy of half a million actual people held in bondage as slaves.[4] The majority of common people, many of whom were the original creditors having had taken paper IOUs in exchange for their good and services, were now expected to suffer a second time. Their taxes were being used to repay speculators the face value with interest of war debts they bought at steep discounts.

Taxes also sparked the elite counter-revolution. Congress directed the states to assess the value of their land so it could calculate their share of the revenue. However, these requisitions proved to be both extremely difficult to estimate and unpopular to collect. The states had discretion to collect taxes in any way they could, resulting in taxes on land, people (or "poll" tax), exports, imports, slaves, and other things of value. When the Revolution ended, most states paid a steadily declining share of their requisitions or none at all, while some were paying most or all of their debts directly. Unable to pay its bills and in default with France in 1785, Congress and a number of states began reissuing paper money. Paper money relieved the coin shortage, expanded the currency supply, and could be used to pay state taxes which were used to retire outstanding debts. Pennsylvania's state legislature even passed a law in 1780 refusing to repay a debt at face value because it would amount to paying the debt twice.[5]

While farmers demanded paper money so that they could borrow from state land banks, such plans did not reappear except in Pennsylvania. Because not all the currencies declined in value, paper money was not automatically inflationary as is commonly claimed.[6] Paper money lost value where merchants refused to accept it as legal tender in protest. The value of paper money remained stable in some states such as Pennsylvania.[7]

Because Congress lacked the power to tax directly, several efforts were made to give it the power to impose tariffs on imports which failed in 1781 and again narrowly in 1783 when New York approved it with conditions which were rejected by Congress. Its defeat, according to historian Jackson Turner Main, was due to opposition by those "who feared a consolidation of power in the central government."[8] Giving Congress the power to tax land, slaves, income, and wealth was seen as a form of tyranny leading to standing armies, emoluments for the rich, destruction of the states, and expensive wars.

Ironically, New York was one of the few states that paid its requisition in full during the Confederation. It did that by taxing most imports, a power it would not easily let go. Virginia and a few other states were also able to repay their debts by a combination of tax revenue and paper money. The ongoing negotiations to solve the problem of internal tariffs also disproved nationalists' claims that the Confederation had failed and needed to be replaced.[9] New York proposed no longer taxing goods for re-export if they remained packed. New Jersey and Pennsylvania agreed to concurrent jurisdiction over Delaware River traffic as did Virginia and Maryland over the Potomac and Chesapeake Bay. These efforts weakened one of the major arguments for a new Constitution.[10]

The struggle over taxation led the Framers to design a Constitution which empowered the elites to govern by making the economic majority pay for it. Limiting revenue to direct taxes, such as the tariff, was a minority check built into the Constitution by imposing "a limitation on the power of majorities to decide how to tax." Direct taxes shielded elites from the burden while passing it on to the consumer in higher prices.[11]

Joined at the Hip: Slavery and Taxes

The relationship between the tariff and slavery did not begin at the Convention. The debate over how to apportion the states' tax burden led to the passage of a real estate apportionment clause in 1777. This became Article XI, allowing government funds to "be defrayed out of a common Treasury, which shall be supplied by the several Colonies in Proportion to the Number of Inhabitants of every Age, Sex and Quality, except Indians not paying Taxes, in each Colony, a true Account of which, distinguishing the white Inhabitants." The words

"who are not slaves" following the second use of the word "Inhabitants" were removed and replaced with the modifier "white" to make
it clear that slaves would not be counted in the system of taxation.

Despite this language, the states disagreed about whether to count
the value of slaves. The Southern states preferred assessing real estate
values, as long as their slaves were not included, because their lands
were less valuable than in the North. Northern delegates wouldn't go
along with it for obvious reasons. Rather than tax property or heads
(i.e., a poll tax) it adopted what became Article VII in 1781 so that
"[e]ach Colony may assess or lay such Imposts or Duties as it thinks
proper." No federal impost was ever implemented and states were
unable to assess the value of property or impose a poll tax, relying
instead on a combination of assorted taxes, paper money, and tariffs
to meet their requisitions from Congress. Apportionment was the
device for preventing a national tax on the population while instead
favoring one on foreigners. As Einhorn noted, "Congress ... could
levy the impost without talking about slavery."[12]

The nationalists' project gained momentum once they got to
Philadelphia. The power to tax was extended to Congress in I.8.1,
which reads the "Power To lay and collect Taxes, Duties, Imposts
and Excises, to pay the Debts." It is further limited by forbidding to
Congress, "No Capitation, or other direct, Tax shall be laid unless in
Proportion to the Census or Enumeration herein before directed to
be taken" (I.9.4). These clauses transferred the power to tax exclusively from the states to the Congress. Over the next century, a system
of dual jurisdiction over taxation emerged in which state and local
governments taxed houses and land while the federal government
was effectively limited to the impost on specific imports rather than
all imports.[13]

During the debate over whether to allow Congress to impose taxes
on land and people, the disagreement over whether to count slaves
as people, or literally as an equivalent of non-human farm animals,
was resolved by the infamous "compromise." In exchange for a direct
tax on people rather than property, the slave states were obligated
to accept poll taxes that included their slaves but only by counting

them as the notorious "three fifths of all other Persons" (I.2.3), "other Persons" serving as a weasel word for slave.

The infamous three-fifths clause in the Constitution originated in Congress's 1783 request that the states approve an amendment to the Article's reading: "the whole number of white and other free citizens and inhabitants, of every age, sex and condition, including those bound to servitude for a term of years, and three-fifths of all other persons not comprehended in the foregoing description, except Indians, not paying taxes, in each state."[14]

The three-fifths clause was hardly a "compromise," as historians tend to call it, since it favored only one side. As historian Robin Einhorn explains, "at the very moment of its birth, the United States was already almost 'half slave and half free.'"[15] The big slave states inflated their political representation by counting three-fifths of their slaves, and only temporary direct taxes were ever implemented for the next 74 years. Because no taxes were ever imposed on slaves, the slaveocracy got the better end of the deal, receiving more federal revenue, possessing the same number of Senate seats regardless of population, adding seats in the House, and exaggerating their electoral college votes.

The tariff became the only form of taxation because it allowed the Confederation Congress and later the federal Congress to entirely avoid the issue of taxing slaves and all other forms of wealth and income.[16] Since it wasn't apportioned based on population or value assessments, but instead imposed on imports, it entirely bypassed the need to count slaves. This was a considerable issue, as we saw earlier, primarily because only about 4 percent of the population in Northern states were slaves while 37 percent of the population in Southern states were slaves. The tax debate had been about whether to count the *number* or the *value* of slaves. In the end, it did neither. According to historian David Waldstreicher, "in the new American order, taxation with representation and slavery were joined at the hip."[17]

Land Taxes: Redistribution from Below
Tax policy is not about funding a neutral government but about how it can most effectively manage class conflict and redistribute wealth

upwards. By basing taxation on population, the Framers transferred the costs to those who would be controlled and managed. The inevitable outcome of the direct apportionment criteria would be that states with a larger population would pay a higher proportion of federal taxes. This restriction created immediate resistance.

In 1782, Superintendent of Finance Robert Morris had proposed a poll tax based on the number of people as well as on land, houses, farms, tools, liquor, and adult male slaves ages 16 to 60. Without a sense of irony, Morris, who was a large absentee landowner and slave owner himself, proposed a land tax as an "agrarian law" from above that "would relieve the indigent and aggrandize the State by bringing property into the hands of those who would use it for the Benefit of Society."[18] He preferred a tax on landed estates in order to minimize taxes on the population that he feared would spark an insurrection.

Morris also proposed a poll tax of $1 on all freemen and male slaves and an eighth of a dollar on distilled liquor.[19] He appointed federal agents to assess the value of taxable property and collect the taxes in the states, hiring Hamilton as one of his New York agents. His extremely unpopular tax proposals likely contributed to the defeat of his plan and weakened him as Superintendent.[20] Morris was not alone. During the debate about how to generate revenues to meet the demands of the mutinous Newburgh officers for an immediately payment in 1783, Framer John Rutledge suggested a poll and land tax and Hamilton added a house and window tax.[21] Every state already had some type of land tax, some based on assessed value and others on a flat rate per acre, which were unpopular and difficult to collect.[22]

Morris's tax plan had a second objective "of encouraging settlements and population."[23] He also foresaw funding a muscular national government with a military and bureaucracy with revenue from tolls on roads and turnpikes and, without any apparent irony, a stamp act.[24] The attempt to collect the taxes provided futile, Hamilton informed him, because elected tax assessors, collectors, and county treasurers in New York refused to collect the unpopular taxes. Morris' tax policies were made stillborn by class conflict.[25]

Although land sold at low prices, small farmers lacked the cash or credit to buy it. Rather than redistributing land, Morris' plan would drive up the value of the vast supply of unsold lands and further concentrate them in the hands of the elites. Auctioning government lands and increasing taxes to generate revenue to repay bondholders would make them richer by redistributing wealth from below in two ways.[26]

As prices for land rose, fewer and fewer would have the cash to buy, further accelerating the sale of land as a speculative investment. And as small subsistence farmers would be hit with unpayable higher state and new federal taxes, they would be increasingly forced off their lands and into waged labor. The tax plan would simultaneously expand the vast holdings of elites like Morris, who was co-owner of a land company with vast western holdings, while providing them with a larger pool of cheap exploitable waged labor.

The consequences of Morris's tax plan didn't escape Massachusetts Supreme Court Justice William Whiting, who warned that they would transfer property from the "Labourous Members of Society" to "the non-productive class," who were "useless and idl who [were] living on the common stock."[27]

The Framers sought to block states from setting up more land banks from which farmers could borrow while establishing a government-backed private credit system such as the one Morris had been promoting since the formation of his own Pennsylvania bank. In 1782, Morris told Congress that his plan for a land tax was about more than "the establishment of permanent revenues." Rather, it was intended to raise the revenue to "do justice" to the creditors while unifying the elites and the states into a national system. "A public debt, supported by public revenue, will prove the strongest cement to keep our Confederacy together," he wrote.[28]

The type of "justice" Morris was advocating was allowing creditors to earn their expected return on money lent to the states and Congress to fight the Revolution. It didn't matter that most creditors bought the debts for pennies on the dollar and now demanded to be paid for the full amount printed on the paper.

Morris's land auction never took place due to machinations by the land speculation companies tied to states competing for a share of the western lands until a settlement was reached in 1787. It was ultimately settled by the Constitution in III.2.1, which enumerated supremacy power over "Controversies ... between Citizens of the same State claiming Lands under Grants of different States," and was later expanded by the 11th amendment.[29]

The Trouble with Direct Taxes

The states and Confederation Congress found it extremely difficult to calculate and collect direct taxes on land. According to historian Gary Nash, eighteenth-century tax lists "grossly underestimated" the wealth of the rich and did not tax many types of wealth held by the urban elites such as mortgages, bonds, debts, ships, and rural lands.[30] The census recorded the number of slaves but did not report the value of property, acres, or houses owned until 1850.

Requiring that taxes be direct only created a minority check that doomed the first effort to collect them. After becoming Secretary of the Treasury in 1789, Hamilton included a tax on land sales in his public credit plan to supplement tariff revenue. His May 1790 proposed tax bill included a very similar list of taxes, such as on rooms in a house, later dropped in favor of an excise tax on whiskey.[31] After the first bill was voted down in the House, Hamilton issued a report on public credit in December 1790 in which he preferred excise taxes over tariffs (also known as the impost), reversing his support for them in *Federalist #12*. In the midst of declining tariff revenues due to British attacks on US ships, the later 1794 Revenue Act further expanded new taxes to stamps, stock transfers, and increased tonnage duties as well as excises on snuff, sugar, and carriages.[32]

The proposed excise tax on whiskey was particularly explosive. It sparked protests known as the Pennsylvania Whiskey Rebellion, beginning in 1791, that spread across five states by 1794.[33] Ultimately, Hamilton lost when the centerpiece of the tax system to fund his financial plan was defeated in Congress. Over these decades, efforts to impose excise taxes on an array of items were tried and revoked a few times. The earlier excise taxes and system to collect them were abolished in 1801, only to be brought back between 1813 and 1817 to pay the costs of the War of 1812. These were proposed by Madison's Secretary of the Treasury Albert Gallatin, who was one of the highest-profile participants in the Whiskey Rebellion. Now channeling his adversary Hamilton, Gallatin's successful 1813 tax plan included not only a tax on whiskey and tariffs but also licenses for sellers of imported liquor, excise on sugar, a carriage tax, a direct tax on land, houses, and slaves, and a stamp tax on legal documents like that the British imposed which helped spark the Revolution.

Despite his lifelong efforts, Hamilton's financial plan proved to be a partial victory. He got the publicly backed credit system but not the entire tax system he needed to fund it. Congress had the power of the purse but that purse was still mostly empty.

For example, a 1798 direct tax to collect $2 million from the states based on the value of homes, slaves, and land was oddly modeled after the earlier requisition system of the Confederation Congress. The results were eye opening. Only 2 percent of homes accounted for 25 percent of all value, with the top 10 percent comprising half of home values.[34] The effort to directly tax tangible property faced tax evasion and resistance by elites and the 1798–99 Fries Rebellion which killed the tax. Despite the states making assessments of property values, President Jefferson had Congress repeal the tax in 1802. By 1808, 6 percent of the taxes were still uncollected.

After this tumultuous period, Congress relied almost exclusively on the regressive tariff as the only source of tax revenue until the Civil War. In 1895, property ascended to new heights in the constitutional system when the income tax was thrown out in the *Pollock v. Farmers' Loan and Trust Company*, when the Supreme Court found the income tax was a direct tax which required that it be apportioned by population. That same year the Supreme Court also exempted manufacturing from anti-trust law in *United States v. E.C. Knight Company* and upheld the use of a court injunction to break the Pullman strike in *In re Debs*. It took the 1913 16th amendment to allow that "The Congress shall have power to lay and collect taxes on incomes, from whatever source derived, without apportionment among the several States, and without regard to any census or enumeration." But this was made moot by the rule of property, which didn't merely exempt itself from the Constitution but maintained its position outside, above, and shielded by it.

Tax-Free Elites

While it is well known that the three-fifths rule protected slavery, what is less well understood is how it profited all propertied elites. The power to impose taxes as long as they were exclusively "direct" and "in Proportion to the Census" (I.9.4) has a dual role. It was explicitly designed with the intention of impeding or preventing the power of Congress to tax the property of elites. The requirement that "Representatives and direct Taxes shall be apportioned among the several States" (I.2.3) excluded income and all forms of wealth from taxation unless both imposed directly and apportioned according to population. As Charles Beard pointed out, "[d]irect taxes may be laid, but resort to this form of taxation is rendered practically impossible, save on extraordinary occasions, by the provision that they must be apportioned according to population—so that numbers cannot transfer the burden to accumulated wealth."[35]

I.8.1 grants Congress the "Power To lay and collect Taxes, Duties, Imposts and Excises." However, this is specifically restricted to direct taxes that correspond to the proportion of the population of each state. As discussed above, this empowered the big slave states while excluding the slave owners from taxation. In exchange for a partial counting of slaves as three-fifths of a person, the big slave states were now subject to proportional taxation in I.9.4 so long as "No Capitation, or other direct, Tax shall be laid, unless in Proportion to the Census or Enumeration herein directed to be taken." These same powers were denied to the states in I.10.2, which mandated that "No State shall, without the Consent of the Congress, lay any Imposts or Duties on Imports or Exports," and I.10.3 extended it to "any duty on Tonnage" as pertains to shipping.

Apportionment of direct taxes was first tested in the 1796 Supreme Court case *Hylton v. United States*, in which the court struck down the tax on luxury carriages as indirect, the same criteria used a century later in *Pollock*.[36] While the 16th amendment removed the limit to direct taxation, no tax on financial wealth has ever been issued, although failed efforts have been made to impose federal taxes on land and other forms of tangible wealth. Today, elites of the richest country in human history do not pay a single cent on their wealth unless they withdraw it either as income or realize their "capital gains" on profits made by the sale of an asset, both of which are currently taxed at a lower rate than income from work. There is currently no federal tax on tangible property other than a luxury tax on consumer items purchased by the rich.[37]

Anti-Federalists had warned that stripping the states of the power to tax would result in the imposition of federal taxes on land and other regressive taxes rather than on imports.[38] Yet, they proved only partially right. There are *local* and *state* taxes on land and real estate, and regressive taxes on prepared food and body care items. But to this day there is no *federal* tax on any form of wealth, land or otherwise.

In effect, the three-fifths clause not only perpetuated and strengthened the atrocity of slavery, it also strengthened the power of property produced by the exploitation of all human labor. The minority checks embedded in the constitutional power to tax served to prevent all types of leveling. In doing so, the Constitution serves to perpetually shield the elite's wealth from economic democracy.

Putting an End to That Evil

The Constitution was designed to realize what Robert Morris had failed to accomplish during his tenure. Along with giving Congress the power to tax, issue currency, regulate commerce, and pay debts it redistributed vast government lands to the elites while using the earnings from the sales to pay interest on their outstanding loans. This restarted and accelerated westward settler colonial expansion that had been blocked by the presence of the British, French, and Spanish, as well as another century of armed native resistance.

For Madison, there was a clear connection between the sale of public lands and the payment of debt. The federal government "will render the vacant territory a more necessary, as well as more productive fund for discharging" the debt while also reopening the Mississippi to US expansion.[39] He wrote that it would now be possible to take the western forts, "which will not cease to instigate the Savages, as long as they remain in British hands. It is said also that the Southern Indians are encouraged and armed by the Spaniards for like incursions on that side. A respectable Government would have equal effect in putting an end to that evil."[40]

Paying one's debts ensured the ability to borrow. This proved critical for defending the country's property and interests from enemies both at home and abroad while making it possible to take more.[41] Without an army and navy, foreign creditors might seek to seize compensation for unpaid debts directly, which is exactly what the USA would later do across Latin America during the Wilsonian Era of the early twentieth century to help banks and investors by seizing tariff offices to claim unpaid debts.[42]

Taxes were needed to raise the money to repay the debts and establish a government-backed credit system which would provide the financial resources to fund the military. Once established, the military would carry out repression of the "evil" of native resistance, the dangers of slave rebellions, and white rural resistance to land theft and debt peonage, putting down three interlinked struggles that tragically never recognized one another as such.

This was yet another tragic missed opportunity to merge the insurrections between white small farmers, laborers, mechanics, slaves, and native peoples, each of which were another side of the same struggle. While slaves were resisting their domination and exploitation that enriched the elites who evaded taxation, native peoples were arming themselves against a growing army funded by taxes, and small farmers and laborers were organizing against the taxes that funded it. The tragedy is that an opportunity was missed by these waged and unwaged workers to cross the barriers of race and join their struggles to change the outcome of the Revolution. We can only speculate how things might have turned out differently if they had.

Making the working class pay the cost of government reinforced the reality that government doesn't just serve elite interests: it is inseparable from the elites. This is the fundamental flaw in the liberal and social democratic critique of so-called "government capture." One hardly need to "capture" what one already possesses. No candidates, parties, or organized interest groups will be able to alter the fundamental design of the Constitution and its function to serve the elites.

6
The Executive: The Rule of One

Civil government, so far as it is instituted for the security of property, is in reality instituted for the defence of the rich against the poor, or of those who have some property against those who have none at all.

Adam Smith, *An Inquiry into the Nature and Causes of the Wealth of Nations*, 1776[1]

The radical American Revolution ended with a conservative, even reactionary, outcome.[2] Less than a decade after the Revolution against the tyranny of a British king, the Constitution created an effectively unelected president who could serve an unlimited number of terms, wield a veto, and was empowered to enforce the law and use the military against enemies both foreign and domestic. An undemocratic national government with concentrated powers replaced a decentralized confederation and its mostly more democratic state governments.

We learn that the Framers designed the presidency with two objectives in mind. First, checks and balances empower each branch of government to restrain and prevent one branch from overpowering the other two and the states, thereby preventing the President from becoming a tyrant, a king or a new caesar. Second, the Framers kept Article II extremely short and listed far fewer enumerated powers for the President and Vice President in order to prohibit the executive from using its power to emasculate Congress and transform the republic into a dictatorship.

Today the presidency looks nothing like what we are told was intended by the Framers. The expansion of presidential powers is blamed on power-hungry presidents who abuse the Constitution to pickpocket the powers of the other branches, causing our constitutional system to go off the rails, checks and balances to break down, and democracy to be imperiled.

Rather than an unintended outcome, the nearly unlimited power of the executive today is actually built into Article II. The President, and the executive branch that emerged around it, was designed with few enumerated limits on what it can do to police representative democracy. The President is not directly elected by voters, was eligible to serve for life for 163 years until 1951 when the 22nd amendment established a two-term limit, is nearly impossible to remove by impeachment, appoints its own cabinet, is secure against having its vetoes overridden, and nominates the very judges who might shine a light onto the executive's power.[3]

Unlimited Power

Article II presents a conundrum for political scientists and constitutional scholars. Although the Constitution delegates the power of the pen and sword exclusively to Congress, in practice it is the President who wields them. Using their executive powers, presidents interpret and pick winners and losers when administering the law, and decide life and death during wartime, powers presumed to belong to the courts. Presidents have claimed the power to appropriate and spend government funds and deploy the military without Congressional approval. The discretionary powers have only become more expansive with time as a result of the vagueness of Article II and the election of the President independently from the legislature. With little power to control and remove the President and other executive officers except by the nearly impossible threshold of impeachment, Congress can do no more than legislate and issue polemics. The immense growth in the power of the President is the result of the separation of powers, not despite them. When Congress cannot carry out its functions in times of crisis or so-called "partisan" divide, presidents are left to wield power with unlimited discretion.

While the list of the President's constitutional powers is relatively short, Article II is nearly silent on what the President *cannot* do. The Constitution lacks checks on powers that are not enumerated or explicitly prohibited, such as in I.9's list of "POWERS FORBIDDEN

TO CONGRESS." All but one enumerated power of the President, the "Power to Grant Reprieves and Pardons for Offense against the United States, except in Cases of Impeachment" (II.2.1), include checks on them. By not making other powers explicitly prohibited, the presidency was designed to have virtually unlimited power.

The separation of powers and strong presidential system was created to solve the problem of the pseudo-parliamentary system of the Articles of Confederation which gave Congress the power to both make and execute the law.

Despite being a single branch government, in which the Congress formed the executive and judicial branches, the Articles did not establish a parliamentary system in which the legislative branch forms the executive branch based on the majority in the "lower" house. Parliamentary systems subject not only the making but also the administration of law to the demands of the majority.

The state systems described in Chapter 4 came closer to democratizing both the making and administration of law. For this reason they were unacceptable to the Framers, who sought to constrain democracy by separating the power to legislate from the power to execute.

The Unitary Executive

From the first days of the Washington administration the power of the presidency has expanded without limits in two ways. Presidents have acted unilaterally during times of economic crisis and war, thereby institutionalizing their actions as precedent, a problem compounded by the failure or refusal of Congress and the courts to counteract them. As journalist Ferdinand Lundberg keenly observed, "the President often fills interstices in the law. He often acts where there is no law, and Congress later formally makes the law. Or it does not. In this role the President is obviously a one-man legislator."[4] After the attacks of 9/11, the Bush II administration described the President as the "unitary executive" unrestrained by ordinary checks and balances.

Bush operationalized the long list of extra-constitutional powers claimed by previous presidents. To go to war, spend money never appropriated, imprison and execute citizens, issue executive orders by fiat, and carry out line item vetoes in the form of signing statements, are just a few of the many powers presidents have claimed. Once these powers are pickpocketed from the other branches and the states they become sticky, remaining with the presidency, never to return to their rightful owners.[5]

II.3 says precious little about how the President "shall take Care that the Laws be faithfully executed," providing an unlimited discretionary power to interpret and enforce the law. The lack of specificity implies, according to Hamilton, that "[h]e who is to execute the laws must first judge for himself of their meaning."[6] Presidents have assembled a vast array of power merely by exercising their implied power to interpret the law when turning them into rules and regulations.

Congress has only the remotest check on the President. The criteria for "high Crimes and Misdemeanors" (II.4) is ill-defined and the supermajority vote threshold to remove is so high that impeachment has yet to be successfully used to remove and ban a president from office.

A Few Designing Men

The problem of the presidency is not just about the electoral college. Once the position has been attained without a direct popular vote, the President is empowered to constrain political democracy and prevent economic democracy in four critically important ways.

The electoral college, by which a group of "electors" selected by the party casts the official vote based on the outcome of the popular vote in each state, was designed as a minority check on the unpredictable will of the majority. It was designed at the very end of the Convention after five previous attempts to decide how the President would be selected. The Framers debated whether to restore a monarch for life or elect a weak executive who would serve long terms, until finally modeling it after a parliamentary system with Congress selecting the President.

On September 4, 1787, during the final weeks of the Convention, the Committee of Eleven on Postponed Matters, which met in secret and included James Madison, John Dickinson, Roger Sherman, and

Gouverneur Morris (the latter of whom appeared to have his hand in nearly every aspect of the final text), made one lasting change. The committee had electors selected by state legislatures pick the President, an idea proposed by James Wilson and modeled after the German system of princely electors. Passed by a vote of nine states to two,[7] the new process made the President "elected" by the eligible voters every four years in non-binding ritual crowning.

The debate was focused on how the executive would be selected and how long they would serve, not whether or not to have one. The consensus was that a president was needed to constrain democracy because the people out of doors could not be trusted to govern themselves. Elbridge Gerry echoed many of the Framers when he declared that "the people are uninformed, and would be misled by a few designing men." He opposed direct popular election as "the worst of all" the methods.[8]

Hamilton supported the electoral college in *Federalist #68* because it protected the majority from harming themselves by voting incorrectly. Separating the popular vote from the actual selection was an "effectual security against this mischief" so as to prevent "tumult and disorder." Voting in separate states "will expose them much less to heats and ferments, which might be communicated from them to the people, than if they were all to be convened at one time, in one place." The electorate would also be divided into different groups and interests in order to create what Hamilton called "obstacles" in the way of the majority combining to elect a president who would serve their shared class interest. The electoral college was a manifestation of the strategy of divide and conquer.

The system works only too well to deny the majority their desired candidate. The electoral college creates 51 distinct and disconnected elections for president, one for each state and the colony of Washington, DC. For decades, about 80 percent of states and DC have been "safe states" which consistently vote for one or the other of the two dominant parties. Truly competitive election campaigns only happen in between 5 and 15 "swing states" while the remaining states are mostly ignored by the major parties. This means that a tiny number of the most motivated voters in these close races, who tend to be white, wealthier, and with more education, determine who will win the electoral college.

Twenty presidential elections have delivered a president who either did not win a majority of the popular vote, won with only a plurality (e.g., the most votes), had the recount stopped by the Supreme Court, or were picked by the House of Representatives.[9]

It was apparent almost immediately that the electoral college serves to constrain majority will. After the 1800 election did not deliver a winner in the electoral college and 36 inconclusive votes in the House, Jefferson was elected president along with Aaron Burr as Vice President. They did not get along. The situation was so tense that Madison feared the military would be called out to put down a popular revolt if Jefferson was blocked.[10]

The 12th amendment was supposed to fix the electoral college so that voters would cast a single vote for both the President and Vice President. Instead, the electoral college has continued to deliver presidents who didn't win the popular vote. Today, the USA is one of the few representative democracies with a separately elected president who is not elected directly by the voters.

The Executive Veto

The veto in I.7.2 is one of the few enumerated presidential powers, but it has no conditions or limits on how or when a president may wield it. The Framers rehabilitated the English king's veto to overturn the laws of parliament, although it had not been used since 1707.[11] Ben Franklin thought the executive veto was subject to abuse so that "no good law whatsoever could be passed without a private bargain with him." His fellow Framers favored it for just that reason: empowering the President could extort changes from Congress as an intentional constraint on democracy. The veto was included as a weapon of executive power to impede political democracy while shielding property from the threat of economic democracy.[12]

The veto was rarely used until President Andrew Jackson vetoed the rechartering of the 2nd US Bank in 1832, for which he was widely attacked. His veto nevertheless created a precedent that the President possessed unchecked power to veto a bill for any reason.

By 2020, the last year President Trump was in office, presidents have issued 2,584 vetoes of which only 112 were overridden—a meager 4 percent.[13] The tiny number of overrides demonstrates that the veto is almost completely effective in the President blocking the majority will of Congress, not Congress checking the President. The record demonstrates that the opposite of what we have learned about checks on the President is true—these powers were given to the President as a minority check of one *on* Congress.

The Framers were explicit about why they included the veto. Madison celebrated that "[o]ne object of the National Executive, so far as it would have a negative on the laws, was to control the National Legislature."[14]

Although the veto can be overridden, the override mechanism appears near the end of a long sequence of minority checks that effectively make it unusable. Requiring a two-thirds majority in both houses, it was designed as a "double check on the democratic House"[15] by what Hamilton and Madison called "a well-constructed Senate" in *Federalist #63*. Today a mere 33 senators can prevent a veto from being overridden even against a consensus in the House. If these 33 senators come from the 17 smallest states in population size, totaling only 25 million people—or about 8 percent of the 2021 population of 328 million—they would prevent the representatives of 92 percent of the population from constraining the President.

Combined with the federal court's power of judicial review (see Chapter 8), the Framers effectively prevented the House from acting on its own while giving the Senate and President unlimited discretion to block it. The high threshold for both overriding vetoes and removal by impeachment, along with the ability of the courts to strike down laws, means that the overwhelming power lies in the hands of either a single indirectly elected executive or five unelected justices.

Anti-Federalist warnings that the presidential veto would lead to the concentration of power in the hands of a single person were prescient. About a dozen times as many vetoes have been issued by presidents than the number of federal laws that have been struck down as unconstitutional by the Supreme Court.[16]

Rule by One

The executive was designed to be run by a single rather than a plural executive like that used in Pennsylvania. The Framers threw out the system in which Congress was a unitary branch with the authority to execute its own laws by using committees composed of its own members. In doing so, they severed the direct relationship between Congress and the President in the interpretation and execution of the law.[17]

In 1781, Congress had already begun replacing its committee system on the advice of Hamilton and his ally James Duane. Administrative boards and offices for war, foreign affairs, naval issues, and finance headed by individuals appointed by Congress wielded extensive discretionary executive authority as a de facto separate executive branch. Hamilton thought that "an executive ministry ... would speedily restore the credit of government abroad and at home ... would inspire confidence in monied men in Europe as well as in America to lend us [those] sums of which it may be demonstrated we [stand] in need from the disproportion of our national wealth to the expences of the War."[18]

The proto-executive branch was an unmitigated disaster, riddled with conflicts of interests, corruption, secrecy, waste, self-dealing, and authoritarian rule. Robert Morris was the poster boy for everything wrong with this system. "Morris was made dictator by Congress," according to historian Merrill Jensen, when he was appointed in early 1781 as chair of the Secret Committee of Trade, later becoming the Superintendent of Finance.[19] Although he refused to vote for the Declaration of Independence, Morris became the most powerful executive officer of the Revolutionary Congress, wielding a financial veto power much like a "financial emergency manager" today. Believing that government should be an "administration by single men,"[20] Morris consolidated control over other departments and boards, including quartermaster, commissary, department of the marine, and the army medical department. He even bypassed Congress by directing American diplomats abroad.

Morris's own financial interests became blurred with Congress, often using government ships to import goods for himself, his firm

(Willing and Morris), his partners, and Congress while financing them with government accounts. Writing to Silas Deane, his business partner and agent in Europe, Morris said: "I shall continue to discharge my duty faithfully to the Public and pursue my Private Fortune by all such honorable and fair means as the times will admit of." He lived up to his promise by using the government's short supply of coinage to line his pockets and those of his business associates, sustaining his global supply chain of goods during the Revolution.[21]

Morris had become the richest man in the country by the time he resigned in 1784 and was replaced by the Treasury Board. His wealth was produced by doing the business of Congress as his own behind a shield of secrecy and opaque accounting. The Congressional committee that spent years investigating Morris after he left office as the Superintendent of Finance concluded that he owed the US government $93,000 for two bonds he never repaid. Rather than being the "financier of the American Revolution," the committee reported that his wealth was likely financed by the Revolution.[22] When the Treasury Department was formed in the new federal government on September 11, 1789, Congress also passed a conflict of interest law prohibiting public officials from engaging in private trade.[23]

Despite the corruption, Morris' short tenure as Superintendent of Finance became the organizational model for the executive branch. Authority over the government's finances was transferred back from the plural executive Treasury Board to a single Secretary of the Treasury, Morris's protégé Hamilton. This time, however, the Secretary of the Treasury became a critical part of an executive branch designed as the singular protector of all property, not only of the personal property of the Secretary.

Between the end of the Revolution and the Convention, no one institution possessed sufficient authority, power, and resources to protect property from the threat of democracy. The Confederation and the states were challenged by an organized people out of doors demanding debtor-friendly policies and political power, slaves rising up for their liberation, armed native peoples defending their lands from incursion, anxious creditors, and foreign enemies on the continent. A single unified authority with the power to "execute" the power of government was needed to collect and spend the tax revenues required to set up and run the military, expand overseas trade, repay the debt, control the currency, protect property, regulate commerce, and protect government and the economy from being democratized.

Faithfully Execute

Requiring that the President "shall take Care that the Laws be faithfully executed" (II.3) provides vast discretionary power to respond to emerging threats to property posed by the majority. The Constitution is silent on exactly what "faithfully" means. Although Congress establishes, funds, and confirms the appointment of the rest of the leadership of the executive branch to implement its laws, the President possesses extensive discretion in interpreting, administering, and enforcing the law.

Despite passing significantly fewer laws in the past half century, those that do pass are both longer and more complex. This has resulted in the executive branch using its executive authority to not only interpret law into federal regulations but make it in the process of doing so.[24]

Laws are getting longer and more complex because, as we saw in Chapter 4, to get anything done Congress must overcome a nearly impassable gauntlet of roadblocks and impediments to pass a bill. On the rare occasions when a bill passes it must face the executive, designed with few enumerated constitutional powers and unlimited discretionary power to undermine the will of the majority of Congress and the voters. Today the President possesses a treasure trove of legislative powers entirely removed from not merely control by the majority of the population but accountability to Congress, and sometimes unchecked by judicial review due to deference to executive privilege in national security matters.[25]

Over the centuries the law has been interpreted into federal regulations that determine who is responsible for carrying out the will of Congress. Without going into the complicated and extensive history of the emergence of the administrative state, the law is fragmented immediately into three types: statutory law made by Congress, administrative law made by the executive branch while interpreting the law, and case law issued by the courts in precedent setting rulings. The list of ways in which administrative law can be used to trump statutory law is far too long to recount here, but a few examples will suffice.

Presidents can simultaneously wage dozens of wars, some in secret, that are never declared by Congress. Congress nevertheless funds them and other national security priorities, often in classified legislation, that gives presidents a virtual blank check to run them. Alternatively, the President can declare a national emergency, allowing them to spend money never appropriated for that purpose. In the past century, border and immigration policies have been changed at whim to incarcerate entire ethnic groups in concentration camps, denying their constitutional due process and equal protection rights, censoring the media, and shielding its own agencies from public transparency.

During the ordinary regulatory process, companies and industries are commonly exempted from the law and given a free hand to pollute, fire workers for unionizing, and engage in religious discrimination, evading punishment altogether or paying a small fine to avoid federal criminal prosecution. Presidents sell weapons and carry out trade with countries engaged in heinous atrocities, despite being sanctioned by law, because they are "strategic allies." When banks crashed the global economy, the President and Secretary of the Treasury directed the Federal Reserve to bail them out. Money was printed and lent to the banks at negative interest rates, effectively paying them to borrow.[26] These are but a few of the many ways the executive branch uses its constitutional powers to shield the economy from democratic control.

While most battles to change policy are fought out on the public stage of Congress, little light shines into the deep recesses of the numerous administrative departments, agencies, commissions, and councils of the executive branch that make regulations. The appointment of regulatory officials itself can be used to shape the making of regulations and their enforcement. Top department officials, members of boards and commissions, and White House staff are appointed by the President and confirmed by the Senate along with Article III federal judges who serve "during good Behaviour," interpreted to mean for life. II.2 establishes that "[h]e shall have Power, by and with the Advice and Consent of the Senate … and he shall nominate, and by and with the Advice and Consent of the Senate, shall appoint Ambassadors, other public Ministers and Consuls, Judges of the supreme Court, and all other Officers of the United States." This was a dramatic departure from the Articles and most of the state constitutions, few of which granted the governor the power to appoint officials and judges.

After winning in Congress and marching down the Capitol steps to celebrate their legislative victories, most supporters then go AWOL. Few stay on the job to ensure that the law is enforced "faithfully" according to the intent of Congress when it is interpreted by the administrative body tasked with writing and administering the regulations, a process that can takes years if not a decade or more to complete. As attention from supporters falls away, those with deep-pocketed interests remain on the job. A loss in Congress can be turned into a win on the regulatory side, as opponents rotate on and off the regulatory bodies which write the regulations, lobby them in hours-long hearings that continue for months, and campaign for their favored "preferred option." If opponents lose again on the regulatory side, they can still turn to the Office of Management and Budget inside the White House to issue an administrative veto and start the entire regulatory process over from the beginning.[27] This process contains countless roadblocks and impediments that serve as extra-constitutional powers not enumerated in the Constitution and minority checks on bills that have already passed into law. These checks ensure that regulations that limit or restrain the capitalist economy can be prevented, and that those that do enter into force are acceptable to those who own the economy.[28]

The vagueness of the "shall take Care" (II.3) clause leaves its meaning, scope, and the consequences of failing to do so difficult to ascertain. Rather that limit such power, Article II unleashes it, shielding the execution of the law from democratic demands. Staggered terms between the executive and legislative branches, the lack of term limits until the 22nd amendment, and the impossibility of both impeachment and overriding vetoes gave the President staying power during conflicts with Congress. The executive branch was designed to execute the law with minimal interference of the other branches of the government, states, or the majority of the people.

Presidential Fiat Power

The "shall take Care" (II.3) clause has been used by presidents to invent new powers to interpret and executive the law, even writing their own laws without going through Congress. When treaties are blocked by the Senate, presidents design executive agreements to carry out foreign and trade policy obscured by the necessary murkiness of national security and commercial secrets.[29] Despite Congressional oversight powers, presidents redirect funds, issue executive orders, call out the National Guard against the domestic population and foreign armies alike, and issue signing statements that declare their reasons for not enforcing the very laws they just signed.[30]

Executive orders are perhaps the most expansive presidential power in the hands of the presidency. When presidents sign a bill or, far rarer, it passes over their veto, presidents issue executive orders that direct their subordinates to interpret the law into new regulations, or interpret its meaning in ways that contradict the law. Such executive orders have evolved over the centuries to become a process of making law by fiat, a power of kings against which the Revolution was presumably fought. It is unknown exactly how many executive orders have been issued because they were not recorded until 1907, when the State Department began back-numbering to 1862. Although 14,036 known executive orders had been issued by 2021, estimates of the true figure run as high as 50,000.[31]

Presidential discretion grows with each creative interpretation of the Constitution. President Bill Clinton went as far as to obtain the line item veto from Congress although it was thrown out by the Supreme Court in the 1998 case *Clinton v. City of New York*. Since President Monroe, presidents have issued about 1,000 total signing statements that announce that they have no plans to execute part or even all of the very law they just signed. Although none exists, these effectively serve as a line item veto.[32]

Those with the Purse Strings Must Rule

Presidents have also usurped Congress's "power of the purse" by "impounding" (e.g., refusing to spend), spending less, or reallocating money to other purposes without Congressional approval, even spending secret monies never disclosed to the public. Presidential power of the purse gives presidents immense additional power to rule by fiat. As Hamilton made clear, those "which holds the purse strings absolutely, must rule."[33]

The Framers intended that expenses and other executive actions be reported to Congress according to the requirement that "He shall from time to time give to the Congress Information of the State of the Union" (II.3). However, no specifics were given about what and when the information should be provided, giving presidents broad discretion to decide what is reported. In a debate with Madison, George Mason suggested that "[i]n matters relative to military operations, and foreign negotiations, secrecy was necessary sometimes." Recognizing this necessity, he suggested that although "the people ... had a right to know the expenditure of their money [...] it might be concealed forever from them," unless there was a specific time period required other than "from time to time."[34]

The impounding of funds finally led Congress to pass the 1974 Impoundment Control Act. However, presidents evade it by declaring a national emergency (as we will see in Chapter 7) to get around the law, or by appointing administrators who wish to abolish or impede their own agency by not spending funds appropriated by Congress.[35]

Secret spending by the executive was first used in 1790, although it remained infrequent until 1935. This all changed during World War II, when President Franklin D. Roosevelt appropriated billions of dollars to build the nuclear weapons program, which included entirely secret labs and towns to house the workers, scientists, and their families.

Today, presidents exempt spending related to policing and intelligence agencies such as the CIA, which is exempt from Government Accountability Office oversight and the 1966 Freedom of Information Act. Members of Congress without proper security clearance cannot be briefed about how much is included in the appropriation bills they are voting on.[36] Following whistleblower Edward Snowden's revelations about US government mass surveillance, it was reported that nearly $53 billion was spent in 2013 on a range of secret intelligence functions among 16 agencies and contractors employing 107,000 people.[37] Snowden's disclosures have demonstrated just how permanent, extensive, and opaque the scope of presidential power of the purse is today.

Permanent Wartime Necessity

Beginning with Washington, presidents have continued to seize and accumulate more power by appealing to non-existent claims of exclusive authority over foreign policy to "guarantee to every State in this Union a Republican Form of Government, and shall protect each of them against Invasion; and ... against domestic Violence" (IV.4). To carry this out, Washington appointed army officers during the Indian war in the Ohio Valley without consent of the Senate.[38]

Washington also used presidential claims of war power to suppress the 1794 Whiskey Rebellion, which began in four counties of Western Pennsylvania against Hamilton's excise tax on domestic alcohol producers, a key revenue source for his financial plan. It arose at the same time Washington was troubled by squatters on his own lands in the same area.[39] Rather than repealing the excise tax, Hamilton shifted it from imported to domestic liquor. Following the failure of commissioners sent to the region to convince the rebels to surrender, Washington asserted authority under IV.4 to send into the area between 13,000 and 15,000 militia men from Pennsylvania, New Jersey, Maryland, and Virginia.[40] For Hamilton, the Whiskey Rebellion was a direct challenge to not only the excise on domestic alcohol production but his entire public credit plan and the constitutional authority of the executive. The Whiskey Rebellion became a pretext for Washington to use his war powers against what Hamilton had him believe was a threat to the very survival of the federal government.[41]

By labeling it an insurrection, the Whiskey Rebellion served as an early test of executive war power.[42] Responsibility to guarantee a republican form of state government by protecting against invasion and domestic violence found in IV.4 had just been enshrined in the

1792 Militia Act, which passed during the early stages of the protests in Pennsylvania. It would later be extended after the fact in the 1795 Enforcement Act, allowing the President to use the army and militia for ordinary law enforcement. This law, and an 1807 amendment, continued to be updated in federal statutes and has been used for a wide range of purposes, including breaking strikes, putting down urban rebellions, and patrolling the border.

Washington's military response to the Whiskey Rebellion protests in Pennsylvania was not merely intended to protect the Capitol or secure his own personal land interests in the area. It also created a pretext for creating a standing army, which was extremely unpopular at the time. For Hamilton, the rebellion made "a vigorous exertion of the powers of government indispensable," and made possible by the excise tax and public credit system then under attack. Using it for such purposes justified the expense and established a precedent for using the military against domestic dissent, protest, and insurrection.

Today, the "necessary and proper" implied power in I.8.18 has been used, often with Congressional approval, to remove constraints on presidential war power, allow money never appropriated by Congress to be spent, write new "laws" by fiat, and determine guilt and carry out a sentence of death without a trial. As long as the courts continue to defer to the President on national security issues and Congress fails to pass new laws or attempt to amend the Constitution to constrain such powers, presidential power will continue to expand without limit.[43] As constitutional scholar Louis Fisher warns, after an executive uses such powers "temporarily" in an emergency, the "temporary departure became a permanent condition."[44] Congress and the courts continue to ignore Locke's admonition that a legislature "cannot transfer the power of making laws to any other hands." Because the Constitution is silent on whether power can be permanently delegated, it will remain unrecoverable.[45]

The dangers of unlimited authoritarian presidential power did not escape the Anti-Federalists, who railed against the unelected president who could serve for life and impose new taxes to fund oppressive military powers. It was apparent to many in 1787 to 1788 that the Framers had included a master switch of presidential dictatorship if the survival of the state and economy were at stake.

Washington would come to warn about the rapid growth of executive power. In his last speech to the nation, he seemed to concede his direct responsibility for this development. He bluntly warned the country to "avoid the necessity of those overgrown military establishments, which under any form of government are inauspicious to liberty, and which are to be regarded as particularly hostile to republican liberty."[46]

Washington also warned about "combinations and associations" which serve their own particular elite class interests—a class to which he obviously belonged—that "become potent engines by which cunning, ambitious, and unprincipled men will be enabled to subvert the power of the people and to usurp for themselves the reins of government."[47]

In this extraordinarily honest farewell message, Washington appeared to accept responsibility for establishing the precedent of presidential "wartime necessity" that virtually every president has used.

President Abraham Lincoln vastly expanded the necessity claim to revoke *habeas corpus* several times, despite I.9.2 giving that authority only to Congress, and to spend money never appropriated to him during the Civil War. He asserted that the survival of the state depended on "measures, otherwise unconstitutional, [which] might become lawful, by becoming indispensable to the preservation of the constitution."[48]

Lincoln likely channelled Madison, who wrote in *Federalist #41* that "it is in vain to oppose Constitutional barriers to the impulse of self-preservation ... because it plants in the Constitution itself necessary usurpations of power, every precedent of which is a germ of unnecessary and multiplied repetitions."[49] In other words, to borrow Justice Robert Jackson's phrase, the Bill of Rights is not a "suicide pact" that prevents the President from taking the necessary unilateral action for the survival of the constitutional system.[50]

The Constitution finally enumerates the power of unlimited presidential rule by enabling the President to send Congress packing.[51] In II.3, the President is authorized to, "on extraordinary Occasions, convene both Houses, or either of them, and in Case of Disagreement between them, with Respect to the Time of Adjournment, he may adjourn them to such Time as he shall think proper." The germ of the US constitutional system of government now appears to be a latent dictatorship, by which the police and national security powers have been used to crush legal protest, dissent, whistleblowing, and strikes, put down armed insurrections, contradict the will of Congress, go to war across the planet, and even protect property to the detriment of the survival of humanity and the rest of the planetary ecosystem.[52]

7

The Executive: Unrestrained Global Guardian of Property

It is said that the "shall take Care" (II.3) clause of the Constitution delegates "police powers" to the executive branch to administer, regulate, and enforce the law. Of all the President's police powers, perhaps the most important is enforcing the economic aspects of the Constitution in I.8–10 discussed in Chapters 1 to 3. When Congress uses its enumerated powers to protect property by ensuring contracts, regulating interstate commerce, and coining money, etc., it falls upon the executive to police these laws. To carry out this responsibility, myriad powerful institutions have grown up around the executive. While Congress made the law to set up, manage, and protect property, it was delegated to the President to provide the strong arm that would suppress internal dissent, insurrection, and rebellion against theft of native lands, slavery, and settler colonialism, and protect the opening of overseas markets and trade as the country transformed itself into an empire.

Today, the President has virtually unlimited authority and power to control the world's largest military, deploy it anywhere in the world, invade and overthrow other countries, protect US businesses abroad, and to do so entirely in secret with almost no accountability. From such unlimited discretionary power can be traced war powers, fiat legislative and spending power, executive privilege, national security exemptions, classified trade agreements, and executive agreements that, while once infrequent, have now become the *modus operandi* of executive power.

Protecting Property

Displacement of native peoples and the speculative boom in land sales were interconnected aspects of settler colonialism. As we saw in

Chapter 5, selling these lands allowed the government to pay its debts and expand the supply of investment capital. Settlers were pushed into the cash economy and forced to produce for sale to nearby urban and export markets, generating export earnings that fed the government-backed public credit system used to finance industrial development.

As land prices rose and commodity prices fell, small farmers facing foreclosure were increasingly forced off their lands and into the waged labor force while land ownership concentrated into the hands of the few. Treasury Secretary Alexander Hamilton's taxation policies accelerated the transformation of small farmers into waged workers. Resistance to these policies exploded into rural insurrections in Pennsylvania in 1794 and 1798–99 and into the first decade of the nineteenth century in Maine.

Slave rebellions created existential dread for the Framers, leading James Madison to warn Virginia during the Revolution that slavery was "the only part in which the colony was vulnerable, and if we shall be subdued, we shall fall like Achilles by the hand of one that knows that secret."[1] Delegates like planter Charles Cotesworth Pinckney from the big Southern slave states ultimately came to agree with Northerners like Rufus King that they needed to contribute to the immense "compensation for the burden" of putting down slave uprisings.[2]

This joining of differing elite interests demonstrated that property—whether slave, land, credit, or capital—proved to be the unvanquished victor in the Constitution. It prevailed with the protection of a powerful executive with the authority and means to ensure its security.

As the guardian of property, the President became the midwife of the birth of a great empire of property that would grow into a global power today. It was in most part due to Alexander Hamilton's financial plan which, according to historian Michael Merrill, sought "to create what can only be called a capitalist society" by ensuring "the money economy of the coastal entrepôts had to spread to the small towns and settlements in the countryside where most people lived."[3] The Constitution made it possible to create a single economic system that would reign supreme both economically and politically in the USA and globally.

Today, presidents deploy the military abroad, claiming to "protect life and property." "Property" is the operative concept contributing to nearly every one of the estimated 125 deployments from 1798 to 1966, and another 75 by 1991.[4] The presidency, designed by the Framers as the executor of laws and power to protect property, has become a global weapon in its defense. From the war against native peoples to expropriate their lands, the fabricated 1846–8 war that resulted in seizing half of Mexico to speed the westward expansion of slavery, the 1911–12 invasions of Nicaragua to protect the property of US investors, and to the current use of sanctions to strangle countries like Venezuela, the President is not only the world's policeman but also the global landlord.

Insurrection against a Republican Form of Government

Although Congress and the President share war powers in Articles I and II, the President also possesses authority under the "guarantee" clause in Article IV that "The United States shall guarantee to every State in this Union a Republican Form of Government, and shall protect each of them against Invasion; and on Application of the Legislature, or of the Executive (when the Legislature cannot be convened) against domestic Violence" (IV.4).

The desire to protect a "Republican Form of Government" was first offered in the May 29th Virginia Plan.[5] Section 6 granted Congress the power "to call forth the force of the union against any member of the union failing to fulfill its duty under the articles thereof," and Section 11 provided that "a Republican Government & the territory of each State, except in the instance of a voluntary junction of Government & territory, ought to be guarantied by the United States to each State."[6]

Constitutional war powers were a response to the inability of the states and Congress to protect a republican form of government by sufficiently repressing the Regulators, slaves uprisings, and native resistance both during and after the Revolution.[7] The Shays' Rebellion and its later electoral success were on the minds of the Framers concerned about the lack of a standing army to suppress it. In *Federalist #43*, Madison warned about such struggles swapping "republican for antirepublican Constitutions," whether an economic or political democracy.[8]

In the Constitution, however, the threat to republican government was drawn widely to include the threat of economic democracy by the states and people that threatened the economic system.[9] The executive branch and Congress now had the supremacy power to block or overturn any threats to property, by military force if necessary, simply by deeming such efforts as "Insurrections" (I.8.15), "Rebellion" (I.9.2), and "domestic Violence" (IV.4). It is not by accident that Hamilton successfully pushed for designating the Whiskey Rebellion an insurrection even while it was no more than peaceful meetings and protest letters.

Some also feared native resistance, slave insurrections, and the genuine possibility of an alliance between them, as happened in Virginia and elsewhere before and during the Revolution.[10] These dual threats could now be confronted by Congress granted the power of "organizing, arming, and disciplining the Militia" (I.8.16) (today the National Guard), and have the power "To provide for calling forth the Militia to execute the Laws of the Union, suppress Insurrections and repel Invasions" (I.8.15).

While Congress funds and regulates the militias in practice, only the President has called them into action. Washington's deployment of the militia against native resistance established presidential authority over the militias that continues today, with the National Guard and army being used during such emergencies. The past two centuries are replete with presidents calling out these forces against slave rebellions, native uprisings, Confederate secession, mass protests, strikes, and immigrants at the Southern border.[11]

Despite the widespread hostility to standing armies, these powers were added to the Constitution to avoid "the extraordinary spectacle of a government destitute even of the shadow of constitutional power to enforce the execution of its own laws," according to Hamilton in *Federalist #21*. He was thinking about the Shays' Regulators, "[t]he tempestuous situation" in Massachusetts. Without war powers, he warned, "[a] successful faction may erect a tyranny on the ruins of order and law" spread by a charismatic leader to other states.[12]

By outlawing the same revolutionary force that was used for the independence struggle, the Constitution leaves open the possibility of change only through elections limited to a minority of proper- tied white men eligible to vote, and an even smaller number eligible to hold office. In *Federalist #21*, Hamilton offers the maxim, still influential today, that "[t]he natural cure for an ill-administration, in a popular or representative constitution, is a change of men." Thus begins the dead-end strategy that change is only possible by voting for new individuals to hold office in an otherwise unchange- able system.

Against Invasion

The power of the sword was designed to be shared by Congress and the President and be used for two purposes. The first is when Congress declares war and the President then takes command as Commander in Chief (I.8.11) and as the "Commander in Chief of the Army and Navy of the United States, and of the Militia of the several States" (II.2.1) to "protect each of them against Invasion; and … against domestic Violence" (IV.4).[13]

The second use of war powers occurs in the event of "domestic insurrection" and is spread over three separate Articles. I.8.12 estab- lishes Congress's exclusive authority to "raise and support Armies" for no more than two years at a time. In addition to the power over the militias in I.8.15 and I.8.16, I.8.13 gives Congress the power to "provide and maintain a Navy" and I.8.14 to "make Rules for the Government and Regulation of the land and naval Forces." Protec- tion to "suppress Insurrections and repel Invasions" (I.8.15) is also repeated in the shared responsibility to respond to an invasion or domestic violence (IV.4).

The armed resistance of native peoples presented a dual threat of "invasion" and "domestic Violence" that undermined the consolida- tion of the national government and economy. The use of war power against native self-defense hastened the expropriation of their lands which were carved up into private property to be sold and leveraged as financial assets. Congress proceeded to use these lands to bankroll Hamilton's government-backed public credit system in which loans by the first Bank of the United States triggered land speculation, drove up land prices, and escalated the genocidal war on native peoples.[14] Land transformed the public debt into public credit for government to fund the military in order to further displace native peoples and colonize their lands.[15] The war decimated native populations and opened up their lands for settlement, speculation, and most importantly investment capital for commercial agriculture and manufacturing. When foreign trade, tariff revenues, and foreign investment resumed after ratification, land sales became a less important source of revenues to repay debts and fund the government. Instead, they served to attract more immigrants, expanding the pool of "free labor."[16]

Washington's war against native peoples had no basis in the Constitution. There is no enumerated authority in Article II granting the President authority to go to war unilaterally or offensively, or to remain "Commander in Chief" at all times even when war is not declared. Native resistance could hardly be considered an "invasion" since it was their land being stolen. Washington had unilaterally gone to war against several sovereign nations, some of whom the USA had signed treaties with, in violation of the Congress's exclusive power to declare war.

The absence of authority has never deterred presidents from asserting war powers. Washington requested funds to build additional forts and expand the army to take over the genocidal war from the routed state militias. Nearly every President has followed his precedent, whether the threat is actual or a pretext for acting.

Today, presidents continue to refer to themselves as "Commander in Chief," even though Congress has not declared war since June 4, 1942 during World War II. Even the Oath of Enlistment requires that soldiers pledge allegiance such "that I will obey the orders of the president of the United States," although the Constitution gives the President no such authority except when Congress declares war.

Beginning with President Washington and continuing until today, war powers have been used without limit to invade and occupy other countries and destabilize and overthrow unfriendly governments. Since 9/11, the "War on Terror" in Afghanistan and Iraq have cost an estimated $8 trillion without any formal declaration of war.[17] Invoking even the fatally flawed 1973 War Powers Act, which passed over President Nixon's veto and was intended to restore some of the powers that Congress lost since WWII, has failed several times. Today, Congress's role has been so eroded that presidents either ignore it entirely when using military force or obtain an "authorization for the use of military force," such as for the wars in Afghanistan and Iraq. Either way, by exercising their unlimited discretion, presidents have transformed Congress's power of the sword into the much weaker privilege to provide "Advice and Consent" (II.2.2) such as given for treaties and appointments on a decision after the fact.

The first real exercise of presidential war powers was Washington's claim of executive privilege to withhold documents requested by Congress in its first committee investigation into the military defeat at the 1791 Battle of the Wabash River in the Ohio Territory against the native confederation. While Washington later relented and delivered some of what was requested, he established a precedent that is now firmly engrained within the scope of discretionary presidential power.

The defeat of the militias led to their reorganization and the expansion of the army to 1,000 men equipped to fight native resistance, expel squatters, and guard surveyors sent to parcel out western lands for auction under command of the new Secretary of War, Henry Knox.[18] Between 1790 to 1795, the US government spent $5 million on the army, five-sixths of the federal government's operating budget, to fight an undeclared genocidal settler colonialist war against native peoples.[19]

Expropriating native lands accelerated the westward expansion of trade that depended on negotiations with Spain for access to the Mississippi River. Executive power to make treaties, with both native peoples and Spain, was inseparable from the claim to unlimited executive privilege and protecting national security.[20] The Battle of the Wabash River didn't just open the way to consolidating settler colonial control of the continent; it put the power to transform the USA into a global empire into the hands of the President.

Executive Aggrandizement

One source of unlimited presidential power is the declaration of a national emergency which presidents have used to take over a wide range of legislative functions and bypass the Constitution and the law. Congress passed the 1976 National Emergencies Act to impose limits on their use but, like the 1973 War Powers Act and 1974 Impoundment Control Act, the new law had the opposite effect of expanding them, allowing presidents to reappropriate money and direct, if not take over, the operations of private companies when they declare a national emergency. National emergencies are yet another example of how presidents have consolidated power to the office since Washington. We seem to have forgotten George Mason's advice that "[t]he Executive power ought to be well secured agst. Legislative usurpations on it. The purse & the sword ought never to get into the same hands whether Legislative or Executive."[21]

Presidential powers grow with each crisis, war, and emergency as Congress actively and passively hands over more and more of its own constitutional power to the executive.[22] Transferred to the executive under temporary emergencies, these powers become "permanent fixtures."[23] Supreme Court Justice Robert Jackson called Congress's abrogation of its own power a "zone of twilight" in the 1952 *Youngstown Sheet & Tube Company v. Sawyer*, which struck down President Harry Truman's seizure of steel plants threatened by a strike. Jackson chastised Congress's failure to take a position on the President's power grab as an invitation to "enable, if not invite, measures on independent presidential responsibility."[24]

Madison's position on presidential power only began to change during the Washington administration. In a series of Pacificus-Helvidius newspaper debates of 1793–4 with Hamilton, he wrote that "it has grown into an axiom that the executive is the department of power most distinguished by its propensity to war." War causes "executive aggrandizement" that makes self-dealing and war profiteering widespread.[25] A year later, Madison again anonymously warned that "[o]f all the enemies to public liberty war is, perhaps, the most to be dreaded" because it expands discretionary presidential power, leads to the formation of armies, raises debts and taxes, allows war profiteering, and encourages fraud. "No nation could preserve its freedom in the midst of continual warfare," he lamented.[26]

Unitary Foreign Policy

The Constitution transferred the making of foreign policy from the states, which were more subject to democratic pressure from below, to Congress and the President. Although the Articles delegated sole power to negotiate treaties in Article IX to Congress, some states had entered into their own diplomatic agreements with competing European powers that threatened existing treaties and financial ties with France and the Netherlands, relations between Georgia and native nations, and the unity of the Confederation.[27]

The problem was compounded by states defying the 1783 Treaty of Paris by closing their courts to suits by Loyalists seeking replevin orders for the return of their expropriated estates (Article 5th) and slaves (Article 7th), and by British creditors attempting to collect their outstanding debts (Article 4th).[28]

Although they lacked the power to negotiate treaties, several states nurtured cordial relations with competing European empires by adjusting tariffs on both foreign imports and imports from other states. Massachusetts was one of several states engaged in a trade war with England, imposing protective tariffs in 1785 and refusing to open its courts to Loyalist property claims and British creditors. England responded by threatening to negotiate separate treaties with each of the states in 1786.[29]

The lack of a single national trade policy prompted merchants to demand Congress be given the power to regulate trade. Merchants then met at Washington's Mt. Vernon estate in the first of several meetings leading to Philadelphia, where the Constitution put a stop to these state obstructions to trade.[30] I.10.2 mandated that "No State shall, without the Consent of the Congress, lay any Imposts or Duties on Imports or Exports, except what may be absolutely necessary for executing its inspection Laws: and the net Produce of all Duties and Imposts, laid by any State on Imports or Exports, shall be for the Use of the Treasury of the United States." Additionally, II.2 enumerated that "He shall have Power, by and with the Advice and Consent of the Senate, to make Treaties, provided two-thirds of the Senators present concur."

These clauses definitively stripped the states of the power to make or defy treaties. The executive—not the states or Congress—would negotiate treaties and submit them to the Senate for "Advice and Consent" while giving the Congress exclusive power to tax imports but prohibit taxes on exports in I.9.5. In turn, the executive was now tasked to "take Care that the Laws be faithfully executed" (II.3), including treaties, trade, and tariffs.

Exclusive power over foreign policy empowered the national government to promote elite economic interests globally. Both the 1783 Treaty of Paris and the 1794–5 Jay Treaty proved to be a boon for reopening markets in Europe. The USA promised English creditors access to US courts and that they would be repaid in silver if England removed troops from western forts and abandoned their native allies. The USA regained unimpeded access to Atlantic shipping lanes, markets in Canada, and British slave colonies in the Caribbean. Most importantly, the USA would again begin collecting tariffs to fund Hamilton's financial plan.[31]

Giving the unelected Senate and the President shared power over treaties further insulated foreign policy from democratic control by excluding the House. Hamilton argued in *Federalist #75* that the legislature should dominate foreign policy because the "power of making treaties … will be found to partake more of the legislative than of the executive character." In practice, the making *and* implementation of foreign policy has evolved to be primarily the exclusive purview of the executive, leaving only the Senate to vote a treaty up or down with little power to shape its contents.[32]

The lack of public disclosure can stretch for years, if not decades, making foreign policy, national security, and trade opaque. Although members of Congress have actively participated in the making of foreign policy beginning with Washington, even joining President

Truman to negotiate the 1949 North Atlantic Treaty which established NATO, today treaties are delivered as final product to the Senate, when they are introduced at all.[33]

In recent decades, presidents have entirely bypassed the required two-thirds ratification vote in II.2.2 by submitting executive agreements requiring only a simple majority in both houses. The annexations of Texas (1845) and Hawai'i (1898) after treaties were defeated in the Senate were early models. In recent decades presidents have also submitted trade agreements such as the North American Free Trade Agreement (NAFTA, now the 2020 United States-Mexico-Canada Agreement). Barely passing as an agreement on January 1, 1994, NAFTA became the model for globally extending extra-constitutional rights to US corporations and investors. Sometimes Congress delegated power to presidents to unilaterally control international finance, such as in the 1917 wartime Trading with the Enemy Act and later 1977 amendments.

Some executive agreements were not voted on by Congress, the contents not publicly disclosed, or both. These have been used to cement an ongoing alliance with Saudi Arabia in 1944, to end the Vietnam War, and to establish military bases in the USA's gigantic global base network. Today, with about 800 military bases in more than 70 countries and territories, the US military is both the world's largest landowner and burner of fossil fuels. Despite being revealed in a 1972 Senate hearing, the precise number of such status of forces agreements is still unknown.

The historical record shows no necessity for bypassing treaties in favor of executive agreements other than to expand presidential power. By 1971, out of the nearly 1,000 treaties submitted to the Senate for ratification, only 12 percent were rejected (14 percent passed with amendments), resulting in an 88 percent success rate.[34] Today there is no operative definition or limit to extra-constitutional executive agreements and no clear constitutional path to checking, annulling, or overruling them.[35]

In the 2015 *Zivotofsky v. Kerry* case, the Supreme Court threw out a law restricting the President's "exclusive" authority to recognize foreign governments, only further expanding the President's unilateral power to carry out diplomacy, war, and treaty making without Congressional participation. The court cited Hamilton's assertion in *Federalist #70* that the President is best positioned to make foreign policy with the "[d]ecision, activity, secrecy, and despatch" inherent in the "unity" of executive power. Yet, as we already saw in *Federalist #75* Hamilton flipped, warning that "to commit to him the entire power of making treaties, it would be utterly unsafe and improper to intrust that power to an elective magistrate of four years' duration."

8
The Judiciary:
The Servant above His Master

Americans have a paradoxical understanding of the role of the courts in American politics. The courts are seen both as adversary and savior, impediment to and protector of rights, and shield of the elite and protector of the everyday people. These roles are, of course, diametrically opposed and impossible to reconcile.

This paradox is apparent in how both major parties, civil right organizations, law and order advocates, and proponents of private property see the courts. The courts are a friend to liberty and rights when they rule in a way that accords with one's interests and perspective. And when they don't, the courts are a hostile affront to constitutional principles. When a court rules in a way that favors one's interests, the court is ruling according to the "original intent" of the Framers (says the right) or interpreting the Constitution as a "living" document (says the left). This problem is widespread among historians, law professors, and political scientists, who see the courts as neutral umpires that weigh "rights" and "wrongs" right out of a *Schoolhouse Rock* cartoon.

The extremely brief Article III gives the courts immense powers, perhaps the most power of all three branches, to constrain and impede the will of the majority. The Framers didn't just place the judiciary third in order of importance by the sequence of constitutional Articles—they made them the last line of defense in the gauntlet of minority checks set up to protect property, and the final arbiters of elite minority rule.

Article VI and the 4th, 5th, and 14th amendments are also part of the courts' arsenal, providing supremacy power as a minority check to protect slavery, commerce, contracts, currency, debt repayment, and protections for property. Without explicitly doing so, the Constitution granted a single judge and as few as three appellate judges and five justices—all of whom serve for life and are nearly impossible to remove by impeachment—the power of judicial review to override laws. The courts were designed, and continue to serve, as the last line of defense against political democracy and to prevent economy democracy.

From States to "the People"

The Constitution shifted who is governed from the *states* under the Articles of Confederation to the *people* under the Constitution. No groups, classes, organizations, or any other social formation are explicitly identified in the Articles of the Constitution other than "militias," "citizen," "people," and "person," all terms that obscure material differences of class, race, sex, and other hierarchies.

Disempowering the states removed their authority over economic policy to impede the demands of the people out of doors. Because the states were no longer sovereign entities in a voluntary confederation, they could not refuse to comply with the decisions of the federal government.

Despite "the people," or individuals, being the primary subject of the Constitution, they were actually given very little power, or right, to control the actions of the federal government.

Try asking anyone to describe the difference between the Declaration of Independence and the Constitution. Most will repeat the childhood lesson that the Declaration was an assertion of independence. Some will even add that it was also a revolutionary statement of grievances principles such as "Consent of the Governed." You are likely to be told that the Constitution is the source of our rights. But which part of the Constitution? The Articles of the Constitution provide precious few of these much-vaunted rights, other than the rights of individuals to run for office in I.2.2, I.3.3, and II.1.5; the right to *habeas corpus* in I.9.2; to receive "Privileges and Immunities" from the states and not the federal government in IV.2.1;[1] and the right to a jury trial in criminal cases III.2.3. Few realize that the list of rights in the unamended Constitution are this sparse because it was written to establish the organization and power of the federal government and its relationship to the states. The much-vaunted "We the People" are virtually unmentioned and unprotected.

The most cherished right of all—the right to vote, or the "Consent of the Governed"—in the Declaration is nowhere to be found in the Constitution: not in 1787 and not today. The most glaring absence is the justification for the Revolution, the right "to alter or to abolish it, and to institute new Government," asserted in the Declaration— the right of revolution criminalization as "treason" in III.3.2. The omission of rights did not go unnoticed. An effort to add a bill of rights modeled after Pennsylvania's and Virginia's failed at the Convention, was demanded again at a few of the state ratifying conventions, and was taken up by the first Congress. Although we credit James Madison with shepherding them, he didn't always support a bill of rights, having called them "parchment barriers" violated by "overbearing majorities" but conceded to them to help the ratification effort.[2]

The shift to the individual corresponded to the shift from feudalism to capitalism.[3] Feudalism granted some rights to the class of serfs, which the lords could not violate, and to the class of lords, which the monarch could not infringe upon. The shift to a capitalist economy removed the serfs from the land and thus stripped them of their group rights. While the merchants gained rights as a class without aristocratic title, the serfs were no longer bound to the lord, and gained the right to bodily autonomy and to sell themselves, and their labor, to anyone. Rights for the merchants implied obligations for the monarch. In contrast, rights for the former serfs, now as workers, were the result of the stripping away of obligations for the capitalists that purchase their labor. Replacing the states with the people as the primary political actor in the Constitution represented the triumph both of the merchant over the feudal lord and of the economic system based on the exploitation of the labor of workers as individuals.

Judicial Breakdown

Under the Articles, Congress served as a final appeals court and could establish courts to decide cases concerning piracy and the capture of ships. With virtually no judicial power, cases were really decided by state courts which had vast discretion as to whether to abide by treaties and Congressional law. During the economic crisis preceding the Convention, state courts proved to be a threat to property by hobbling the attempts of creditors to collect their debts and secure their assets through delays, the lack of bankruptcy laws, ineffective debtor prisons, and the inability to compel replevin actions to force repayment and collection. State courts asserted state sovereignty that conflicted with Congress and with other states, and impeded efforts to integrate the political and economic systems of the states.

The Framers saw local and state judges as partisan hacks who were too sympathetic to the people out of doors and too willing to concede to the "mob" when attacked or faced with widely unpopular cases. The state constitutions revised during the Revolution allowed for either appointed state and local judges subject to the confirmation by the legislature or direct election by the legislature with term limits. In several states, judges were elected, with local justices of the peace limited to a single year long term. None gave lifetime tenure to the judges or had judicial review of the law. In no state were the courts established to wield immense powers as a co-equal branch of government.

As members of the local communities where they served, local justices of the peace were often responsive to the demands of local debtors. During the 1780s economic crisis, numerous local and state courts in several states refused to hear cases concerning foreclosures for outstanding debt, prevented auctions, and left taxes uncollected. Numerous tax collectors refused or were unable to collect from recalcitrant backcountry farmers and local justices of the peace refused to punish them. In Pennsylvania, New Hampshire, and other states, many locally elected justices of the peace refused to hold trials, delayed enforcing judgments for debt collection, made creditors pay to imprison debtors, and slow-rolled or refused to collect taxes and seize property for unpaid taxes. For their sympathies with the local majority interests, justices and tax collectors were threatened with arrest and removal from office, and were publicly denounced by the elites.

Making matters worse, local communities refused to cooperate or obstructed the courts. Witnesses refused to testify, juries refused to convict, and crowds refused to bid at auction, effectively preventing the courts from being used for debt collections. Many county petitions in the 1780s called for closing courts, banning lawyers, and stopping foreclosures and collections of debts. There were also armed attacks on judges and courts in several states, most famously the 1786–7 Shays' Rebellion which shut courts down and prevented enforcement of foreclosures, debt collections, and enforcement of contracts. This was but the mid-point for a cycle of rebellion across several other states from 1765 in North Carolina to the early 1800s in Maine.

After the experience of the courts during British control, they were the least popular and weakest branch of the state governments. The Declaration protested the king's control of the courts so that he "made Judges dependent on his Will alone."[4] This was likely a reference to colonial judges, the Board of Trade, and the English Privy Council using judicial review to strike down laws and hear appeals. In all, these bodies struck down 469 (or 5.55 percent) of the 8,563 colonial acts that were reviewed.[5] Not surprisingly, judicial review was widely despised and entirely excluded from the state courts.

Local and state courts also proved unfriendly to suits brought by Loyalists to recover their confiscated property and British creditors trying to collect unpaid debts under the authority of the 1783 Treaty of Paris that ended the Revolutionary War.[6] Replevin laws were widely unenforceable.

Article III was designed to counter these disruptions of the courts and provide adequate protection for property missing from the Articles of Confederation and the state constitutions. To understand the role of Article III as a protector of property, it must be situated in the long-running conflicts that preceded the Revolution, Confederation, and Constitution by several decades.

Creditors' Courts

The Treaty of Paris may have been as influential as the Shays' Rebellion for creating a federal judiciary armed with judicial review.

Recognizing the Confederation and reopening British Atlantic markets to American traders is only half the agreement. The treaty also granted access to state courts which obligated judges to grant replevin petitions from Loyalist creditors and landowners for the return of their expropriated land, property, and outstanding debts. The Treaty of Paris, which John Jay, John Adams, and Ben Franklin had negotiated, was an unenforceable replevin order to the states. Many states did not comply with Article IX of the Articles of Confederation granting Congress the power to make treaties. Article 4 of the treaty had stipulated that "Creditors on either Side shall meet with no lawful Impediment to the Recovery of the full Value in Sterling Money of all bona fide Debts heretofore contracted," and Article 5 "that all Persons who have any Interest in confiscated Lands, either by Debts, Marriage Settlements, or otherwise, shall meet with no lawful Impediment in the Prosecution of their just Rights." However, both articles were unenforceable. Few judges were willing to face local wrath for handing back property to the disgraced Loyalists from whom it had been expropriated and redistributed as the spoils of war.

Wondering whether "our courts of justice [are] open for the recovery of British debts," debtor Jefferson lamented that "[t]he principles of that act [the 1783 Treaty of Paris] can be justified: but the total stoppage of justice cannot."[7] Virginians were some of the adamant opponents of the treaty because they had incurred heavy losses from rebellious slaves, had large outstanding personal debts, and possessed large amounts of expropriated Loyalist land. Slavery, land, debt, courts, and international trade were interconnected.

The inability to enforce the treaty resulted in a capital strike. After the Revolution, the broke and indebted states and Congress struggled to obtain new lines of credit from the Dutch and Spanish to cover their defaulted loans to the French. Hard currency became scarce, prices skyrocketed, and imports and exports came to a halt. States adopted "beggar-thy-neighbor" policies, using import and export taxes and other protectionist measures. Seeing British and Loyalist creditors spurned, European lenders refused to get in deeper. Writing from Paris, Jefferson warned that "every one therefore would prefer having his money here rather than on the other side the Atlantic, where distance, want of punctuality, & a habitual protection of the debtor would be against them."[8] The Confederation, the 13 states, and Vermont were denied credit. The markets came to a screeching halt. Although there were some signs of new manufacturing, and subsistence farmers still grew for local markets, nearly everyone was in dire straits. Congress's demands for requisitions came up mostly empty and protests against taxes and debts exploded.

To address the crisis, the elites demanded a new national system that could prevent state and local courts from interfering with the enforcement of contracts, and debt and tax collection that left the property interests of merchants and bankers unprotected. The state courts were denounced by the Framers and fellow elites as examples of the "tyranny of the majority." Having powerful functioning courts was critical to adjudicating criminal prosecutions of Regulator rebels, civil matters of tax and private and public debt collection, and the enforcement of contracts under the Treaty of Paris that were essential to the economy.

Ratification brought the establishment of Article III federal courts armed with supremacy power in Article VI.2, and judicial review after 1803 that ensured the treaty was enforced and the rights of property restored. Those Revolutionaries who ended up in court discovered that while they had won the political war, the British and their Loyalist allies had won the economic war. Reluctant patriots, who began the 1770s as Loyalists or insisted on sovereign rule for the colonies while staying in the British Empire, used the treaty to restore property relations as they had existed prior to 1775.

Judicial Review: Hither Shall You Go but No Further

The inability to ensure the collection of debts in state courts was denounced by the elites as the redistribution of property. The antidote was Article III and the supremacy power in VI.2 that have provided a minority check of last resort for constraining political democracy and impeding economic democracy.

Judges would no longer be elected, would serve for life, and were made nearly impossible to remove by impeachment according to

I.2.5 and I.3.6, although they are not specifically listed. The Framers fixed the problem of democratically selected state judges being subjected to majoritarian pressures by making federal judges nominated by the President and confirmed by the Senate according to II.2.2, and allowing them to "hold their Offices during good Behavior" (III.1), long interpreted as meaning for lifetime terms. These constraints on political democracy mean that federal judges need not concern themselves with popular opinion or pressures, although they often do. The lack of democratic accountability continues to be celebrated as "independence" and "neutrality."

In addition to the Supreme Court, under III.1, Congress can establish "such inferior Courts" such as trial and appellate courts. This also allows specialized administrative law courts—such as for taxes, bankruptcy, tariffs, and trade, to name only a few—to be created which are housed in the executive branch departments and agencies. These judges are civil servants who are hired and fired at will to compel obedience and insulate them from democratic pressures.

Although the Constitution establishes Congress's authority over the courts, it cannot easily check their power. The courts were granted the power to decide the "supreme Law of the Land" in Article VI.2, equivalent to Congress's enumerated powers in Article I, by interpreting state laws, reviewing state supreme court and lower federal court rulings, and deciding the constitutionality of state and federal laws and regulations. The Constitution ensured this by obligating "the Judges in every State shall be bound thereby, any Thing in the Constitution or Laws of any State to the Contrary notwithstanding" to "the supreme Law of the Land" (VI.2).

The power of judicial review—the most important power of the courts to rule all or part of law or executive actions of both the federal and state governments unconstitutional—is not enumerated in the Constitution.[9] There was little discussion by the Framers of the issue. In fact, a legislative veto over state laws was vigorously debated but was voted down on July 17, 1787. Soon after, the Article VI.2 supremacy clause was introduced.[10]

The dominant explanation for why judicial review is explicitly missing from the Constitution is that the Framers never intended to include it, and it would not exist except for a defiant Chief Justice John Marshall who included it in his 1803 *Marbury v. Madison* majority ruling.

This story is in fact not entirely true. According to historian Charles Beard, the Framers expressed widespread public support for judicial review. He found that 17 of the 25 most influential Framers publicly supported judicial review both during and after the Convention, and only four or five Framers were publicly opposed to judicial review.[11] Several Framers spoke in favor of giving what they then called the judicial "negative" to the courts during and after the Convention in letters, state ratifying convention debates, court rulings, and later in Congress. One even chaired the Senate committee that wrote the 1789 Judiciary Act that granted judicial review to the federal courts and was used in several cases preceding Marbury.[12] Some of the Framers opposed to judicial review supported giving either Congress or the President the same power to veto state laws.[13]

The Framers didn't spend much time debating whether to establish judicial review because there was almost no disagreement.[14] There was broad support for empowering the courts to overturn laws passed by the states, which Madison described as "a serious evil," such as the issuing of paper money.[15] Although he first preferred "a negative *in all cases whatsoever* on the legislative acts of the States," Madison also foresaw that "the national supremacy ought also to be extended as I conceive to the Judiciary departments."[16]

Despite its absence from the Constitution, some Framers claimed it was there.[17] Future Supreme Court Justice James Wilson informed the Pennsylvania ratifying convention that:

If a law should be made inconsistent with those powers vested by this instrument in Congress, the judges, as a consequence of their independence, and the particular powers of government being defined, will declare such law to be null and void; for the power of the Constitution predominates. Any thing, therefore, that shall be enacted by Congress contrary thereto, will not have the force of law.[18]

The Framers widely agreed that these wide-ranging powers of the supremacy clause and judicial review were needed to empower the federal courts to prevent forms of economic democracy that threaten the prerogatives of elites and property. Madison spoke for many when he described the judicial veto as a way to "keep the States within their proper limits" and prevent the economic democracy because "the restraints against paper emissions, and violations of contracts are not sufficient."[19]

Before Marbury

Chief Justice John Marshall's majority opinion in 1803 *Marbury v. Madison*, that a law passed by Congress was unconstitutional, wasn't the first case to use judicial review. That was done in four prior federal and 18 state court cases. Although six states and Vermont explicitly prohibited the use of judicial review, five states began to use it by 1787, although not by judges alone. In Connecticut, New York, and New Jersey non-judicial councils wielded the power over the legislature.[20]

The 1786 *Trevett v. Weeden* case in the Rhode Island Superior Court of Judicature was the first use of judicial review by a court to overturn a state law. Their use of judicial review was so controversial all of the judges who joined the ruling were replaced a few months later.

Two of the first three federal cases involving judicial review in 1792 sought to protect property against state interference with contracts and debts. The 1792 *Champion & Dickason v. Casey* case, for example, was the first use of judicial review by a federal circuit court to throw out a state law. A three-judge panel, which included Supreme Court Justice James Wilson, overturned a Rhode Island state law shielding a debtor from prison for violating the contracts clause in I.10.1.[21] The Supreme Court used judicial review in two later cases also dealing with property. The first was the 1794 *Glass v. The Sloop Betsey* rejection of a federal law asserting court jurisdiction in maritime cases and the 1796 *Hylton v. United States*, which included the Framers Oliver Ellsworth and William Patterson, which asserted court authority to determine the constitutionality of the carriage tax.[22]

Ironically, as a lawyer in the 1796 *Ware v. Hylton* concerning whether the Treaty of Paris's debt collection clause trumped a Virginia state law, Marshall argued that the courts *do not* have judicial review "expressly given by the Constitution."[23] Less than a decade later, however, Marshall famously reversed his legal philosophy in *Marbury v. Madison*. Marshall, writing for the majority of the Supreme Court, asserted the principal of judicial review as if it were obviously included in the Constitution, relying on Section 25 of the 1789 Judiciary Act which granted the Supreme Court the power to overrule state laws and parts of state constitutions that violated the Constitution, treaties, laws, or "commissions."[24] The law went so far as to declare that "an act of the Legislature repugnant to the Constitution is void." In such cases, Marshall wrote, "it is emphatically the province and duty of the Judicial Department to say what the law is." "The judicial power of the United States is extended to all cases arising under the Constitution," he later added, without evidence. He didn't have any evidence because it didn't exist. The Supreme Court's authority extends only to the qualified "all" specific to the "all the other Cases before mentioned" (III.2.1).

Marbury opened the way to also overturning state laws for the first time in the 1810 *Fletcher v. Peck* case, in which Marshall found that Georgia could repeal a land grant law but could not violate the right of a property owner by seizing it without compensation.[25] It hadn't taken long for the federal courts to realize the Framers' wish for a power to overturn laws and actions of state governments.

After being little used by the Supreme Court after *Fletcher v. Peck* until the 1857 *Dred Scott v. Sanford* case, the use of judicial review accelerated after the Civil War. Between 1865 and 1970, during a period of growing industrial class conflict, the Supreme Court struck down all or part of 90 laws, most of which dealt with the rights of property. In its first 100 years, the Supreme Court used judicial review in 181 instances concerning a state constitution or law and another 20 involving acts of Congress. About a quarter, 57 in all, concerned violations of the contracts clause. One early twentieth-century observer found that these rulings "have been almost uniformly advantageous to the capital-owning class in preserving property rights and corporate privileges which the unhindered progress of democracy would have abridged or abolished."[26]

In the twelve years between 1889 and 1901, the Supreme Court struck down another 13 federal laws, 63 state laws, and 14 ordinances, and the numbers kept steady for the next few decades. Between 1899 and 1937, 55 federal laws and 401 state laws were struck down—six times more than during the first 75 years of the country's history.[27] From 1953 to 1988, the Supreme Court struck down 356 state laws and 40 local ordinances. By late 1992, an estimated 142 federal laws and 1,200 state laws or parts of state constitutions unconstitutional. The Supreme Court has used judicial review much more extensively than it was used by the UK under colonial rule.

While the Warren Court, renowned for its civil rights rulings, overturned an average of only 8.69 state and local laws each term, the more conservative Burger and Rehnquist courts overturned an average of 13.24 and 10.67 per term. The Warren and Burger courts overturned precedent 2.5 times per term on average while Rehnquist court reported 4.3 per term.[28]

Because judicial review was most frequently used to shield property, it took until 1965 for the Supreme Court to strike down a law of Congress as a violation of 1st amendment free speech rights in the case *Lamont v. Postmaster General* and 1971 for it to throw out a case on the basis of violating freedom of religion in *Tilton v. Richardson*.[29]

Today the courts' use of judicial review has transformed the judiciary into a "third chamber" of every legislature, providing a roadblock and impediment to laws, policies, and lower and state court rulings that threaten property.[30] The Supreme Court has taken an increasingly larger proportion of cases concerning property, ruling increasingly in favor of corporations over smaller business, workers, environmental groups, and even the federal government in matters of anti-trust law enforcement.[31]

Courts for Capital

From the start, the federal courts have used judicial review to place property out of reach of economic democracy. In the 1816 *Martin v. Hunter's Lessee* case the Supreme Court reaffirmed the supremacy of property when it voided a state's confiscation of land from a Loyalist prohibited by the Treaty of Paris. The rights of the individual property owner now trumped "the people's" elected representatives power to make any law concerning property.

In the 1819 *Trustees of Dartmouth College v. Woodward* case, the Supreme Court once more invoked the supremacy of property by prohibiting the state from turning the private college into a public institution and thus interfering with its contractual right to property inherent in the colonial charter.[32] The court's reasoning appeared to draw on Thomas Paine's earlier defense of the charter of the Bank of North America against repeal by the Pennsylvania legislature. A contract "cannot be affected or altered by any act made afterwards," Paine insisted, because "how much more inconsistent and irrational, despotic and unjust would it be, to think of making an act with the professed intention of breaking up a contract already signed and sealed." In other words, a right granted to property may never be altered.[33]

Federal supremacy superseded state authority to even regulate within its own boundaries. In the 1819 *McCulloch v. Maryland* case, the Supreme Court found Maryland's tax on the corrupt 2nd US Bank violated the bank's federal charter. Agreeing with *Federalist #75*, the court asserted its power to determine which laws, while "not prohibited, but consist with the letter and spirit of the constitution, are constitutional."[34]

The states were compelled to extend the same "Privileges and Immunities," such as state rights for residents, to businesses crossing state lines. In the 1824 *Gibbons v. Ogden* case, the Supreme Court asserted federal supremacy power over interstate commerce of businesses crossing state lines or operating under a federal license. The Supreme Court repeatedly invoked federal power to charter corporations, regulate business, oversee interstate commerce, and prohibit states from regulating business. The "Full Faith and Credit" (IV.1) and "Privileges and Immunities" (IV.2.1) principles protected the "right" of property from "discriminatory" state policies.

In only a few short years, the Supreme Court was already integrating the states into a single national economy. For more than a century, judicial review would be used to constrain and prevent state and local governments' power in the economy. In the 1870s, as industrial unionization and strikes grew rapidly, the court used the "freedom of contract" principle to strike down many state and federal reforms improving the treatment of workers.[35] The Supreme Court threw out a state limit on the work day and week in the 1905 *Lochner v. New York* case, a state minimum wage law in the 1923 *Adkins v. Children's Hospital* ruling, and federal regulation of business in the 1935 *A. L. A. Schechter Poultry Corporation v. United States* case, to name but a few.

Freedom of contract was also deployed as a weapon to break growing industrial unions. A ban on forcing workers to join company-run "yellow" unions was thrown out in the 1908 *Adair v. United States* case, bans on shipping goods made with child labor was overturned in the 1918 *Hammer v. Dagenhart* ruling, and a federal 10 percent tax on products made with child labor was struck down in the 1922 *Bailey v. Drexel Furniture Co.* case.

It ultimately took widespread unionization, wildcat strikes, the rapid growth of pro-Soviet communism, and the Democrats' threat to "pack the court" with more Democratic judges to temporarily reverse the course of the Supreme Court's relentless defense of property. The court reversed *Adkins*, upholding a state minimum wage law for women workers, and finally stopped using the freedom of contract clause in 1937 *West Coast Hotel Company v. Parrish* case. The same year the ruling in *National Labor Relations Board v. Jones & Laughlin Steel Corporation* abandoned the 1895 *United States v. E.C. Knight Company* precedent to allow federal regulation of manufacturing under the interstate commerce clause. This proved to be a brief pause until the 1952 *Youngstown Sheet & Tube Company v. Sawyer* ruling that overturned Truman's nationalization of steel plants to head off a threatened strike. In doing so, the Supreme Court effectively blocked the democratic road to state socialism.

This brief sampling demonstrates that judicial review has served, as Beard concluded, "to secure the rights of persons and property against popular majorities, no matter how great."[36] In the hands of the Supreme Court, judicial review has been molded into a powerful minority check to protect property from the incursions of economic democracy. Along the way, these long-lasting precedents shifted the ground to establish constitutional rights for property, insulated from interference by the majority or local, state, and federal governments. The Constitution cannot and will not be used to democratize or replace the capitalist economy.

Checking the Courts

Although easily forgotten, Article III gives Congress five immense enumerated powers over the courts in addition to impeachment. These include Senate advice and consent on judicial appointments in II.2.2 and the power to establish "such inferior Courts as the Congress may from time to time ordain and establish" (III.1 and I.8.9), the implied necessary and proper power to set the size and composition of each court,[37] and the power of the purse to fund the courts.[38] Perhaps its greatest power is to regulate the jurisdiction of the Supreme Court in III.2.2, which reads that "the supreme Court shall have appellate Jurisdiction, both as to Law and Fact, with such Exceptions, and under such Regulations as the Congress shall make." In short, Congress can decide which kinds of cases the Supreme Court can hear on appeal, establish a specialized constitutional court with restricted judicial review, and definite criteria for "during good Behavior" (III.1) including age or mental capacity.

The most notable efforts to rein in the courts was President Franklin D. Roosevelt's support for a 1937 bill that would have "packed the courts" by appointing a new justice when a sitting justice reached 70 years old and didn't resign, up to a maximum of 15 justices. A 1968 bill requiring two-thirds of judges to agree when overturning a law as unconstitutional passed the House but was killed in the Senate.[39]

Despite the nearly insurmountable threshold for passage, amending the Constitution is a possible method to constrain the power of the Supreme Court. The 16th amendment of 1913 checked the court and the elites by putting the income tax directly into the Constitution. It took 117 years to finally establish a form of taxation that was not subject to apportionment or population, thereby overturning both the 1796 *Hylton v. United States* and the 1895 *Pollock v. Farmers' Loan and Trust Company* rulings. The ratification of the 1913 16th amendment stopped the Supreme Court from further preventing the economic majority from taxing the rich and redistributing their income. The 1913 16th amendment stands out as one of the rare instances in which elite property rights lost to the "leveling" demands of economic democracy.[40]

As long as Congress does not use these powers to control the courts, the courts will control the Congress.[41] The Anti-Federalist Brutus[42] foresaw that the "judges under this constitution will control the legislature" when the court would "give the sense of every article of the constitution." The Constitution provided "no power above them, to control any of their decisions," "no authority that can remove them," he warned.[43]

From This Court there Is No Appeal

The Constitution is an extreme outlier among representative democracies, granting unlimited judicial review to the courts which very few countries, even those using common law, allow. The Framers were certainly concerned about what we today call the "Overton window." They tried to not move too fast by contemporary political norms and doom the Constitution. But the record shows they wanted to restore the British monarchy's judicial review to impede democracy. The combination of a judicial veto, lifetime appointments, and the nearly impossible impeachment removal process was understood to be a bridge too far. Their sensitivity to accusations that they were restoring aristocratic rule—a common line of Anti-Federalist attack—left judicial review to be read into the Constitution some time in the future.

Judicial review has transformed the courts into a power above the government, to borrow Hannah Arendt's defining characteristic of a totalitarian government, from which there was no further appeal. Supreme Court rulings are the end of the line and cannot be appealed or easily overturned by Congress or amendment.

Judicial review has served to deny the economic majority the capacity to pursue systemic changes to the system. Although local movements might successfully change local ordinances and state law, they are soon challenged in the federal courts. While it is true that many political innovations are born at the local and state levels, many eventually end up in the graveyard of judicial review.

Judicial review is not an abuse of power but a minority check impeding political democracy and preventing economic democracy. As J. Allen Smith put it so long ago, the judiciary "is not only the most important of our constitutional checks on the people, but is also the means of preserving and enforcing all the other checks. ... Its aim was not to increase, but to diminish popular control over the government."[44]

This is expressed most explicitly in the 1895 case *In re Debs*. American Railway Union President Eugene Debs and other union officers were charged with conspiracy for violating a court injunction obtained by the railroad company prohibiting them from communicating with workers during the 1894 national railroad strike.[45] The Supreme Court unanimously found Debs in contempt of court and sentenced him to six months in prison. Writing for the court, Justice Josiah Brewer believed that the Constitution put the entire government in service to protect business against workers. The court confirmed that "[t]he strong arm of the national government may be put forth to brush away all obstructions to the freedom of interstate commerce or the transportation of the mails. If the emergency arises, the army of the nation, and all its militia, are at the service of the nation, to compel obedience to its laws."[46]

9
Amendments and Ratification: An Act of Force and Not of Right

Even without seeing the last episode of the 2020 TV series *Mrs. America*, portraying the battle to ratify the Equal Rights Amendment (ERA) during the 1970s, we already know how it ends. Women still lack enumerated constitutional rights. The three-line amendment, which reads in part that "[e]quality of rights under the law shall not be denied or abridged by the United States or by any state on account of sex,"[1] is just one of a long list of failed amendments to the Constitution.[2] Women today are in much the same position as Harriet Scott was in 1857, waiting for a Civil War to topple the rule of racial supremacy and abolish slavery.

The defeat of the ERA means that women, who comprise the majority of the US population, continue to lack the enumerated rights, privileges, and protections of the Constitution, except for the 19th amendment negative right to have their right to vote "not be denied or abridged ... on account of sex." Without the same constitutional rights as men, women are still paid less, own less wealth, and lack formal political power. Nearly half a century after my mother brought me to an ERA meeting to organize for its ratification, and nearly 60 years since the passage of the 1963 Equal Pay Act, women continue to be subjected to unequal treatment as citizens.

Despite about 11,000 attempts to amend the Constitution over the past two centuries, we are still operating a twenty-first-century economy and government according to little-changed eighteenth-century rules. A society that had no railroad, no airplanes, no telephone, no public education system, and no knowledge of bacteria and viruses, and that believed nature was inexhaustible, black people could be property, and native peoples should be exterminated, still dictates how we run things. It is little wonder that the USA is one of the most conflict-ridden societies on the planet. We are governed by a virtually unaltered archaic system designed to protect eighteenth-century elites, passed along to their inheritors as a gift from the past.[3] The Framers wrote the rules by which we still operate to make sure it would be virtually impossible for us to change the rules.

The righteous document was neither written nor ratified with a fair fight. Throughout the campaign, Federalist elites rigged the vote in many of the key late states, locked the Anti-Federalist opposition out of most of the newspapers and printing presses, interfered with the mailing of newspapers across state lines, misrepresented and omitted important features of the proposed constitutional system, and prohibited a popular vote to ratify their document.[4]

That the Constitution has survived periods of turmoil, change, war, and insurrection is not a virtue. Rather than surviving these challenges and threats we should rather see the Constitution as their cause. As humanity teeters on the cusp of obliteration it is the Constitution that has brought us there and makes it possible for the propertied elites to push us over the edge. The inability to change or replace the Constitution is preventing us from taking the very action needed to keep our planet from burning—all to preserve the supremacy of property.

If John Locke foresaw a "slowness and aversion in the people to quit their old constitutions,"[5] in our case it is not for the lack of trying. Every effort to transform society leaves us trapped in the grip of the unchangeable Constitution. It is long past time to broach the taboo question of whether to change, sidestep, replace, or abolish the Constitution if we are to survive.

We Make the Rules

The Articles of Confederation had a long and painful birth but thrived in infancy. The Articles took nearly seven years to be ratified due to disputes over which state and land speculation company would control the vast western lands. The Articles proved hard to change because Article XIII required achieving consensus twice, in both Congress and the state legislatures, which stubbornly clung to their enumerated powers.[6] This was intended to preserve the sovereignty of the states and prevent the formation of a national government.

The nationalists used the difficulty of changing the Articles to portray it as flawed and in need of being replaced. After two years of effort, in July 1782, Alexander Hamilton and his father-in-law, Philip Schuyler, got the New York legislature to pass a resolution calling for a convention to strengthen the Articles.[7] A few months later, public creditors meeting in Philadelphia called for stronger powers to be given to Congress.[8] The pressure for a new constitution built up over the next few years. The commercial meeting hosted by George Washington at his slave plantation resulted in the 1785 Mount Vernon Compact to expand Congress's commerce power. After repeatedly failing to ratify amendments to give Congress the power to directly impose and collect even temporary taxes to repay the debt, establish a publicly backed financial system, and fund a national military, the nationalists pivoted to a grander prize.

The next meeting in Annapolis was primarily focused on the issues of paper money, debt, and fixing the Articles.[9] The Convention was supposed to begin on September 11, 1786, with delegates chosen from nine states, but only twelve delegates from five states appeared. To salvage their effort, Hamilton introduced a resolution calling for another convention in Philadelphia in May 1787 that should entertain "the Idea of extending the powers of their Deputies, to other objects, than those of Commerce."[10]

Because the Articles provided no authority to hold a constitutional convention, three states refused to appoint delegates for the Philadelphia meeting until it was officially sanctioned by Congress. Even then, Congress issued instructions limiting the Convention to only proposing amendments to the Articles.[11] The failure to ratify two proposed imposts (e.g., tariffs) helped propel more states to appear in Philadelphia.

The plan shifted dramatically only hours after the Philadelphia Convention began. Delegates ignored Congress's directions and voted to toss out the Articles and replace it entirely. Edmund Randolph and other Virginian delegates, who had been meeting before the Convention, submitted their plan, much of which would end up in the Constitution. According to notes taken by New York delegate Robert Yates, Randolph's motion that "the articles of confederation ought to be so corrected and enlarged" was withdrawn after a challenge by Gouverneur Morris and replaced with a resolution proclaiming "that a national government ought to be established, consisting of a supreme judicial, legislative, and executive."[12] After a long effort, the nationalists' project for a new constitution had hit pay dirt.

Unable to change the system using the rules of that system, they opted instead to throw it out and make a new system governed by their own rules. The Framers expected that their proposed constitution would be impossible to ratify if they followed the amendment ratification process in the Articles. To avoid possible defeat, Article VII bypassed the procedure for amendments, allowing it to be approved by conventions in 9 of the 13 states. Because the Convention defied the will of Congress, "the Constitution was illegal at the time it was drafted, a problem it promptly rectified via the miracle of self-legalization."[13]

We the Absent People

"We the People" was not just a clever turn of phrase. Shifting power from the states to individuals was an essential part of the ratification strategy.[14] Also important was the required vote by popularly elected state conventions, which allowed the Framers to bypass the state legislatures. For Madison, "[t]his will be the more essential as inroads on the *existing Constitutions* of the States will be unavoidable." They expected immense opposition to ratification from prominent state legislators who feared a loss in power and influence, and from those who opposed protections for elite property, a standing army, and other national powers enshrined in the Constitution. The state legislatures were unlikely to vote for giving up their power as the primary political actors.[15] James Wilson thought it necessary because "the House on fire must be extinguished, without a scrupulous regard to ordinary rights."[16]

This shift from the states to the people was reiterated by President Andrew Jackson in his 1832 suppression of efforts by some Southern states to nullify federal law.[17] Jackson insisted that the US government "operates directly on the people individually, not upon the States," and that the people owe their "allegiance" to the US government, the Constitution, and the laws of Congress, not the states.[18] Note that Jackson said the government operates "on" the people not that the people operate the government.[19] This is because the Framers never sought consent from "We the People of the United States," let alone the state legislatures. Even then, they had no intention of obtaining consent from all groups of people then comprising the population of the states—slaves, native peoples, small subsistence farmers, laborers, mechanics, and people with little or no property were glaringly missing at the Convention.

Supreme Court Justice Joseph Story thought that the constitutional system was "formed without the consent, express or implied, of the whole people." The truth is, he wrote, that "many of them have not been permitted to express any opinion, and many have expressed a decided dissent." This leads some to doubt that the Constitution is a "binding compact between them, with mutual obligations to observe and keep it."[20]

The Framers failed to even use what historian William Appleman Williams called the "lowest order of democracy," in which people only get to vote "yes" or "no" on a system that they had no role in making.[21] More than 230 years later, we have yet to consent to the Constitution. Ratification by a higher order of democracy, a direct ratification vote of the population, was not unknown then and was used by about half the states after 1780.[22]

That the Constitution is designed to be eternal remains unquestioned. In 1789, Jefferson thought the opposite, that "[n]o society can make a perpetual constitution, or even a perpetual law. The earth belongs always to the living generation. They may manage it then, and what proceeds from it, as they please, during their usufruct." He thought constitutions should be temporary:

Every constitution then, and every law, naturally expires at the end of 19 years. If it be enforced longer, it is an act of force, and not of right.—It may be said that the succeeding generation exercising in fact the power of repeal, this leaves them as free as if the constitution or law had been expressly limited to 19 years only.[23]

"We the People" never voted on the Constitution and do not have the right to do so in the future because it does not allow for a plebiscite or referendum on either the entire document or amendments.[24] Only New York asks the voters every 20 years to weigh in on their state constitution, asking, "shall there be a convention to revise the constitution and amend the same?" although it has not been approved since 1967. The promise of the 9th amendment that "The enumeration in the Constitution, of certain rights, shall not be construed to deny or disparage others retained by the people" can never be fully realized as long as the right of "consent of the governed" is denied by the Constitution. Despite the 15th amendment ensuring that "The right of citizens of the United States to vote shall not be denied or abridged by the United States or by any State on account of race, color, or previous condition of servitude," we are denied the right to vote for the very system of rules that govern us and to which we are expected to consent. Nineteen states with nearly half the country's population allow a direct or indirect vote on their state constitution but we have no right to vote on the US Constitution unless we first amend the Constitution to extend that right—a nearly impossible task.[25]

"We the People" must rely on government actions, interpretations, and enforcement to interpret what the Constitution means and who is accountable to it.[26] The most important power and right—which according to both John Locke and the Declaration of Independence is to alter, change, or throw off the system of government—is prohibited by law and the Constitution. As we sink ever deeper into a never-ending constitutional crisis we would do well to remember that the Declaration lamented "[s]uch has been the patient sufferance of these Colonies; and such is now the necessity which constrains them to alter their former Systems of Government."

The complete absence of a popular vote to propose or ratify amendments and call for a convention is the ultimate minority check intended to forever lock us into a system designed to protect property from democracy. Even states using Article V to call conventions is not without a possible check by the Supreme Court using judicial review to strike down the state law calling for it.

The Framers' fear of democracy also lies behind the use of state conventions instead of referendums or town meetings, refusal to recognize directions issued to delegates, and preference for rapid state convention votes for fear that prolonged democratic debate might sink the Constitution. As law professor Michael Klarman concluded, "what most Federalists wanted was not a genuine debate on the merits of the Constitution but simply its ratification."[27]

The undemocratic process for ratifying the Constitution perfectly corresponded to its undemocratic content.[28] Alongside the myriad minority checks, the ratification and amendment processes ensure that change would always fall short of economic and political democracy. By making peaceful reform impossible, the Framers inadvertently made violent struggle to overcome constitutional roadblocks and impediments inevitable.

The Lowest Order of Democracy

Despite the shift from the states to the people, only about half the population of free white men who met the state property qualifications were eligible to vote for or serve as delegates to the ratifying conventions.[29] Turnout was low in some states like Pennsylvania, for example, where about 13,000 of the 70,000 eligible voters, about 18.6 percent, voted in the delegate election. The 6,800 total votes received by the winning candidates meant that nearly half as many people voted for delegates who supported the Constitution than supported the 1776 state constitution. In total, only about 9 percent of the eligible white male voters voted indirectly to approve the Constitution.[30] Only three states and Maine, then part of Massachusetts, allowed some direct voting on the Constitution, although it mostly occurred in rural towns with small populations.[31] Nearly all the voting was limited to indirectly voting on delegates and on issuing directions to the delegates.

Pennsylvania was hardly an outlier. According to historian Charles Beard's estimate, only 20 to 25 percent of eligible white men, who comprised only 5 percent of the total population (including slaves), voted indirectly for the delegates to all the state ratifying conventions who decided whether to ratify the Constitution. This meant that only about 160,000 free white men, out of about 650,000 to 800,000 living at the time, voted. Federalist candidates won about 60 percent of the vote, representing 12.5 to 15.5 percent of the eligible voters, and Anti-Federalist candidates won the remaining votes, representing only between 7.5 and 9.87 percent of eligible voters.[32]

The Article VII ratification process fragmented the opposition into 13 different campaigns and conventions, operating at different times according to their own rules. Anti-Federalist organizing and agitation suffered from a late start, censorship, communication difficulties, and internal divisions between the elite leadership and the base. They had to play catch-up, analyzing and critiquing a document written in secrecy over the course of many months, during which the Framers were informing their Federalist allies of their work, and with few Convention records. Despite these obstacles, the majority of voters selected Anti-Federalist delegates in the four states where the final vote was close or they prevailed, and the vote was close in another four.

The Constitution was very popular in the first five states which quickly held their elections for delegates who met and ratified. The final tally in three of these included not a single "no" vote, although they met during the dead of winter in December and January before the Anti-Federalists were organized. Once they mobilized, the Anti-Federalists defeated the first vote in New Hampshire and threatened to defeat the Constitution in the remaining large states of Virginia, New York, and Massachusetts, as well as Rhode Island and North Carolina, which didn't ratify until after the Constitution went into effect. Rhode Island voters defeated it in a plebiscite, one of eleven failed efforts to ratify in two years. North Carolina voted it down in August by a very large margin and then passed it by nearly the reverse vote in November.[33]

The state ratifying conventions were rife with censorship, arm twisting, bribes, and threats to intimidate and pressure delegates.[34] In the few states where the Anti-Federalists won the overall majority of the delegates and threatened to vote "no", Federalists flipped several delegates with offers of jobs, bribes, and promises of business deals and to consider proposed amendments, prevailing in four close votes. Among the prominent Anti-Federalists who switched loyalties were Virginia Governor Edmund Randolph, a Framer who didn't sign the Constitution, and Melancton Smith of New York, a prominent *Anti-Federalist Papers* author.

It didn't help that the Anti-Federalists were internally divided. The letters, pamphlets, and editorials that comprise the *Anti-Federalist Papers*, which have yet to be published in full,[35] show wide disagreement about what they liked and disliked about the Constitution. By agreeing that Congress needed the power to tax, even temporarily, they conceded important ground to the Federalists and blunted their own critique.

Although there were several capable Anti-Federalists leaders, such as the three Framers who refused to sign the Constitution, few were small farmers, and even the wealthiest among them were not as rich as Federalist leaders.[36] The interests of the wealthiest leaders, such as their support for the I.10.1 contract clause, did not align with the movement's base of mostly of small subsistence farmers.[37]

This internal class divide among the Anti-Federalists was reflected in how delegates voted on ratification in the conventions and on paper money, stay laws, and tax relief, etc., in their state legislatures. This difference correlated with profession, level of personal wealth, and position in the economic system.

Poor and middle-income small farmers located further inland produced mostly for subsistence, engaged in non-cash exchanges, and were less integrated into commercial markets. These interests meant they benefited from state policies of economic democracy that could potentially be prohibited in the Constitution.

In contrast, merchants and commercial farmers were more likely to live in or near cities and serve regional and export markets. They were more likely to be disadvantaged by state policies of economic democracy and stood to gain from national control over currency, trade, and debt.

These internal class divisions among the Anti-Federalists ultimately contributed to their defeat in state after state as much of the leadership, who were primarily from the same class as the Federalist leaders, abandoned their opposition and voted to ratify—which an estimated one-sixth of the most outspoken eventually did.[38] Ultimately, the Anti-Federalist elite leadership voted for their class interests over all else.

The obstacles faced by the Anti-Federalists also hampered their analysis and critique of specific features of the Constitution. Their critiques published in newspapers, pamphlets, and letters, and their speeches in the state convention debates, were extremely general. They repeatedly raised vitally important concerns about consolidated power, the lack of a bill of rights, disempowered states, protections for slavery, and exclusion of large numbers of the population from participation, especially in electing the President and Senate, and appointing judges. Their analysis of the Constitution, while rushed due to having little time to study the document before the early convention votes, are still incredibly relevant today. However, few addressed the roadblocks and impediments that served as elite minority checks on the majority.

Even a better organized and more unified Anti-Federalist opposition might not have succeeded. They operated according to rules made up by Framers, such as voting in 13 separate conventions rather than a single plebiscite. It was easier to swing a few key delegates' votes at an isolated ratifying convention than having to persuade thousands of remote, rural, and hard to reach voters.

Despite being poorer, less influential, more disorganized, and having fewer political resources, the Anti-Federalists nearly defeated the Constitution.[39]

Four Dead Ends

Alongside ratification is the problem of amendment. Only 27 of approximately 11,000 proposed amendments to the Constitution have been ratified, a miserable success rate of 0.00245 percent.[40] The inability to amend the Constitution not only allows private power to fill in the gaps when government cannot function. It allows presidents to accumulate power under the guise of necessity, and the Supreme Court to overturn laws passed by elected representatives of the majority.

Fearing demographic change, the Framers made the Constitution virtually static and unalterable. The rules of the system were locked in by two levels of a supermajority vote requirement in the two stages of voting by Congress and the states. According to Article V, if an amendment passes both houses of Congress with a supermajority two-thirds vote it must then be ratified by an even higher supermajority of three-quarters of the state legislatures or conventions. The other two methods similarly allow two-thirds of states to pass an amendment which then requires a three-quarter vote of the state legislatures or conventions to ratify. Except for the use of state ratifying conventions to decide on the 21st amendment in 1933, which repealed the 1919 18th amendment banning alcohol, all the other 26 amendments have been passed by both houses of Congress and ratified by the state legislatures.

These high vote thresholds and the involvement of the states were intended to make the amendment process a "substantial check upon democracy," according to Anti-Federalist Dr. James Hutchinson.[41] The inequality of representation of the states in the Senate means that senators from the 18 smallest states can block passage of an amendment, even if it passes unanimously in the House. Even if it passes the Senate an even smaller number, 13 of the smallest states with a total population of only about 15 million people—or 4.6 percent of the US population of 328 million—can also block the will of nearly the entire US population. Our system is even more undemocratic than was the slaveocracy's Confederate constitution during the Civil War that allowed only three states to recommend an amendment triggering a constitutional convention requiring only two-thirds of the states to ratify any changes.[42]

The historical record of the amendments to date demonstrates the impossibility of meaningfully changing the Constitution. The first ten amendments were ratified by 1791. After the 12th in 1804 no more amendments were ratified for another 61 years. The 13th, 14th, and 15th amendments followed between 1865 and 1870, while all or some of the ex-Confederate states (Mississippi, Texas, and Georgia) were still not readmitted into the union. The 16th amendment followed 43 years later in 1913. The 26th amendment was ratified in 1961, 61 years before this book was published. The last amendment to be ratified was the 27th amendment in 1992, 30 years ago. Because it was one of the original twelve sent to the states, of which only ten were approved, the 27th is actually 203 years old. In total, twelve amendments were ratified in the first 15 years, 15 in the first 81 years, and the last 12 added during the last 152 years. There were many decades with no changes to the Constitution at all. Of the more than 11,000 proposed amendments only 33 have gone to the states with 27 of these being ratified. Beginning in 1999, an average of about 747 amendments were introduced during every two-year Congressional term, of which only 20 ever received a full vote by either House or Senate.[43]

While 27 successful amendments is a very small number, some might argue that it is still 27 more changes than were made to the Articles. However, it is misleading to suggest that it is easier to amend the Constitution than the Articles. While no amendment to the Articles received the required consensus of all 13 states, there were only eight attempted amendments, with two coming very close to being ratified, during the five short years it was in effect.[44] The Articles did not exist long enough to test the amendment process, especially considering that part of that time was during the tumultuous Revolution.

Repairing the Checks

The first and last time a convention met to amend or write a new Constitution was 235 years ago. This is because the amendment process was designed to prohibit the people or the states from repeating the very same process that the Framers used.

Constitutional amendments exist to address a constitutional crisis, fix a flaw, correct a mistake, fill a gap, or update the system to better fit the times. Amendments are most likely to be ratified when they right the sinking ship of state and restore its credibility. But even once ratified, amendments have been distorted for other uses.

The 13th, 14th, and 15th Reconstruction Era amendments reconstructed the union by forcing the Southern states to give citizenship and rights to former slaves and free blacks. The former Confederate states were readmitted once they changed their constitutions. These and other states claimed a 10th amendment reserve clause power to discriminate by using Jim Crow laws to evade these amendments and block further federal intervention in the economy.

Although these amendments were intended to dismantle obstacles to political and economic democracy, what historian W.E.B. DuBois described as "racial democracy," they were designed or soon turned into new roadblocks and impediments.[45] The 13th amendment allows prisoners to be enslaved, and Section 2 of the 14th amendment allows them to be disenfranchised.

The 17th amendment made the Senate directly elected but did not alter the Senate's function as a minority check. The amendment was ratified in response to the growing success of the populist People's Party which had won control of several state legislatures and governors' offices in the plains states and in the South during the 1870 and 1880s and sent a few members to the US Senate to rein in elite power. The Senate is still elected in three staggered two-year phases, and disproportionately represents the population. Rather than democratizing the Senate, the 17th amendment kept it as a roadblock in the path of any upstart third party seeking to send one of its own to serve as a senator.

Article V explicitly prohibits the Senate from ever being eliminated by amendment with the exceptional prohibition that "no State, without its Consent, shall be deprived of its equal Suffrage in the Senate." The Framers clearly prevented any effort to make the amendment process easier by either removing or democratizing the Senate by making the number of seats proportional to the population of the state. That would require an entirely new constitution.

It is not surprising that even efforts to amend the amendment process are routinely defeated. Between 1911 and 1929, 18 proposed amendments to do just that went nowhere after being introduced into Congress.[46] The amendment process is itself a minority check on any attempt to change the Constitution.

This is why Article V is called an "iron cage." It prevents any attempt to further democratize the Constitution by using the Constitution. Rather than illustrating a capacity to change, Article V instead demonstrates what law professor Sanford Levinson calls a "*constitutional stasis.*"[47] Law professor Michael Klarman described Article V as designed "to disable current majorities from escaping constitutional constraints imposed by their predecessors."[48]

Today it is clear that the rule of property must be abolished if we are to save humanity and the myriad other species we are taking down with us. Yet our way is blocked by a Constitution that makes change all but impossible, to the detriment of us all.

10
Beyond the Constitution

It is extremely difficult to reconcile a belief in the Constitution as living, flexible, and changeable with the virtual impossibility of making change in the USA. There is abundant persuasive evidence that the Constitution was designed not to facilitate meaningful systemic change but to prevent anything that does not serve the interests of the propertied elite. Designed to be nearly unchangeable, the Constitution simply cannot be fixed. We have run out of precious time trying to change what was designed to thwart change.[1] After a period of grief for the death of the mythical Constitution, it will be time to accept that we cannot use the Constitution to organize a more democratic system to reverse the trajectory towards planetary ecocide. The constitutional rule of property—made possible by the expropriation of native peoples, slavery, and the exploitation of labor—is a primary threat to the survival of humanity.[2]

As I write in 2022, we continue a half century of endlessly circling around the same pressing issues with no end in sight. The fossil fuel industry continues to block legislation that would initiate a transition from our dependence on its products, women are losing the right to have an abortion, and dozens of undeclared wars continue even after the withdrawal from Afghanistan, just to name a few.

The effort to highlight the shortcomings and dead ends in the Constitution in this book does not provide easy solutions for fixing or bypassing it. Too many of us still cling to the illusion, as law professor Jeffrey Toobin puts it, that "the Constitution, and the structure of government that it established, provides the backdrop, but never the subject, for every controversy."[3] The Constitution is always *affected* by the problems we face, it is never the *cause* of the problems.

Too many of us have trouble letting go of the Constitution as a tool for change. We cling to the fantasy that the Constitution could work if not for corruption, politics, partisanship, big money, and apathy. We fail to realize that these are the *symptoms* of what's wrong with the Constitution, not the *cause*. The source of the problem is the "US Constitution: hiding in plain sight," as journalist Daniel Lazare put it so succinctly.[4] Like an abusive relationship, we struggle to accept that some day we will have to leave.

If you are, like me, ready to move past the Constitution, we have options. Forget about impossible amendments. We should use the Framers' strategy when they too were unable to amend the Articles— bypass it altogether and create a different system. Refusing to play by its rules, as the Framers also did, will transform the Constitution into an irrelevant and obsolete relic that no longer has power to control us.

We are more than capable of writing our own rules for how we govern ourselves that can change when change is needed. The survival of all life on our planet depends on us getting beyond the Constitution as quickly as possible. As the global hegemonic power, the USA stands in the way of the urgently required international action needed to reverse climate catastrophe. Either the Constitution or humanity must go.

We Have Options

We have options for getting past the Constitution in the short term. Whether these can survive the minority checks they will certainly face is uncertain. To ensure some success we can move along several tracks at once, abandoning failed or blocked efforts so that we can refocus attention, power, and resources on winning strategies.

One current strategy on the right is to use the nearly insurmountable Article V to call a constitutional convention of the states. The Convention of States Project, funded by the last surviving right-wing billionaire Koch brother, is currently attempting to do this with tediously slow progress due to widespread distrust. Few expect that this convention would result in anything but a new elite-serving constitution. Even if it resulted in a more democratic government, failing to end the rule of property would soon undermine it.

An alternative is to ignore Article V and change state law. Once the laws are passed by a majority of the states, Congress can approve them as a state compact according to I.10.3. Because the text is open-ended, Congress alone decides whether to approve them. There is currently an effort to pass a state compact in which states totaling at least 270 electoral votes award all their electoral votes to the winner of the national popular vote. Unfortunately, after about a decade, only states totaling about half the required number of electoral votes have approved it.

State compacts are an imperfect option. They move slowly, may not pass enough states or Congress, and could be repealed by either or both. Without a strict exit clause, states could break a compact by withdrawing when the state's majority party changes. Congress or the President could also decide that the compact threatens national security and then use the "guarantee" clause in IV.4 to suppress them. Because they do not change the Constitution, they can be ruled unconstitutional by the Supreme Court.

We could also try the Framers' strategy of bypassing the states and Article V altogether by launching an independent effort by the majority to write a new agreement or constitution, publicly debate it, and directly vote on ratification. Because it only applies to "the Establishment of this Constitution," Article VII would be entirely moot. Our agreement, or constitution, would be an entirely different one.

Madison provided the rationale for disposing of the Articles of Confederation in *Federalist #43*. Rather than a constitution, he thought the Articles were "founded on ordinary acts of legislative authority" creating a league or treaty. Because "a breach of any one article is a breach of the whole treaty," he had the audacity to "pronounce the compact violated and void."

We could make a case that the Constitution is also self-breaching. It has never lived up to its first three words, "We the People," because we the people have never directly given consent to be governed by it nor does it grant us the right to ever do so. Denied the right to give consent to the Constitution we could pronounce the Constitution "violated and void" for denying another principle for which independence was declared: "the Right of the People to alter or to abolish it, and to institute new Government."

Some countries require regular constitutional revision, as New York requires (see Chapter 9), or have devised new democratic methods for revising their constitution or writing a new one. The Constitute Project's database of world constitutions shows that many have either been thoroughly revised or replaced in recent decades.[5]

We can learn from the Athenian assembly and contemporary participatory budgeting to do constitutional revision from the ground up.[6] Local neighborhoods could meet in regular public assemblies, as happened in the 2011–12 Occupy Wall Street encampments, to write a list of priorities. Everyone aged twelve and older could take turns serving short terms representing their neighborhoods in the assemblies and be subject to recall by a plurality of residents.

They would send their lists to a regional assembly composed of rotating delegates from all the local assemblies. They would discuss all the priorities and synthesize them into several draft versions that are sent back to the local assemblies. All assemblies would be open and allow anyone to speak on the proposed drafts, decide their own procedures, and vote on their priorities. They would be live streamed and televised in real time allowing for moderated chats, open comments, proposals, questions, and voting, and ultimately write and revise their own priorities. The local and regional assemblies would continue the process with a deadline to achieve modified consensus. At every stage, these drafts would be published widely by printing them on receipts and food packages, distributing free copies in print and online, and by mailing, emailing, and texting copies to every person and household to discuss, debate, and propose ideas.

Once the neighborhood and regional assemblies approve a draft text, a streamed and televised "national" assembly would meet to reconcile each regional draft in a similar manner, this time with the regional assemblies. Members of the "national" assembly would be randomly selected from each region, serve short terms, and be subject to instant recall by a plurality of regional delegates. The assembly would also debate openly in real time and vote until a final modified consensus document is approved by the deadline. Assembly days would be a weekly national holiday with paid leave for anyone serving in an assembly, attending the meetings, engaging in short-term specialized roles, or organizing a recall. This will allow many to participate at all levels. Funding would be provided for education, outreach, promotions, and publicity.

There are several risks to this strategy of participatory constitutional revision from below. Because it is an end run around the Article V process, writing an entirely new agreement, or constitution, this way would likely run into fierce opposition by those opposed to change from below. The USA is a violent country with widespread false consciousness, far too much propaganda and misinformation, far too many guns, and far too much money concentrated in the hands of the very few. Preparations will be needed to counter the inevitable front groups of deep-pocketed billionaires, both plutocratic political parties, non-profits, non-governmental organizations, and chambers of commerce that will attempt to co-opt, harness, professionalize, redirect, take over the process to serve their interests, or have the courts rule it unconstitutional. Some of these may attempt to stir up ultra-nationalist sentiment to disrupt the effort.

Another threat would come from below, from both far right and sectarian left groups and parties that would likely try to hijack the process. Even supportive members of our divided, conflict-ridden, and misinformed population would likely bring the factionalism, prejudices, and turmoil already enveloping society into the process and bring it to a grinding halt. We should be prepared for vicious battles over differing and competing interests that would drive away many who genuinely desire changes that would serve the interests of direct political and economic democracy.

Any process must also be insulated against the "tyranny of structurelessness" that puts control of the process in the hands of the few who have the time, resources, money, and motivation to be involved in the fight to further their own concerns, interests, groups, and class.[7] For this reason, all participants should rotate in and out of the assemblies, be subject to instant recall, and receive paid leave to serve.

Those pursuing this strategy must be prepared for, even if they are uncertain how to prevent, these inevitable threats. Because it is self-organized it should not be an official government-sanctioned process to avoid another set of inevitable risks.

These strategies ultimately offer little chance of removing the supreme rule of property. We must accept the likelihood that we are simply unable to change or replace the Constitution. There is simply too much at stake for the ruling elite to allow any process to succeed, which is why few are seriously talking about constitutional change. Most of those who recognize the predicament of being governed by an unchangeable Constitution have resigned themselves to futilely pursuing impermanent short-term reforms.

Constitutional Dead Ends

The right and left are torn over whether the Constitution prevents or allows for change. Conservatives approach the Constitution as realists, using its myriad minority checks as weapons to prevent, dilute, or undo reforms that oppose their interests. As its base of support shrinks, conservatives, backed by a growing far right in the streets, have turned to creating new obstacles to voting, participation, and even the basic functions of governing. Their tenuous ally, the fast-growing far right, uses constitutional myths to justify violently smashing those who want change. This conservative/far-right alliance now presents a very real risk of corporate-backed fascism based on a romanticization of the Constitution's granting of supremacy to property.

Liberals and social democrats are united in their repeated futile attempts to salvage what is good in the Constitution for the short term. This electoral center left has been captured by the myth of constitutional change through voting, protest, and majority rule, and is unwilling to acknowledge the minority checks that impede them every time. With each new election cycle those demanding systemic change repeatedly embrace "progressive" and leftist candidates who promise to take over the Democratic Party and implement change. They expend immense energy toiling to elect these candidates, help elite foundation-backed advocacy groups to push for new laws, influence a friendly administration, and win in the courts. With each election cycle voters send these candidates to office only to see their promises blocked or altered beyond recognition by the need to "compromise" the best features of their proposals just to get them passed, approved, or protected in court. Each new defeat emboldens the center left to push on, temper their ambitions for systemic change, and continue channeling their efforts into a dead end.

Despite the long historical record of reform efforts running aground on the shoals of innumerable minority checks, these missionaries of change continue their push. Their efforts are renewed each election cycle like a political melodrama with the same predictable outcome. They lack the irresistible force of mass movements, insurrections, uprisings, armed struggles, mass strikes, and civil wars that provide the necessary leverage to give them the upper hand.

Year after year, generation after generation, these insider progressives are unable to turn the impossible into the plausible, toiling away with little to show for their efforts. After achieving the smallest reforms, activists shift gears to become advocates, consolidate their resources, and harden their base to defend a hard-won fragment of their demands from the inevitable ravages of reaction.

Advocates seek funding, stage media events, and lobby, thereby investing the system with the legitimacy needed to protect their minuscule gains. In this process, the organizer, insurgent, or revolutionary becomes an advocate, "stakeholder," executive in a non-profit interest group, or a candidate for office. And in an instant, the activist for change is subtly transformed into a vigorous defender of the very system that gave rise to their movement, continues to block systemic change, and never delivers on its promises.

Despite the long series of defeats and failures, many on the center left still cling to the mistaken idea of the Constitution as a *tabula rasa*, a blank slate, onto which we can pour our strivings for change no matter how remote. We continue to cleave to the disempowering myth that the Constitution is changeable despite the mounting evidence to the contrary.

On the center left are many who agree with historian Howard Zinn that, "the Constitution is of minor importance compared with the actions citizens take, especially when those actions are joined in social movements." While Zinn is correct that "liberties have not been given; they have been taken," this process can and has been reversed.[8] Zinn rightly saw that the power of organized people is the only source of all fundamental and lasting change in the USA, but he was mistaken to say that the Constitution doesn't matter as much as we think because pluralist groups can organize, make demands, and force elites to concede to demands for change.

It turns out that the Constitution matters a whole lot. It was designed to constrain the ability of self-organized struggles to enshrine into law and the Constitution the changes conceded in struggle. Most importantly, it preemptively declares all attempts to fundamentally alter the rule of property to be criminal and subject to prohibition and severe penalty, including detention, military force, and death.

Zinn is hardly alone in underestimating just how much the Constitution matters. He has been joined by many unions, every third party, and many radical social movements in US history. For advocates and organizers for change, the assumption is that, if only enough force could be applied, the system will change. Nothing expresses this more than the chant, "when we fight, we win," the slogan of my own union. That most fights result in defeat is obvious enough, but that many "victories" are ultimately defeated by co-optation, institutionalization, or death by a thousand cuts is not. The constitutional system almost never moves more than what is minimally required to restore control, and then finds a new equilibrium when the threat is gone.

On the other side stand those who, like the Framers, fear change.[9] A substantial portion of the non-elite population is comforted by the inability to change things quickly or at all. Such comfort is rooted in the same distrust in humanity that shaped the thinking of the Framers, who feared the consequences of putting political power into the hands of the majority.

The difference is that the Framers feared the consequences for their property and their rule if the economic majority used its power to "level" society by seizing and redistributing their property to all. Non-elites who seek safe harbor in the Constitution are undermining their own majority interests to retain the limited privileges of their subjugated alliance with the elites.

Constitutions Are the Problem

If we are to ensure the future survival of humanity and the rest of the ecosystem to which we belong, we need to quickly sever property from its constitutional foundation. The objective is not to replace it with another system of rule but to organize society for direct democratic self-rule and a shared commons protected in trust for all.

Even writing a new constitution is problematic because the logic of governance is one of domination. Our system is rooted in the theft of the commons, exploitation of human labor, racial supremacy, gender and sex domination, and the supremacy of property above people and other non-human life. This cannot be undone with a new piece of paper. Delegating political power to "representatives" leaves the governed in a state of permanent subjugation. Representative systems can only work by suppressing political autonomy and economic self-determination and transferring power to a select few individuals. Economic and political democracy cannot be realized through a set of rules but through a set of daily lived practice of collaborative and cooperative self-governance of all life as part of the commons that belongs to all beings.

Representative democracy is a historically specific governance system for capitalism that must be transcended. Because representative democracy emerged as inseparable from property, we must dismantle both the constitutional and property systems at the same time. The political economy of the Constitution cannot be reformed away. Moving past the Constitution will be a necessary step in removing the impediments to change around the world that are enforced by the US empire.

We have been ruled long enough. It is time to govern ourselves. If we are to get past the Constitution and all systems based on constitutions, we need to move past the nation state as the means by which we are governed from above.

To do that we need to understand that the nation state arose alongside the capitalist economy. Modern nation states, and the ideology of nationalism, were founded nearly 375 years ago at the 1648 Treaty of Westphalia which fixed state boundaries apart from the church. The nation state facilitated the transition from monarchy and feudalism to democracy and capitalism by first dividing power between the king, the aristocracy, and the merchant class. In the past several hundred years we have transitioned from an authoritarian system in which the monarch had absolute rule, owned everything in the realm, and ruled by fiat to an authoritarian system in which property rules.

The modern nation state was formed during this transition as the administrative body responsible for setting up, managing, and defending the capitalist economy by interpreting and executing the law while adjudicating disputes. The nation state is a product of the historical political economic development of the first half-millennium of capitalism. It belongs to the era of global capitalism because the nation state was designed to establish, manage, and protect that economic system.

The problem humanity faces is not just with the US Constitution, it is with *all* constitutions. Constitutions imply a power separate from the people that governs on behalf of and in place of the people. Constitutions are based on an expression of government authority and rule over a defined territory with borders, rules, and sanctions for disobedience. This persists even as borders are eroded and eclipsed by the global elites who manage and own the global capitalist economy.

Constitutions are written by the elites to set the rules by which everyone within its border must operate while deciding what the constitution means. When disputes and conflicts emerge, rights are abused, or powers exceeded, elites sit in judgment, decide what to permit or sanction, and write new rules. In this way a constitution is a top-down instrument for imposing the rule of elites in the form of the state. Because the myriad crises we face are the result of decisions made by elites from above, changing this instrument of state power without altering the balance of power will not solve our problems.

Constitutions disempower people from being able to act, cooperate, self-organize, and self-govern. They allow the few to rule, through passive compliance, consent by inaction, or coercive violence using guns, prisons, and pain. Humanity's dire situation today is the direct result of decisions made by the few who made the rule of property the supreme law of the land while locking out the many from having any say.

Beyond Constitutional Government: The One Gives Way to the Many

What are our options beyond constitutions, the nation state, and representative democracy? Direct democracy, modeled after the systems established by ancient Athens, Iceland, the *shura* councils during the life of Mohammed, and in Rojava in Syrian Kurdistan, are inspiring but ultimately insufficient for the task because they mistakenly separate political from economic self-governance.

Survival means all of our communities need to become schools of self-governance by determining the basic needs of the community and how they are fulfilled through direct democratic decision making. This is a project of not merely shifting our thinking from a paradigm of growth to degrowth, or from production for accumulation to reproduction for care, but shifting our thinking from governing to the self-organized meeting of collective needs. When the economy is democratically governed, our community is democratically governed. The opposite has proven untrue.

Murray Bookchin's idea of "libertarian municipalism," in which local self-governing communities collaborate with one another in horizontal alliances and confederations, is a promising model for transcending constitutional governance.[10] Because Bookchin's concept shares the same word as current free market economic "libertarianism," and the word municipalism is close to the word for local "municipal" governments, it might better be called *autonomous localism*.

Libertarian municipalism is based on self-organized autonomous local communities using direct democracy to decide what to make, how to make it, who makes it, and how to distribute it. But how exactly can we get there from here? For Bookchin, it was a matter of using local voting in the same system he wanted to replace, to form what he called "dual power" in which a confederation of local communities would gradually displace government. Unfortunately, Bookchin never explains how that could happen using the rules of the very system he wanted to replace.

Most significantly, Bookchin didn't say much about how to organize for power over work. Without the leverage to bring this transition about, his strategy amounted to electing friendly local politicians who would establish community assemblies and confederal councils with authority over the economy.[11] Without democratic control of the economy, the community assemblies and confederal councils function more like non-profit advocacy groups. Bookchin's strategy mistakenly separates the economic from the political.

Another strategy is needed. During the next global economic crisis, workers at critical global choke points are already well situated to shut down, take over, and democratically run the operations. Once management is removed and access is secured, the workers can decide how and what to decommission, dismantle, or transition over to non-polluting uses, while deciding with local communities what to replace it with.[12] During this first phase, strategically situated workers can spread the effort to every critical sector by supporting strikes at critical choke points that shut down key sectors of the global economy, wrench control over the workplace, and put it under the democratic control of those who do the work and rely on what is produced. While this is happening, community groups could also begin to take over community resources and democratically reorganize them to serve community needs.

Workers and community members can now begin to discuss what they can do to operate the facilities differently in order to serve immediate human needs in a non-destructive manner. Workplace and community occupations could be run by joint community assemblies in which all local residents take turns participating for short periods with instant recall. These assemblies could facilitate guided discussions and democratic decision making about the capacity, desires, needs, vulnerabilities, and wishes of the community. Workers, who have set up councils to run their workplaces, and community members involved in democratically reorganizing community assets for local needs, could collaborate in the assemblies to decide how the workplaces and community assets will be cared for, distributed, managed, produced, and shared.

The joint assemblies can set up councils responsible for continuing essential work and services, and appoint those who will run them to rotating positions with complete transparency and the possibility of immediate recall. Assemblies could decide which destructive and wasteful work and services to discontinue and which new operations should be launched to serve unmet local needs, sharing the responsibility required to produce essential goods and services. To the degree that they are capable, those attending the assemblies should be encouraged to rotate out of their council positions after a short period and into other councils, to learn different aspects of how to carry out the autonomous local projects.

In the next phase, assemblies can select rotating delegates to visit other nearby assemblies to provide updates on their own operations, bring back news of others' efforts, and propose collaborations and cooperation. Efforts to share experiences, skills, goods, and services with the other assemblies for the purpose of mutual aid and solidarity can be pursued. Assemblies at close distances to one another can extend their reach even further by establishing a rotating council of delegates, with short terms of service and subject to immediate recall, to establish relations with individual assemblies or groups of assemblies elsewhere for the purposes of mutual aid.[13]

Over time, these networks of assemblies can form themselves into confederations or leagues for collaboration, cooperation, and mutual security. The ultimate objective of this democratic cooperative self-organization of society is to reduce the amount of work while expanding free time for improving the well-being of all humanity and the rest of the ecosystem.

Today there are several existing models of self-organized communities. The Zapatista autonomous municipalities and *caracoles* in the Mexican state of Chiapas, in which decision making and control of the economy lies in the hands of the community, and the Federation of Neighborhood Councils in El Alto, Bolivia, are informative models. According to Raúl Zibechi, the self-organized neighborhoods of El Alto do not need representative government because the community councils "lead by obeying" according to the logic of Aymara indigenous principles. The decentralized coordination of reciprocally cooperative councils demonstrates how "the one gives way to the multiple."[14]

This short hypothetical scenario provides just one possible strategy for dismantling the nation state and transitioning past capitalism. The needs of local communities can be served by seizing and directly democratically deciding what should and should not be produced, and how it should be distributed and shared. This reintegrates democratic control of the economy with democratic control of society by returning property to the commons under the protection of and in the service of all.

This can be done immediately, without presenting demands or grievances to the government and then attempting to pressure it to act on our behalf. Organized direct action at both the site of production and consumption is hyper-democratic because it is carried out by the self-organized community and requires no government or rules governed by a constitutional system. Direct self-organization makes a constitutional system unnecessary while simultaneously dismantling the rule of property. Such urgently needed action can begin restoring control over our lives and reverse the course of certain widespread destruction of the ecosystem. It is possible because it does not rely on or attempt to use the rules of a system designed to protect property and prevent change. Direct action breaks our reliance on the very system that has caused global catastrophe so that we can begin to solve the problem ourselves.

This is one of several strategies needed in the immediate present if humanity and myriad other species are to survive. Urgently needed change has not and will not be forthcoming by using the rules of the system. Swedish climate organizer Greta Thunberg is correct in stating that our systems of government have utterly failed us and that we must carry out a global strike for the climate and for the future. But such a strike must be much more than a symbolic walkout into the streets. It must harness and build our power where it lies in the economic system to take it over and reorganize it to meet the needs of humanity and the rest of the global ecosystem to survive.

This strategy will generate immediate and massive violent retaliation. But by staying put and taking control, and doing it everywhere at once or in a staggered array which forces of repression cannot predict, we will be able to minimize the loss of life and increase the possibility of success. This is the "whack-a-mole" strategy, so that when any takeover is attacked two more pop up in other unexpected places, four more appear when those two are attacked, and so on, until the takeover irreversibly and unstoppably reverberates across many simultaneous locations and circulates globally.

Self-organizing beyond the Future in the Present

We have two critically important lessons to learn from the ongoing global pandemic. The first is that humanity can expect governments to abandon us in our time of greatest desperation, deprivation, and danger, in order to protect the rights and survival of property. Despite the resources and innovations to decisively end the pandemic around the world, states have allowed it to grind on, by 2022 killing more than 15 million people simply to protect the property rights of the vaccine companies and the rest of the medical industry.

The second lesson is that our existing models of political change are so bankrupt that corporate-backed non-profits, loyal opposition parties, and unions were bypassed and relegated to obscurity as workers all over the world continue to self-organize and engage in wildcat strikes against unsafe work and police violence during the first two years of the pandemic. Countless numbers of people have self-organized to replace absent governments and take care of those in need, develop new personal protective equipment, distribute food and other necessities in mutual aid networks, and come to the defense of those murdered by the police. As I write, a widespread refusal of workers to return to low-paying, dangerous, and deadly work has disrupted global supply chains and put business and employers on notice that they will not be coming back to work until things change.

The pandemic has showed once more that people not only have the capacity and willingness to self-organize globally but already know how. We self-organize all the time in our own families, among our friends and neighbors, and across vast expanses of terrain and borders. Self-organization is something we already do in our everyday lives when neighbors watch one another's children, feed their pets when they are out of town, fundraise to build a local community center, erect a basketball court or new playground, organize a local festival, write about local news on a blog or social media, strike with co-workers demanding changes at work, and build virtual networks of people across the globe to act in solidarity with one another.

Self-organization is not about resistance, which implies protest to demand that those with power make concessions that allow them to preserve their credibility and maintain control. When organized people shut down the workplace and organize in their communities in response to a crisis, they are carving out pockets of what C. L. R. James called "the future in the present." They are acting to take care of one another and plan for a future without property, constitutions, and government.[15] We see evidence of self-organized mutual aid during hurricanes, floods, and other "natural" catastrophes as well as during mass movements, strikes, and when government is unresponsive to widespread deprivation such as hunger.[16]

We don't need a constitution to tell us how to organize ourselves because we already do it without realizing it. We are already more than capable of organizing ourselves without government and meeting our shared needs without capitalism.

I don't have the answer for transcending the Constitution and the supremacy of property. But together, we all do.

Notes

Introduction

1. In the late 18th century, it was common to think of every system that wasn't a monarchy as "republican."
2. D. Lazare, "US Constitution: Hiding in Plain Sight," *Cosmonaut*, September 29, 2020; D. Lazare, *The Frozen Republic: How the Constitution Is Paralyzing Democracy.* New York: Harcourt Brace & Company, 1996, pp. 9, 45, 111, 114. See also M. Klarman, *The Framers' Coup: The Making of the United States Constitution*, New York: Oxford University Press, p. 245.
3. J. Wilson, July 14, in M. Farrand (ed.), *The Records of the Federal Convention of 1787 (RFC)*, Vol. 2. New Haven: Yale University Press, 1911, p. 1.
4. Then President of Congress in 1779, Jay was already concerned about repaying the debt and making creditors whole. J. Jay, *Journals of the Continental Congress*, Vol. 15, September 2–December 31, 1779, p. 1062.
5. The problem is commonly portrayed as a more recent distortion of the Constitution. See the otherwise excellent N. MacLean, *Democracy in Chains: The Deep History of the Radical Right's Stealth Plan for America.* Melbourne: Scribe, 2017, pp. 80–1.
6. "Negative" was the Framers' term for the veto. J. Madison, July 14, 1787, in M. Farrand, *RFC*, Vol. 1, 1911, pp. 464, 816.
7. Quotes from J. Madison, *Federalist #51*; A. Hamilton, June 18, 1787, in M. Farrand, *RFC*, Vol. 1, 1911, p. 289; J. Adams to J. Taylor, December 17, 1814; and J. Adams to T. Jefferson, December 6, 1787. Note that all letters and private notes that can be widely found online and are not cited in full in the footnotes. Adams spoke for the common belief that "humane Nature" tended "towards Tyranny." J. Adams to R. H. Lee, November 15, 1775.
8. G. Washington to J. Jay, August 15, 1786.
9. D. Hume, *Essays Moral, Political, Literary*, Part II: Essays Moral, Political, and Literary, Essay I: Of Commerce. Indianapolis: Liberty Fund, 1987 [1777], p. 256.
10. G. Washington, Farewell Speech, September 19, 1796.

11. J. Toobin, "Our Broken Constitution: Everyone Agrees that Government Isn't Working. Are the Founders to Blame?" *New Yorker*, December 9, 2013.

12. A. T. Hadley, "The Constitutional Position of Property in America," *The Independent*, 1848, pp. 834, 837–8.

13. J. Purdy, "Beyond the Bosses' Constitution: The First Amendment and Class Entrenchment," *Columbia Law Review*, Vol. 118, No. 7, 2021.

14. In M. Klarman, 2016, p. 133.

15. C. L. Becker, *The History of Political Parties in the Province of New York 1760–1776*. Madison: University of Wisconsin Press, 1909, p. 22. Historian Michael Merrill put it another way: "The American Revolution was history's most sustained and most successful peasant revolt" that didn't end with the peace treaty. M. Merrill, "Completing the Revolution: The Constitution and the Triumph of Radical Republicanism. Beyond Beard," *Radical History Review*, Vol. 42, 1988, p. 23.

16. R. Dahl, *How Democratic Is the American Constitution?*, 2nd ed. New Haven: Yale University Press, 2003, pp. 24–4.

17. H. Aptheker, *Early Years of the Republic: From the End of the Revolution to the First Administration of Washington (1783–1793)*. New York: International Publishers, 1976, p. 47.

18. D. Lazare, 1996, pp. 2–3.

19. D. Lazare, 1996, p. 5.

20. I. Katznelson, M. Kesselman, and A. Draper, *The Politics of Power: A Critical Introduction to American Government*, 7th ed. New York: W. W. Norton & Company, 2013, p. 188.

21. H. Arendt, *Origins of Totalitarianism, Origins of Totalitarianism*. Orlando: Harvest Books, 1973, pp. 255, 259, 265, 420.

22. G. Morris, July 5, 1787, in M. Farrand, *RFC*, Vol. 1, 1911, p. 533.

23. C. Beard, *An Economic Interpretation of the Constitution of the United States*. New York: Free Press, 1986 [1913], p. 154. See also K. Coulter, *The Rule of Property*. New York: Apex Press and Program on Corporations, Law and Democracy, 2007, pp. 25–33.

24. See also L. René Beres, "The Masses Were Never Intended to Rule: The 'American People' have long been viewed with suspicion by politicians," *U.S. News & World Report*, March 20, 2018, accessed June 8, 2022, https://www.usnews.com/news/the-report/articles/2018-03-20/commentary-the-masses-were-never-intended-to-rule.

25. V. L. Parrington, *Main Currents in American Thought*, Book III. Norman: University of Oklahoma Press, 1987 [1927–30], p. 410.

26. Italics in original. T. Jefferson, *Notes on the State of Virginia*, 1784, W. Peden (ed.). Chapel Hill: University of North Carolina Press for the

Institute of Early American History and Culture, Williamsburg, Virginia, 1954, pp. 120–1.

27. J. T. Main, *The Social Structure of Revolutionary America.* Princeton: Princeton University Press, 1965, p. 270.

28. G. Wood, "Democracy and the Constitution," in R. A. Goldwin and V. A. Schambra (eds.), *How Democratic Is the Constitution?* Washington and London: American Enterprise Institute for Public Policy Research, 1980, p. 1.

29. Sir W. Blackstone, *Commentaries on the Laws of England in Four Books.* Oxford: Oxford University Press, 1771 [1893], p. 61.

30. C. Beard, *The Supreme Court and the Constitution.* New York: Paisley Press, 1912, pp. 76–7.

31. C. Beard, 1912, p. 79. Brown also argues that the Framers' "class-specific views" of taxation also influenced their design of the Constitution. See R. Brown, *Redeeming the Republic: Federalists, Taxation, and the Origins of the Constitution.* Baltimore: Johns Hopkins University Press, 1993, p. 5.

32. Wilson thought at the time that both Congress and the President had been engaged in a struggle for power. We now know that Congress lost. W. Wilson, *Congressional Government: A Study in American Politics.* New Brunswick, NJ: Transaction Publishers, 2017 [1900], pp. 4, 6–7.

33. R. Brown, 1993, pp. 153–5.

34. See also W. Wilson, *Divisions and Reunion, 1829–1889*, 10th ed. New York: Longmans, Green, & Co., 1898: "a strong and intelligent class possessed of unity and unformed by conscious solidarity of interest."

Chapter 1

1. Beard estimated that only about 25 men played any significant role in writing the Constitution because the rest either didn't participate or were often absent. See C. Beard, "The Supreme Court: Usurper or Grantee?" *Political Science Quarterly*, Vol. 27, No. 1, March 1912, p. 3–4; C. Beard, *Supreme Court and the Constitution.* New York: Paisley Press, 1912, pp. 16–17.

2. E. Greenberg, "Class Rule under the Constitution," in R. A. Goldwin and V. A. Schambra (eds.), *How Capitalistic Is the Constitution?* Washington, DC: American Enterprise Institute for Public Policy Research, 1982, p. 33.

3. J. Madison to T. Jefferson, October 24, 1787.

4. M. Parenti, "The Constitution as an Elitist Document," in R. A. Goldwin and V. A. Schambra (eds.), *How Democratic Is the Constitution?* Washington, DC: American Enterprise Institute, 1980, p. 53.

5. J. Manley and K. Dolbeare (eds.), *The Case against the Constitution: From the Antifederalists to the Present.* Armonk, NY: M. E. Sharpe, Inc., 1987, p. x, italics in the original. They are part of a very small crowd that make the same argument. See also L. Cutler, "To Form a Government," in R. A. Goldwin and A. Kaufman (eds.) *Separation of Powers: Does It Still Work?* Washington, DC and London: American Enterprise Institute for Public Policy Research, 1986, pp. 1–17.

6. For example, Gouverneur Morris warned that without checks "the Rich" will seize power and oppress the majority in a "violent despotism." Of course, it is the system of minority checks that made elite rule possible. G. Morris, July 2, 1787, M. Farrand, *The Records of the Federal Convention of 1787 (RFC)*, Vol. 1. New Haven: Yale University Press, 1911, p. 512.

7. Cicero, *De Republica*, translation cited in D. Adair, *The Intellectual Origins of Jeffersonian Democracy: Republicanism, the Class Struggle, and the Virtuous Farmer*, Yellin, M. E. (ed.). Lanham, MD: Lexington Books, 2000, p. 87.

8. J. A. Smith, *The Spirit of American Government*, Strout, C. (ed.). Cambridge, MA: Belknap Press of Harvard University Press, 1965, p. 12; F. Lundberg, *Cracks in the Constitution.* Secaucus, NJ: Lyle Stuart, Inc. 1980, p. 104.

9. J. Madison, "Notes on Ancient and Modern Confederacies," April–June, 1786; and J. Madison, "Additional Memorandums on Ancient and Modern Confederacies," November 30, 1787.

10. Montesquieu, Book IX: Of Laws, in the Relation They Bear to a Defensive Force, Chapter 1: In What Manner Republics Provide for Their Safety, *The Complete Works of M. de Montesquieu*, Vol. 1. London: T. Evans, 1777, p. 166.

11. J. Adams, *A Defence of the Constitutions of Government of the United States of America.* New York: Akashic, 2004, pp. 61, 67.

12. See Hamilton's title for *Federalist #9*, "The Union as a Safeguard Against Domestic Faction and Insurrection."

13. Historians think Brutus was most likely New York Supreme Court Justice and dissident Framer Robert Yates. Brutus, "Essay #3," *New York Journal*, November 15, 1787, "Observations on the New Constitution, and on the Federal and State Conventions by a Columbian Patriot," in J. Birnbaum and B. Ollman (eds.), *U.S. Constitution: 200 Hundred Years of Anti-Federalist, Abolitionist, Feminist, Muckraking, Progressive, and Especially Socialist Criticism.* New York: NYU Press, 1990, p. 89. See also P. Henry, Speech before Virginia Ratifying Convention, June 5, 1788. Madison also sought to design checks for the minority to protect

itself from majority oppression. J. Madison, Constitutional Convention Debates, Term of the Senate, June 26, 1787.

14. J. A. Smith, 1965, p. 165.

15. Ibid., p. 18.

16. Senator John Kerry, January 30, 2013, Text of John Kerry's farewell speech, www.boston.com/uncategorized/noprimarytagmatch/2013/01/30/text-of-john-kerrys-farewell-speech.

17. G. Morris, "We Shall Be under the Domination of a Riotous Mob": Letter to Thomas Penn, May 20, 1774.

18. C. Beard, *An Economic Interpretation of the Constitution of the United States*. New York: Free Press. 1986 [1913], pp. 73 and 188. According to historian Jackson Turner Main, perhaps not more than 10 percent of the delegates in the three largest states were personally influenced by their status as significant creditors. J. T. Main, "The Antifederalists," in J. Birnbaum and B. Ollman (eds.), 1990, p. 66. On the lack of complete records, see J. Ferguson, *The Power of the Purse: A History of American Public Finance, 1776–1790*. Chapel Hill: The University of North Carolina Press, 1961, p. 338–9.

19. C. Beard, 1986 [1913], pp. xvi and 294. For example, Hamilton acknowledged the creditors' substantial role in the Convention and may have been the shadow leader of the effort to organize the creditors to push for changes leading to the Convention. A. Hamilton, "The Defence of the Funding System," July 1795. See also E. J. Ferguson, "The Nationalists of 1781–1783 and the Economic Interpretation of the Constitution," *The Journal of American History*, Vol. 56, No. 2, 1969, p. 260.

20. W. A. Williams, *The Contours of American History*. Chicago: Quadrangle Books, 1961, p. 150.

21. See also M. Parenti, "The Constitution as an Elitist Document," in J. Birnbaum and B. Ollman (eds.), 1990, p. 144; J. Rasmus, *Alexander Hamilton and the Origins of the Fed*. Lanham, MD: Lexington, 2019, p. 19; M. Jensen, *The Making of the American Constitution*. Huntington, NY: Robert E. Krieger Publishing Company, 1964, p. 127; and E. Greenberg, 1982, pp. 33–4.

22. F. Lundberg, 1980, pp. 139–41.

23. Ibid., p. 141.

24. Several Framers, including Washington, acknowledged that the Convention succeeded in reconciling these diverse interests. See G. Washington to D. Humphreys, October 10, 1787. McDonald futilely used this evidence in an effort to discredit Beard by overlooking his larger thesis about recognition of shared class interests. In fact, McDonald resorts to his particularist personal interests to explain

Anti-Federalist opposition since some had used paper money to pay off purchases of expropriated Loyalist estates. In reality, McDonald was commissioned to write a McCarthyite attack on Beard's economic analysis. F. McDonald, *We the People: The Economic Origins of the Constitution.* Chicago: University of Chicago Press, 1958, pp. 105, 154. For a contemporary observation of this class interest see L. G. Otto to Comte de Vergennes, New York, October 10, 1786 in J. P. Kaminski and R. Leffler (eds.), *Federalists and Antifederalists: The Debate over the Ratification of the Constitution.* Madison: Madison House Publishers, Inc., 1998, pp. 180–3.

25. J. Ferguson, 1961, p. 338.
26. See M. Tigar and M. Levy, *Law and the Rise of Capitalism.* New York: Monthly Review Press, 2000, pp. 9, 283.
27. S. Lynd, *Class Conflict, Slavery, and the United States Constitution.* Indianapolis: Bobbs-Merrill Company, Inc., 1967, p. 113.
28. A. Hamilton, "Conjectures about the New Constitution," September 17–30, 1787.
29. Such fears about the majority threat to property were common among the Framers. See, for example, J. Madison to T. Jefferson, IV; Madison's Observations on Jefferson's Draft of a Constitution for Virginia, October 1788; R. King to J. Madison, January 20, 1788; and R. King to J. Madison, January 27, 1788.
30. Wilson argues that the design of the Constitution was predicated on constructing a new monetary system based on paper money. See T. Wilson, *The Power "To Coin" Money: The Exercise of Monetary Powers by the Congress.* Armonk, NY: M. E. Sharpe, 1992, p. ix. See also E. Greenberg, 1982, p. 23; and J. Bouie, "The Constitution Was Made for Us, Not the Other Way Around," *New York Times*, October 29, 2021. In 1781, Hamilton was already proposing a public credit system using paper money. He, like other elites, only had a selective dislike for paper money when it was publicly controlled and used for majority interests. A. Hamilton to R. Morris, April 30, 1781.
31. J. Locke, *The Second Treatise of Civil Government*, C. B. McPherson (ed.). Indianapolis and Cambridge: Hackett Publishing Company 1980 [1690], pp. 53–4, 77. James Wilson saw the "exclusive and permanent possession and use" of property as emerging in the transfer of property from common possession to agriculture. J. Wilson, "On the History of Property," 1790, in K. L. Hall and M. D. Hall (eds.), *Collected Works of James Wilson*, Vol. 1, collected by M. Garrison. Indianapolis: Liberty Fund, 2007, p. 395.
32. D. Waldstreicher, *Slavery's Constitution: From Revolution to Ratification.* New York: Hill and Wang, 2009, pp. 9, 18, 154.

33. D. Waldstreicher, 2009, p. 14.

34. J. Madison, June 30, 1787, in M. Farrand, *RFC*, Vol. 1, 1911, p. 486.

35. J. Madison, Constitutional Convention Debates, August 22, 1787. Both Northerners and Southerners concurred. See O. Ellsworth, August 21, 1787, in M. Farrand, *RFC*, Vol. 2, 1911, pp. 364; C. C. Pinckney, Speech in the South Carolina House of Representatives, January 17, 1788; and D. Ramsey, "An Address to the Freemen of South Carolina on the Subject of the Federal Constitution, Proposed by the Convention, which met in Philadelphia, May 1787," in P. L. Ford (ed.), *Pamphlets on the Constitution of the United States. Published During its Discussion by the People, 1787–1788*. New York: Burt Franklin, 1888, p. 378.

36. S. Lynd, 1967, p. 14; see also A. Young, in A. Young and G. Nobles (eds.), *Whose American Revolution Was It?: Historians Interpret the Founding*. New York: New York University Press, 2011, p. 83.

37. Luther Martin was one Framer who refused to do so, particularly on slavery and the need for debt relief. L. Martin, Genuine Information VIII, January 22, 1788.

38. See R. Dunbar-Ortiz, *Loaded: A Disarming History of the Second Amendment*. San Francisco: City Lights Books, 2018, p. 65.

39. See W. E. B. DuBois, "Slavery and the Founding Fathers," in J. Birnbaum and B. Ollman (eds.), 1990, pp. 97, 102–3.

40. E. Greenberg, 1982, pp. 24–5, 29.

41. J. T. Main, *The Anti-Federalists: Critics of the Constitution 1781–1788*. New York: W. W. Norton & Company, 1961, pp. 10–11.

42. In T. Gordon and J. Trenchard, Cato's Letters, No. 91. Saturday, August 25, 1722. How Exclusive Companies Influence and Hurt Our Government. (Trenchard), in the Online Library of Liberty, a Project of Liberty Fund, Inc. John Trenchard, Cato's Letters, Vol. 3, March 10, 1722 to December 1, 1722.

43. Manley and Dolbeare are entirely correct that "class was then, and remains today, the best analytic concept with which to understand the provisions and purposes of the Constitution." J. Manley and K. Dolbeare, 1987, p. x. Manley added, "[t]he Framers saw society in terms of class, government in terms of protecting property, and the people as a threat." J. Manley, "Class and Pluralism in America: The Constitution Reconsidered," in J. F. Manley and K. M. Dolbeare, 1987, pp. 115.

44. J. Madison, "Vices of the Political System of the United States," April 1787. See also J. Madison, Constitutional Convention Debates, June 6, 1787; and J. Madison, Constitutional Convention Debates, Term of the Senate, June 26, 1787.

45. J. Madison, "Vices of the Political System of the United States," April 1787. Madison repeats this elsewhere, such as J. Madison, Constitutional Convention Debates, June 6, 1787; J. Madison to T. Jefferson, October 24, 1787; and J. Madison to T. Jefferson, October 24, 1787. Madison was perhaps the most articulate in giving this warning but he was hardly alone. Hamilton made a similar point in *Federalist #85*. Thomas Paine found himself embracing Madison's thinking when he rented his pen in defense of Robert Morris' Bank of North America in 1786. Paine denounced the Pennsylvania legislature's attempt to withdraw its charter as the majority acting as "the despotism of numbers." See T. Paine, "Dissertations on Government; the Affairs of the Bank; and Paper Money," February 18, M. D. Conway (ed.), *The Complete Writings of Thomas Paine*, Vols. 1 and 2, New York and London: G. P. Putnam's Sons, 1906 [1786], p. 374. See also C. Rappleye, *Robert Morris: Financier of the American Revolution*. New York: Simon & Schuster, 2010.

46. J. Madison, June 26, 1787, in M. Farrand, *RFC*, Vol. 1, 1911, pp. 422–3. Late in life Madison explicitly warned about class conflict between the minority of "wealthy capitalists" and majority of "indigent labourers." See J. Madison, "Note to His Speech on the Right of Suffrage," *Documentary History*, Vol. 5, 1821, pp. 440–9.

47. The elites were already concerned during the Revolution. See G. Morris to T. Penn, "We Shall Be Under the Domination of a Riotous Mob," May 20, 1774; J. Sullivan to J. Adams, May 9, 1776; and F. L. Lee to L. Carter, Philadelphia, May 21, 1776, Lilly Library, Indiana University; T. Ingersoll, "'Riches and Honour Were Rejected by Them as Loathsome Vomit': Fear of Levelling in New England," in C. Pestana and S. Salinger (eds.), *Inequality in Early America*, Hanover, NH: University Press of New England, 1999, pp. 46–66. See also H. Aptheker, *Early Years of the Republic: From the End of the Revolution to the First Administration of Washington (1783–1793)*. New York: International Publishers, 1976, p. 62.

48. H. Knox to G. Washington, December 17, 1786. See also G. Washington to J. Madison, November 5, 1786.

49. W. Randolph, May 29, 1787, Notes from McHenry, in M. Farrand, *RFC*, Vol. 1, 1911, pp. 26–7. Other similar sentiments were expressed by R. Sherman, May 31, 1787, in M. Farrand, *RFC*, Vol. 1, 1911, p. 48; E. Gerry, May 31, 1787, in M. Farrand, *RFC*, Vol. 1, 1911, p. 48; and T. Sedgwick to N. Dane, July 5, 1787, cited in J. Ferguson, 1961, p. 220.

50. Attributed to E. Randolph by J. McHenry in his notes of the Constitutional Convention dated May 29, 1787, in M. Farrand, *RFC*, Vol. 1,

1911, p. 26, 1937. On the same note see A. Hamilton, Monday, June 18, 1787, in M. Farrand, *RFC*, Vol. 1, 1911, p. 203. John Adams had been making the same point for a decade. See J. Adams to A. Adams, July 3, 1776.

51. J. Madison, "Vices of the Political System of the United States," April 1787.

52. Madison, *Federalist #10*, November 23, 1787. We can understand "regulation" to mean minority checks on the majority. While the Federalist Papers could rightly be called political propaganda and dismissed as serious theory, we should recognize that Madison, like Hamilton, did not first express their ideas there but had been developing them for years in letters, debates, and proposals. It is possible to see Madison working out the same ideas on June 6 at the Convention, where he made the same argument about class division between rich and poor and that the minority is threatened by a united majority. J. Madison, June 6 and 26, 1787, in M. Farrand, *RFC*, Vol. 1, 1911, pp. 135–6, 422–3. He also expressed the same ideas in various letters. In 1821, when preparing his notes on the convention for publication, Madison again warned about the leveling ambitions of majority rule and the threat to property. J. Madison, Note to His Speech on the Right of Suffrage, in M. Farrand, *RFC*, Vol. 3, 1911, pp. 450–5. Hamilton repeated much the same points about the class division of the country and the threat of the rule of the "many." A. Hamilton, June 18, 1787, in M. Farrand, *RFC*, Vol. 1, 1911, pp. 288; and J. Madison, Constitutional Convention Debates, Term of the Senate, June 26, 1787.

53. J. Madison, June 26, 1787, Yates' Notes, in M. Farrand, *FRC*, Vol. 1, 1911, p. 431.

54. In *Federalist #43*, Madison warns of the consequences of population growth and immigration when "the minority of CITIZENS may become a majority of PERSONS" (capitals in original). See also J. Madison, Term of the Senate, June 26, 1787; J. Madison, in M. Farrand, *FRC*, August 7, 1787, Vol. 2, 1911, pp. 203–4; G. Morris, August 7, 1787, in M. Farrand, *FRC*, Vol. 2, 1911, pp. 201–3. The Framers had seen the demands for regulating the labor supply, raising wages, strikes, and organized laborers, journeymen, and mechanics, and wanted to constrain or prevent further self-activity. See Chapter 2, and R. Morris, *Government and Labor in Early America*. New York: Harper & Row Publishers, 1946, pp. 145, 152, 163–5, 183–4, 186, 192, 200.

55. J. Madison, in M. Farrand, *FRC*, August 7, 1787, Vol. 2, 1911, p. 4.

56. A. Hamilton, Notes, June 18, 1787. There are two other versions of Hamilton's infamous speech. Robert Yates' notes report that Hamilton said "all communities divide themselves into the few and the many. The

first are the rich and well born, the other the mass of the people. ...
Give therefore to the first class a distinct, permanent share in the government. They will check the unsteadiness of the second, and as they
cannot receive any advantage by a change, they therefore will ever
maintain good government." See A. Hamilton, June 18, 1787, Yates'
Notes. Madison's notes show a slight variation on Hamilton's speech
while capturing the essence: "In every community where industry is
encouraged, there will be a division of it into the few & the many.
Hence separate interests will arise. There will be debtors & creditors
&c. Give all power to the many, they will oppress the few. Give all
power to the few, they will oppress the many. Both therefore ought to
have power, that each may defend itself agst. the other." See A.
Hamilton, June 18, 1787, James Madison's Version.

57. F. Lundberg, 1980, p. 152.

58. M. Jensen, 1964, pp. 29–33.

59. A. Smith, *An Inquiry into the Nature and Causes of the Wealth of Nations*,
Book V: On the Revenue of the Sovereign or Commonwealth, Chapter
I: On the Expenses of the Sovereign or Commonweal, Part Third, At
the Expense of Justice, 1776, p. 715.

60. This point is made by political scientist M. Parenti, who wrote that "the
Constitution, then, was a product not only of class privilege but of class
struggle—a struggle that continued and intensified as the corporate
economy and the government grew." See M. Parenti, "The Constitution as an Elitist Document," in R. Goldwin and W. Schambra (eds.),
1980, p. 158.

61. J. Jay to W. Wilberforce, *Correspondence and Public Papers of John Jay.*
New York: G. P. Putnam's Sons, October 25, 1810, p. 336. John Adams
wrote that "Power always follows Property," which was why propertyless men, along with women and children, could not be trusted to vote
or have any political power. J. Adams to J. Sullivan, May 26, 1776.
During the Revolution, Hamilton had also proposed limited voting to
the propertied. A. Hamilton, The Farmer Refuted, &c., February 23,
1775.

62. For a more detailed history of this motive, see W. Holton, "Did Democracy Cause the Recession that Led to the Constitution?" *The Journal of
American History*, Vol. 92, No. 2, 2005, pp. 442–4.

63. See J. Madison to T. Jefferson, IV. Madison's Observations on Jefferson's Draft of a Constitution for Virginia, October 1788; and M.
Jensen, 1964, p. 40.

64. E. C. Smith and H. Spaeth, *The Constitution of the United States.* New
York: Harper Collins, 1991, p. 23.

Notes

65. H. Aptheker, 1976, p. 65. Aptheker, while acknowledging this, also simultaneously celebrates it as "progressive" according to the Soviet line concerning bourgeois revolutions as a necessary stage preceding state socialism.

66. "[V]ices of democracy." For example, see the debate on June 16, 1787, in M. Farrand, *RFC*, Vol. 1, 1911, pp. 272–3; and Hamilton's extremely long speech on his plan on June 18, 1787. There are three versions of notes on Hamilton's plan. See A. Hamilton, Notes, Speech of a Plan of Government, June 18, 1787; A. Hamilton, Speech of a Plan of Government, Yates' Notes, June 18, 1787; and A. Hamilton, Speech of a Plan of Government, J. Madison's Version, June 18, 1787 in M. Farrand, *RFC*, Vol. 1, 1911, pp. 282–93.

67. M. Klarman, *The Framers' Coup: The Making of the United States Constitution*. New York: Oxford University Press, 2016, p. 249. Perhaps only John Adams was so explicit form a distance. J. Adams cited in F. Lundberg, 1980, pp. 164–5.

68. While commonly called Whig theory, it can be originally traced back to Aristotle's division of government into three parts: deliberators, magistrates, and judicial functionaries. See M. Sharp, "The Classical American Doctrine of 'The Separation of Powers'," *University of Chicago Law Review*, Vol. 2, No. 3, 1935, p. 387. See also J. T. Main, *The Sovereign States, 1775–1783*. New York: New Viewpoints, 1973, p. 115.

69. J. Locke, 1690, pp. 53–4, 77–8. The Constitution is a realization of what historian E. P. Thompson called the Whig principle of the "elevation of property above all other values." E. P. Thompson, *Whigs and Hunters: The Origin of the Black Act*. New York: Pantheon Books, 1975, p. 197.

70. See M. Parenti, 1980, pp. 46, 56; and the extraordinary essay by Yale President A. T. Hadley, "The Constitutional Position of Property in America," *The Independent*, 1848, p. 836.

71. J. Madison to Unknown, re. majority governments, December 1934; A. Hamilton, *Federalist #73*; and C. Beard, 1986 [1913], p. 158.

72. A. Hamilton, The Farmer Refuted, &c., February 23, 1775; and J. Madison, June 6, 1787, in M. Farrand, *RFC*, Vol. 1, 1911, pp. 134–5 and June 26, 1787, in M. Farrand, *RFC*, Vol. 1, 1911, pp. 421–3.

73. See A. T. Hadley, 1848, p. 838; H. Aptheker, 1976, pp. 43–4; and T. Bouton, *Taming Democracy: "The People," the Founders, and the Troubled Ending of the American Revolution*. New York: Oxford University Press, 2007, pp. 177–8.

74. J. Manley and K. Dolbeare, 1987, p. xii. See also, E. Bernstein, "Has the U.S. Constitution Reached Its Expiration Date? A Review and Crit-

icism of the World's Longest Lasting Constitution," *Inquiries Journal*, Vol. 12, No. 11, 2020.

75. I. Katznelson, M. Kesselman, and A. Draper, *Politics of Power: A Critical Introduction to American Government*, 7th ed. New York: W. W. Norton & Company, 2013, pp. 187, 247.

76. For example, law professor Sanford Levinson writes that "substantial responsibility for the defects of our polity lies in the Constitution itself." S. Levinson, 2006, pp. 6, 9, 11. While he is right to critique the Constitution, he takes the mainstream "breakdown" view that government no longer functions because of the "defects" and "failings" of the Constitution not because of its design to protect elite rule and the economy they own. See also S. Levinson, *Our Undemocratic Constitution: Where the Constitution Goes Wrong (and How We the People Can Correct It)*. New York: Oxford University Press, 2006, pp. 26–7, 52. See also M. Parenti, 1980, pp. 49.

77. T. Jefferson, "Report of Committee on Instructions to Indian Commissioners," March 4, 1784.

78. W. Holton, *Forced Founders: Indians, Debtors, Slaves, and the Making of the American Revolution in Virginia*. Chapel Hill: University of North Carolina Press, 1999, pp. 18–20; R. Kohn, *Eagle and Sword: The Beginnings of the Military Establishment in America*. New York: The Free Press, 1975, pp. 94–5.

79. J. Madison to T. Jefferson, October 24, 1787. Madison also worked out these ideas about the necessity of a strategy of divide and rule at the Convention. J. Madison, June 6, 1787, in M. Farrand, *RFC*, Vol. 1, 1911, p. 136.

80. M. Sharp, "The Classical American Doctrine of 'The Separation of Powers'," *University of Chicago Law Review*, Vol. 2, No. 3, 1935, p. 393.

81. J. Madison to T. Jefferson, October 24, 1787. Italics in the original. Hamilton also thought it necessary to also "[g]ive therefore to the first class a distinct, permanent share in the government." See A. Hamilton, June 18, 1787, Yates' Notes, in M. Farrand, *RFC*, Vol. 1, 1911, p. 299.

82. Friedrich Engels wrote that "bourgeois legal rules merely express the economic life conditions of society in legal form." F. Engels, "From Ludwig Feuerbach and the End of Classical German Philosophy," in J. Birnbaum, and B. Ollman (eds.), 1990, p. 269.

83. W. Manning, "Constitution of the Laboring Society," in M. Merrill and S. Wilentz (eds.), *The Key of Liberty: The Life and Democratic Writings of William Manning, "A Laborer," 1747–1814*. Cambridge, MA: Harvard University Press, 1993, p. 60. Abraham Lincoln would make this same point in his first annual message on December 3, 1861.

84. W. Manning, "The Key of Liberty: Showing the Causes Why a Free Government Has Always Failed and a Remedy against It. Addressed to the Republicans, Farmers, Mechanics, and Laborers in America by a Laborer [1799]," in M. Merrill and S. Wilentz, 1993. p. 127.

85. Ibid., p. 141.

86. See M. Merrill, "The Anticapitalist Origins of the United States," *Review*, Fernand Braudel Center, Vol. 13, No. 4, 1990, p. 493; A. Kulikoff, in A. Young (ed.), *Beyond the American Revolution*. DeKalb: Northern Illinois University Press, 1993, p. 28; D. Szatmary, *Shays' Rebellion: The Making of an Agrarian Insurrection*. Amherst: University of Massachusetts Press, 1980, p. xiv.

Chapter 2

1. The quotation in the title, "intoxicating draughts of liberty run mad," is from C. Petit to J. Wadsworth, May 27, 1786, in W. Holton, "'From the Labours of Others': The War Bonds Controversy and the Origins of the Constitution in New England," *The William and Mary Quarterly*, Third Series, Vol. 61, No. 2, 2004, p. 275.

2. W. Holton, *Forced Founders: Indians, Debtors, Slaves, and the Making of the American Revolution in Virginia*, Chapel Hill: Omohundro Institute and University of North Carolina Press, 1999, pp. xxi, 184; W. Holton, *Black Americans in the Revolutionary Era: A Brief History with Documents*. Boston: Bedford/St. Martin's, 2009, p. 2.

3. Henry Knox used Shays' Rebellion and a secession movement and armed organized land squatters in Maine who threatened elites such as himself to justify the need for a strong central government. See H. Knox to S. Higginson, February 25, 1787. S. Patterson wrote that "if Shays's Rebellion had not occurred, the Federalists would have had to invent it." See also S. Patterson, "The Federalist Reaction to Shays's Rebellion," in R. A. Gross (ed.), *In Debt to Shays: The Bicentennial of an Agrarian Rebellion*. Charlottesville: University Press of Virginia, 1993, pp. 115–17.

4. R. King to J. Madison, January 27, 1788; Harrington, "To the Freemen of the United States," *Pennsylvania Gazette*, May 30, 1787; and J. Adams, *A Defence of the Constitutions of Government of the United States of America*, in *The Works of John Adams, Second President of the United States: With a Life of the Author, Notes and Illustrations, by his Grandson Charles Francis Adams*. Boston: Little, Brown and Co., 1856 [1787], Vol. 6, pp. 7–9.

5. See W. Holton, *American Revolution and Early Republic*. Washington, DC: American Historical Association, 2012, p. 7. At the start of the Revolution, R. H. Lee wanted "[a] wise and free government may

now be formed" to "prevent the numerous evils to be apprehended from popular rage & licence whenever they find the bonds of government removed." See R. H. Lee to R. C. Nicholas, April 12, 1776. Historian Staughton Lynd saw that these "original sins of the nation" were being challenged from below. S. Lynd, Foreword in R. Alexander, *The Northwest Ordinance: Constitutional Politics and the Theft of Native Land.* Jefferson, NC: McFarland & Company, Inc., 2017, pp. 1–6. Historian Peter Linebaugh wrote that "the twin absurdities, property in land (real estate) and property in persons (slavery) became the economic and social foundation of civilization." P. Linebaugh, "A Foul Field Full of Foolish Fascist White Folk," unpublished letter, February 14, 2021.

6. J. Madison, Notes on Debates, 28 January 1783. Later in the debate Madison repeated his point that "doing justice to the Creditors alone wd. restore publi[c] credit, & the restoration of this alone could provide for the future exigencies of the war." See also J. Madison, "Note to His Speech on the Right of Suffrage," *Documentary History*, Vol. 5, 1821, pp. 440–9.

7. See W. Holton, *Unruly Americans and the Origins of the Constitution.* New York: Hill and Wang, 2007, p. 88. In the 1793 case *Chisholm v. Georgia,* James Wilson in a separate opinion explicitly defined "to establish justice" with I.10.1 prohibiting states from passing laws "impairing the Obligation of Contracts." The ruling was nullified by the 1795 11th amendment. Law professor James W. Ely called the contract clause one of the most important in the Constitution. See J. W. Ely, "Origins and Development of the Contract Clause," *Vanderbilt Public Law Research Paper*, No. 05-36, November 1, 2005, pp. 220–1.

8. J. Ferguson, *The Power of the Purse: A History of American Public Finance, 1776–1790.* Chapel Hill: University of North Carolina Press, 1961, p. 149.

9. Ibid., pp. 115, 234. Congress owed France $6.4 million, $3.6 million to private Dutch bankers, and more to Spain. The principal of the Dutch loan was being repaid by 1787. See R. Brown, *Redeeming the Republic: Federalists, Taxation, and the Origins of the Constitution.* Baltimore: Johns Hopkins University Press, 1993, p. 19; and R. Buel, "The Public Creditor Interest in Massachusetts Politics, 1780–86," in R. A. Gross (ed.), 1993, p. 52.

10. Letter on Hamilton's funding proposals dated New York, February 3, 1790 in J. Ferguson, 1961, p. xiii. Hamilton thought that fellow elites "wish a government of the union able to protect them against domestic violence and the depredations which the democratic spirit is apt to

make on property." A. Hamilton, "Conjectures about the New Constitution," September 17–30, 1787.

11. See J. Ferguson, 1961, p. xv.

12. J. T. Main, *The Anti-Federalists: Critics of the Constitution 1781–1788*. New York: W. W. Norton & Company, 1961, p. 7.

13. Holton estimates that most states used two-thirds of tax revenue to pay creditors. W. Holton, 2004, pp. 277, 312–15; W. Holton, 2007, pp. 32, 37.

14. W. Holton, 2004, p. 276.

15. G. Nobles, "Historians Extend the Reach of the American Revolution," in A. Young and G. Nobles (eds.), *Whose American Revolution Was It? Historians Interpret the Founding*. New York: New York University Press, 2011, p. 213.

16. G. Nash and historians P. Linebaugh, S. Lynd, M. Rediker, H. Aptheker, and H. Zinn documented a range of insurrections and rebellions from below, such as the 1689 overthrow of New York City by Jacob Leisler and his group who governed for about two years. The Leisler insurrection brought about an almost permanent state of emergency against working-class insurrection that prompted the building of textile mills, prisons, and almshouses to control the poor. see G. Nash, *The Urban Crucible: The Northern Seaports and the Origins of the American Revolution*, abridged edition. Cambridge, MA: Harvard University Press, 1979, pp. 24–7, 218, 247. S. Lynd highlighted the growing influence of the mechanics on New York state politics prior to the Constitution; what merchants saw as a grave threat to their interests. See S. Lynd, *Class Conflict, Slavery, and the United States Constitution.*, Indianapolis: Bobbs-Merrill Company, Inc., 1967, pp. 96–7, 108.

17. M. McDonnell, *The Politics of War: Race, Class, and Conflict in Revolutionary Virginia*. Chapel Hill: Omohundro Institute and University of North Carolina Press, 2007, p. 14–15.

18. The nationalist project was inspired by the efforts of Dutch, Italian, and other European elites in recent centuries to unify their disparate city states and principalities into single national states with centralized supremacy powers that could set up, protect, and promote a capitalist economy. On political centralization see K. Marx and F. Engels, *Manifesto of the Communist Party*, in K. Marx and F. Engels, *Selected Works*, Vol. 1. Moscow: Progress Publishers, 1848 [1969], pp. 98–137.

19. Massachusetts lawyer Fisher Ames issued a "protest against the transfer of my property to my debtor." See Lucius Junius Brutus #6, F. Ames, *Independent Chronicle*, at Boston, October 1, 1786, *Works of Fisher Ames Compiled by a Number of His Friends*, T. B. Wait Court-Street (1786 [1809]).

20. D. Szatmary, *Shays' Rebellion: The Making of an Agrarian Insurrection.* Amherst: University of Massachusetts Press, 1980, p. 49. See also J. Adams to T. Jefferson, November 30, 1786.

21. Morris admitted later in life to having been the person that literally wrote the Constitution. See G. Morris to T. Pickering, December 22, 1814. See also W. Holton, 2004, pp. 294–5; R. Kohn, *Eagle and Sword: The Beginnings of the Military Establishment in America.* New York: The Free Press, 1975, p. 76.

22. See R. Kohn, 1975, pp. 80, 95, 120.

23. S. Lynd, "Revisiting Class in Early America: Personal Reflections," *Labor: Studies in Working-Class History*, Vol. 1, No. 4, 2004, p. 30; S. Lynd, 1967, pp. 125, 128–32. Paul Revere was perhaps the most famous mechanic of his time, eventually becoming a merchant industrialist after the Revolution with an iron foundry and copper-rolling mill that produced canons among other items. See also M. Rediker, "The Revenge of Crispus Attucks, or, the Atlantic Challenge to American Labor History," *Labor: Studies in Working-Class History of the Americas*, Vol. 1, No. 4, 2004, pp. 36, 38. On organizations of mechanics reorganizing themselves into societies of manufacturers, see W. A. Williams, *The Contours of American History.* Chicago: Quadrangle Books, 1961, pp. 142–3.

24. J. Lemisch, "Jack Tar in the Streets: Merchant Seamen in the Politics of Revolutionary America," *The William and Mary Quarterly*, Vol. 25, No. 3, 1968; P. Linebaugh and M. Rediker, *Many Headed Hydra: Sailors, Slaves, Commoners, and the Hidden History of the Revolutionary Atlantic.* Boston: Beacon Press; and G. Nash, 1979.

25. J. F. Jameson, *The American Revolution Considered as a Social Movement.* Boston: Beacon Press, 1925, p. 12.

26. R. H. Brown, 1993, pp. 17–19. See also R. Morris, August 5, 1782, *Journals of the Continental Congress 1774–1789*, 34 Vols., published by the Library of Congress, 1904–1937, January 1, 1782 to August 9, 1782, Vol. 22, p. 438.

27. D. Ramsey made this point. See M. Klarman, *The Framers' Coup: The Making of the United States Constitution.* New York: Oxford University Press, 2016, p. 339; see also L. Hacker, "The Establishment of a National Union," in J. Birnbaum and B. Ollman (eds.), *U.S. Constitution: 200 Hundred Years of Anti-Federalist, Abolitionist, Feminist, Muckraking, Progressive, and Especially Socialist Criticism.* New York: New York University Press, 1990, p. 27.

28. According to Malcolm Sharp, "[s]olicitude for liberty and property, and not unreasonable fear of what unchecked majority rule might do to them, seem the forces which did most to embody the principle in our

constitutions." M. Sharp, "The Classical American Doctrine of 'The Separation of Powers'," *University of Chicago Law Review*, Vol. 2, No. 3, 1935, p. 434.

29. Paper money bills passed in three of the six states—New Hampshire, Maryland and Delaware—but it was blocked by the senate. W. Holton, 2007, p. 174.

30. J. Ferguson, 1961, p. 32.

31. P. T. and J. P. Kaminsky (eds.), *The Constitution and the States: The Role of the Original Thirteen in the Framing and Adoption of the Federal Constitution*. Wisconsin: Madison House, 1988, pp. 228–31.

32. Despite I.10.1, at least eight states continued to attempt to pass stay and debtor relief laws after ratification, sometimes under the cover of martial property laws, but they were struck down by the courts as unconstitutional under the I.10 impairment of contract clause and the 1843 *Bronson v. Kinzie* Supreme Court decision. See W. Holton, "Equality as Unintended Consequence: The Contracts Clause and the Married Women's Property Acts," *The Journal of Southern History*, Vol. 81, No. 2, 2015, pp. 321, 335; and M. Jensen, *The New Nation: A History of the United States during the Confederation, 1781–1789*. New York: Vintage Press, 1959, p. 278. States continued to pass stay, installment, and bankruptcy laws until 1815. See S. R. Boyd, "The Contract Clause and the Evolution of American Federalism, 1789–1815," *The William and Mary Quarterly*, Vol. 44, No. 3, 1987, pp. 537, 548; and J. W. Ely, 2005, pp. 201, 203.

33. See W. Holton, 1999, pp. xv, 112, 117, 129.

34. J. Ferguson, 1961, p. 123–4; for more on its capitalization see G. D. Rappaport, "The First Description of the Bank of North America," *The William and Mary Quarterly*, Vol. 33, No. 4, 1976, pp. 661–7; and M. Jensen, 1959, pp. 66–7.

35. W. Manning, "Some Proposals for Making Restitution to the Original Creditors of Government and to Help the Continent to a Medium of Trade Submitted to the Consideration of the Member of the State Legislature of Massachusetts, February the 6th, 1790," in M. Merrill and S. Wilentz (eds.), *The Key of Liberty: The Life and Democratic Writings of William Manning, "A Laborer," 1747–1814*. Cambridge, MA: Harvard University Press, 1993, p. 113.

36. In fact, a group of creditors wrote to Washington in 1789 asking for a public credit system to "promote the public Welfare" that sounded much like that which Hamilton would propose shortly after. From the Public Creditors of Pennsylvania to G. Washington, August 21, 1789.

37. J. Madison to J. Monroe, October 5, 1786; Madison repeated this point about the oppression, enslavement, and tyranny of the majority

on numerous occasions, including *Federalist #10*; his letters to T. Jefferson on October 17 and 24, 1787; and J. Madison, "Note to His Speech on the Right of Suffrage," *Documentary History*, Vol. 5, 1821, pp. 440–9. See also J. Conniff, "The Enlightenment and American Political Thought: A Study of the Origins of Madison's *Federalist Number 10*," *Political Theory*, Vol. 8, No. 3, 1980, pp. 381–402; and D. Adair, "The Tenth Federalist Revisited," *The William and Mary Quarterly*, Vol. 8, No. 1, 1951; J. Madison, 1751–1836: Bicentennial Number, p. 54.

38. M. Klarman made this point by titling his book with this phrase. M. Klarman, 2016.

39. I.4 also fails to specify that the voters would have the right to continue to submit "memorials" (an eighteenth-century form of petitions) to Congress, recall their representatives, initiate or repeal laws, call for a constitutional convention, and vote directly on amendments or a new constitution. While a few states continued to allow some of these measures, they fell out of favor until the late nineteenth century when some states started to adopt the initiative, referendum, and recall. These, however, are in use only for state and local elections. We have yet to obtain them for the federal government.

40. E. Gerry to J. Adams, November 23, 1783. Gerry was no democrat but opposed the Constitution because he thought elites were better served by their state governments.

Chapter 3

1. See M. Jensen, *The Making of the American Constitution*. Huntington, NY: Robert E. Krieger Publishing Company, 1964, p. 41.

2. Quoted in R. Morris, "Class Struggle and the American Revolution," *The William and Mary Quarterly*, Vol. 19, No. 1, 1962, pp. 11. This was John Adams' motivation for designing what he had hoped would be a standardized form of government imposed on the states.

3. G. Morris, O. Ellsworth, and J. Wilson, August 16, 1787, in M. Farrand, *RFC*, Vol. 2, 1911, pp. 309–11. Because he had his own loans and bills for imported slaves repaid with significantly devalued paper money, Jefferson faced financial ruin due to the inability to collect from those who purchased his father-in-law's imported slaves, debts he tried to collect as the executor of his estate. His financial troubles may have motivated Jefferson to include an extraordinary attack on the slave trade by England in a draft of the Declaration of Independence, even if he supported slavery itself. That text was removed by Congress in the next edit. See W. Holton, *Forced Founders: Indians, Debtors, Slaves, and the Making of the American Revolution in Virginia*. Chapel Hill: Omohundro Institute and University of North Carolina Press, 1999, p. 66;

W. Holton, *Unruly Americans and the Origins of the Constitution*. New York: Hill and Wang, 2007, p. 59.

4. Supremacy of the federal debt was enumerated a second time in the 1868 14.4, which was originally intended to address debts resulting from the cost of fighting the Civil War. The clause reads: "The validity of the public debt of the United States, authorized by law, including debts incurred for payment of pensions and bounties for services in suppressing insurrection or rebellion, shall not be questioned." It should also be noted that I.8.2 establishes Congress's enumerated authority "[t]o borrow Money on the credit of the United States" which, in conjunction with VI.1, implies the supremacy of repaying the debt.

5. J. T. Main, *The Anti-Federalists: Critics of the Constitution 1781–1788*. New York: W. W. Norton & Company, 1961, p. 64.

6. While here he is reciting the critics argument he says it is "a thing intrinsically good" that can be abused. A. Hamilton, "The Defence of the Funding System," July 1795.

7. M. Klarman, *The Framers' Coup: The Making of the United States Constitution*. New York: Oxford University Press, 2016, p. 152.

8. A. Hamilton, "Final Version of the Report on the Subject of Manufactures," December 5, 1791; and A. Hamilton (The Continentalist), No. 5, April 18, 1782. Hamilton made the case not only for the power to charter banks but even for corporations that would be considered "artificial" persons that "have no country," "cannot commit a crime," and "cannot die." See A. Hamilton, "Opinion as to the Constitutionality of the Bank of the United States," 1791.

9. See W. P. Adams, *The First American Constitutions: Republican Ideology and the Making of the State Constitutions in the Revolutionary Era*. Lanham: Rowman & Littlefield, 2001.

10. Karl Marx described this process of creating a class of workers by "primitive accumulation"and the theft of land by "enclosures". See K. Marx, *Capital: A Critique of Political Economy*, Vol. 1. New York: Vintage Press, 1867 [1977], pp. 431–8, 876, especially Part VIII where he describes native peoples and peasants "suddenly and forcibly torn from their means of subsistence, and hurled onto the labour-market as free, unprotected, and rightless proletarians."

11. This was the central concern of Hamilton in making the case for his public credit system. See Chapter 7. See, among others, K. Marx, 1977, Part VIII, chapters 26–33, pp. 873–940; M. Rediker, "Good Hands, Stout Heart, and Fast Feet: The History and Culture of Working People in Early America," *Labour/Le Travail*, Vol. 10, 1982, pp. 123–44; and H. Cleaver, *33 Lessons on Capital: Reading Marx Politically*. London: Pluto, 2019, pp. 16–97.

12. While the militias and army were not sent on murderous assaults carrying out mass slaughter of white farmers, the economic policies slowly eroded the power of the small farmers, ending with the last eruption of mass protests during the populist era which was divided by racism and defeated. The theft of land for the purpose of creating a class of waged workers is part of the same process although in different degrees of violence. That white farmers saw that the level of threat was reflected in their polemical warnings about being thrown into debt peonage and slavery. See W. Holton, "Rebuttal," *Labor: Studies in Working-Class History of the Americas*, Vol. 6, No. 3, 2009, pp. 55–6. Elsewhere Holton points out that "even as the Framers lamented that excessive democracy … had turned the United States into a farmers' paradise, many of the farmers themselves complained that they could redress their many grievances by only taking up arms." W. Holton, 2007, p. 13.

13. P. Linebaugh, "A Foul Field Full of Foolish Fascist White Folk," unpublished essay, February 14, 2021.

14. Staughton Lynd argues that the three-fifths clause was the result of a multidirectional series of bargains. Congress banned slavery in the 1787 Northwest Ordinance at the same time the Convention was taking place, which allow Southern Framers to support the Constitution. S. Lynd, Foreword, in R. Alexander, *The Northwest Ordinance: Constitutional Politics and the Theft of Native Land*. Jefferson, NC: McFarland & Company, Inc., 2017, pp. 1–6.

15. M. Klarman, 2016, p. 269–70.

16. Ibid., pp. 287, 291.

17. L. Martin, Genuine Information VIII, January 22, 1788.

18. D. Ramsey, *An Address to the Freemen of South Carolina on the Subject of the Federal Constitution, Proposed by the Convention, which met in Philadelphia, May 1787*, in P. L. Ford (ed.), *Pamphlets on the Constitution of the United States. Published During its Discussion by the People, 1787–1788*. New York: Burt Franklin, 1888, p. 378.

19. C. C. Pinckney, January 17, 1788; and M. Jensen, 1964, p. 94.

20. Brown lists nine major rural rebellions but he appears to be missing at least four major rural insurrections. These took place in Virginia during the tenant and debtors rebellions, a state he said lacked an uprising, the South Carolina debtors revolt, the 1786 New Hampshire insurrection against laws favorable to British creditors, and the 1760–1815 Maine "white Indians" squatters revolt. He also entirely leaves out native and slave rebellions and resistance. R. M. Brown, *Redeeming the Republic: Federalists, Taxation, and the Origins of the Constitution*. Baltimore: Johns Hopkins University Press, 1993, pp. 73, 81. For Virginia, see W.

Holton, "Did Democracy Cause the Recession that Led to the Constitution?" *The Journal of American History*, Vol. 92, No. 2, 2005, pp. 442–69; M. McDonnell and W. Holton, "Patriot vs. Patriot: Social Conflict in Virginia and the Origins of the American Revolution," *Journal of American Studies*, Vol. 34, No. 2, 2011, pp. 230–56; M. McDonnell, "Class War? Class Struggles during the American Revolution in Virginia," *The William and Mary Quarterly*, Third Series, Vol. 63, No. 2, Class and Early America, 2006, pp. 305–44. For South Carolina, see R. A. Becker, "Salus Populi Suprema Lex: Public Peace and South Carolina Debtor Relief Laws, 1783–1788," *The South Carolina Historical Magazine*, Vol. 80, No. 1, 1979, pp. 65–75. For the "Exeter Riot" at the state legislature in New Hampshire, see W. Holton, "'From the Labours of Others': The War Bonds Controversy and the Origins of the Constitution in New England," *The William and Mary Quarterly*, Third Series, Vol. 61, No. 2, 2004, pp. 272, 298–300; A. Taylor, "Regulators and White Indians: The Agrarian Resistance in Post-Revolutionary New England," in R. A. Gross ed., *In Debt to Shays: The Bicentennial of an Agrarian Rebellion*. Charlottesville: University Press of Virginia, 1993, pp. 147–50. For Maine see R. E. Moody, "Samuel Ely: Forerunner of Shays," *The New England Quarterly*, Vol. 5, No. 1, 1932, pp. 105–34; A. Taylor, "Agrarian Independence: Northern Land Rioters After the Revolution," in A. Young (ed.), *Beyond the American Revolution*. DeKalb: Northern Illinois University Press, 1993, pp. 222–4. A significant oversight is that he's missing the frequent rural struggles of slaves. See H. Aptheker, *American Negro Slave Revolts*. New York: International Publishers, 1983 [1936]. Taylor described land revolts in even more places, sometimes more than one, from the 1740s until 1810, including in New Jersey, South Carolina, New York, Maine, Pennsylvania, Vermont, Ohio, Massachusetts, and Connecticut. See A. Taylor, in A. Young (ed.), 1993, pp. 227–8. Aside from the squatter and secession movement in Maine, the secession movements to create the states of Franklin and Westsylvania should also be included. See T. Slaughter, *The Whiskey Rebellion: Frontier Epilogue to the American Revolution*. New York: Oxford University Press, 1986, pp. 56–7.

21. C. L. Becker, *The History of Political Parties in the Province of New York 1760–1776*. Madison: University of Wisconsin Press, 1909, p. 22, also iv. This is also known as the "dual revolution" thesis. See S. Rosswurm, *Arms, Country, and Class: The Philadelphia Militia and the "Lower Sort" during the American Revolution*. New Brunswick: Rutgers University Press, 1989, p. 3.

22. M. McDonnell and W. Holton, 2011, pp. 233–4; W. Holton, 2007, pp. 11–12.

23. M. Merrill and S. Wilentz, *The Key of Liberty: The Life and Democratic Writings of William Manning, "A Laborer," 1747–1814*. Cambridge, MA: Harvard University Press, 1993, p. 22.

24. H. Knox to H. Jackson, December 17, 1786 in D. Szatmary, *Shays' Rebellion: The Making of an Agrarian Insurrection*. Amherst: University of Massachusetts Press, 1980, pp. 37–41, 57–9, 97.

25. G. Washington to D. Stuart, December 6, 1786. Although the Congress approved funding for 1,300 soldiers to put down the rebellion, it never received the necessary requisition from the states to pay for it and the force ended up being bankrolled by donations from Massachusetts elites solicited by Knox. See also G. Washington to J. Madison, November 5, 1786.

26. G. Washington to H. Knox, December 26, 1786. See also G. Washington to D. Humphreys, October 22, 1786. General Benjamin Lincoln, commanding the troops sent to crush the Regulators, warned of "Agrarian law" if they failed. See B. Lincoln to G. Washington, December 4, 1786 to March 4, 1787. The insurrection was so threatening that John Adams insisted to Thomas Jefferson that "this Commotion will terminate in additional Strength to Government." See J. Adams to T. Jefferson, November 30, 1786. Historian Peter Linebaugh described their warnings as a fear of "the agrarian law of antiquity which, like the jubilee, equalized land distribution." See P. Linebaugh, 2021.

27. J. Madison warned of this outcome to G. Washington. See J. Madison to G. Washington, April 16, 1787.

28. See M. Merrill, "The Anticapitalist Origins of the United States," *Review*, Fernand Braudel Center, Vol. 13, No. 4, 1990, pp. 465–97; and M. Merrill, "Capitalist State, Anticapitalist Economy: Social Relations of Production and Exchange in the Era of the American Revolution," unpublished paper presented at the Workshop of the Atlanta Seminar in Comparative History of Labor, Industry, Technology and Society, "State and Economy: Shaping Capitalism 1750–1914," March, 1996.

29. H. Lee asserted that "their object together with the abolition of debts, the division of property." M. Klarman, 2016, p. 73.

30. G. Nash, "Urban Wealth and Poverty in Pre-Revolutionary America," *The Journal of Interdisciplinary History*, Vol. 6, No. 4, 1976, p. 581. See also D. Humphreys, D. Barlow, J. J. Trumbull, and Dr. L. Hopkins, *The Anarchiad: A New England Poem*. Edited with notes and appendices by Luther G. Riggs. New Haven: Thomas H. Pease. Originally published in *The New Haven Gazette and Connecticut Magazine* of October 26, 1861 [1786]; R. Brown, 1993, p. 73; and A. Hamilton, Speech at the New York Ratifying Convention, June 27, 1788.

31. While he initially opposed her speculation and preferred she bought land, in 1790 John Adams celebrated that Abigail's speculation in government debt would earn them more than 400 percent profit. See W. Holton, 2005, pp. 457–60; W. Holton, 2007, pp. 34–6; A. Adams to J. Adams, January 3, 1784; and W. Holton, *Abigail Adams: A Life*. New York: Free Press, 2009.

32. J. Madison to T. Jefferson, October 24, 1787.

33. The evidence shows that Morris used his position as Superintendent of Finance to expand his global business relationships, opportunities, and profits for himself and his partners. In addition to his bank, vast speculative land holdings, and slaves, Morris also controlled the French tobacco trade as a result of his dealings to obtain new loans for Congress. From 1784, the last year he served in his position, until 1787, 11 vessels in which he either owned or had an interest in left US ports for Europe, India, and the West Indies, and he counted 15 US ships in Canton, China by 1789. Perhaps the richest man in the country at the time of the Convention, Morris was a creditor both as co-owner of the Bank of Pennsylvania and to the Congress. But he was also highly leveraged and buried deeply in debt, to Congress among others; so deeply in fact that he was sentenced to debtor's prison late in life and died penniless. The source of his troubles was engaging in failed overseas trading ventures and speculative purchases of land totaling $6 million by borrowing money he couldn't repay. See F. McDonald, *We the People: The Economic Origins of the Constitution*. Chicago: University of Chicago Press, 1958, pp. 55–6. These business operations are also exhaustively detailed in the biography by C. Rappleye, *Robert Morris: Financier of the American Revolution*. New York: Simon & Schuster, 2010, although he rejects the idea that he was self-dealing.

34. F. McDonald, 1958, pp. 58–9.

35. M. Jensen, *The Articles of Confederation: An Interpretation of the Social-Constitutional History of the American Revolution 1774–1781*. Madison: University of Wisconsin Press, 1959, p. 128.

36. A. Hamilton to J. Duane, September 3, 1780.

37. Virginia had previously tried twice to double the tariff and even ban the importation of slaves but was vetoed by the British Privy Council. Both the 1769 and 1774 Continental Associations banned the slave trade and South Carolina actually did ban the import of slaves between 1787 and 1802. W. Holton, 1999, pp. 70–1, 104–5.

38. Ibid., pp. 52, 60, 67–8.

39. Ibid., p. 107.

40. Article 2 of the 1787 Northwest Ordinance, which included protection of property and private contracts from interference, was used as a model

for this clause in the Constitution. See J. W. Ely, "Origins and Development of the Contract Clause," *Vanderbilt Public Law Research Paper*, No. 05-36, November 1, 2005, pp. 204–8; and Northwest Ordinance (1787). An Ordinance for the government of the Territory of the United States northwest of the River Ohio, transcript.

41. As Superintendent of Finance, Robert Morris warned the states not to violate their contractual obligation to the creditors. See R. Morris, "To the Governors of Massachusetts, Rhode Island, New York, Delaware, Maryland, and North Carolina, Philadelphia," July 27, 1781, in J. Sparks (ed.), *The Diplomatic Correspondence of the American Revolution*, Vol. 11. Boston: Nathan Hale and Gray & Bowen; New York: C. & C. H. Carvill; Washington, DC: P. Thompson, 2009. In his public credit plan, Hamilton argued that debts were unalterable contracts which could not be violated without putting all property at risk. A. Hamilton, "Report Relative to a Provision for the Support of Public Credit," January 9, 1790; and A. Hamilton, "The Defence of the Funding System," July 1795. See also W. Holton, 2007, p. 184; and F. McDonald, 1958, pp. 107–8.

42. Although the contract clause only applied to the states, some continued to evade it until 1815, leading to some of the first uses of judicial review to strike them down. S. R. Boyd, "The Contract Clause and the Evolution of American Federalism, 1789–1815," *The William and Mary Quarterly*, Vol. 44, No. 3, 1987, pp. 537 and 539–40.

43. As we will see in Chapter 8, some states did continue to use some of these economic powers, such as establishing state banks, issuing paper currency, and providing debt relief, until they were struck down by the Supreme Court as unconstitutional.

44. In making the case for Congress having the power to regulate commerce, Madison warned that free trade weakened national power because it allowed other countries to regulate their trade. See J. Madison, Speech to Congress, Commercial Discrimination, January 14, 1794.

45. M. Klarman, 2016, p. 102.

46. A. Hamilton, The Defence of the Funding System, July 1795.

47. Some of Wilson's debts were to the Bank of North America from which he borrowed heavily to finance speculative land purchases. See G. D. Rappaport, "The First Description of the Bank of North America," *The William and Mary Quarterly*, Vol. 33, No. 4, 1976, p. 662.

48. W. Holton, "Equality as Unintended Consequence: The Contracts Clause and the Married Women's Property Acts," *The Journal of Southern History*, Vol. 81, No. 2, 2015, p. 319.

49. Holton makes this same point. See W. Holton, 2007, p. 229–30.

Chapter 4

1. See also T. Bouton, *Taming Democracy: "The People," the Founders, and the Troubled Ending of the American Revolution*. New York: Oxford University Press, 2007, pp. 177–8.

2. G. Morris, July 21, 1787, in M. Farrand, *RFC*, Vol. 2, 1911, p. 76. See also J. Madison in *Federalist #68*, who warned of "the same tyranny as is threatened by executive usurpations."

3. P. Whoriskey, D. MacMillan, and J. O'Connell, "Doomed to Fail: Why a $4 Trillion Bailout Couldn't Revive the American Economy," *Washington Post*, October 5, 2020, accessed June 8, 2022, www.washingtonpost.com/graphics/2020/business/coronavirus-bailout-spending/.

4. J. DeParle, "Pandemic Aid Programs Spur a Record Drop in Poverty," *New York Times*, July 28, 2021, accessed June 8, 2022, www.nytimes.com/2021/07/28/us/politics/covid-poverty-aid-programs.html.

5. C. Beard, *An Economic Interpretation of the Constitution of the United States*. New York: Free Press, 1986 [1913], p. 176.

6. G. Thrush, "'We're Not a Democracy,' Says Mike Lee, a Republican Senator. That's a Good Thing, He Adds," *New York Times*, October 8, 2020, accessed June 8, 2022, https://www.nytimes.com/2020/10/08/us/elections/mike-lee-democracy.html.

7. Brutus, Essay #3, *New York Journal*, November 15, 1787, in J. Birnbaum and B. Ollman (eds.), *U.S. Constitution: 200 Hundred Years of Anti-Federalist, Abolitionist, Feminist, Muckraking, Progressive, and Especially Socialist Criticism*. New York: New York University Press, 1990, p. 86.

8. On this point, see M. Sharp, "The Classical American Doctrine of 'The Separation of Powers'," *University of Chicago Law Review*, Vol. 2, No. 3, 1935, pp. 385–436.

9. S. Levinson, *Our Undemocratic Constitution: Where the Constitution Goes Wrong (and How We the People Can Correct It)*. New York: Oxford University Press, 2006, pp. 39, 46. He calls the President a "one-person third legislative chamber" but overlooks how judicial review also transforms the courts into a chamber of the legislature like the Council of Revision used by three states during the Critical Era before the Constitution.

10. J. T. Main, *The Sovereign States, 1775–1783*. New York: New Viewpoints, 1973, pp. 127–9, 141.

11. Cited in B. Konkle, *George Bryan and the Constitution of Pennsylvania 1731–1791*. Philadelphia: W. J. Campbell, 1922, pp. 311–12.

12. S. Lynd, *Class Conflict, Slavery, and the United States Constitution*. Indianapolis: Bobbs-Merrill Company, Inc., 1967, pp. 40–7.

13. W. Adams, *The First American Constitutions: Republican Ideology and the Making of the State Constitutions in the Revolutionary Era.* Lanham: Rowman & Littlefield, 2001. Massachusetts was an outlier to these efforts at democratization by raising the property requirements to run for and hold office in its 1780 constitution. See D. Szatmary, *Shays' Rebellion: The Making of an Agrarian Insurrection.* Amherst: University of Massachusetts Press, 1980, p. 49. Approximately a quarter of North Carolina's 1776 constitution incorporated the demands of the 1760s regulators. M. Jensen, *The Articles of Confederation: An Interpretation of the Social-Constitutional History of the American Revolution 1774–1781.* Madison: University of Wisconsin Press, 1959, p. 26.

14. For the history of the senate, see M. Jensen, *The Making of the American Constitution.* Huntington, NY: Robert E. Krieger Publishing Company, 1964, pp. 13–14, 20–1.

15. Towns in Berkshire County, Massachusetts were the first to propose electing judges in late 1775. W. Adams, 2001, p. 46.

16. See M. Jensen, 1959, pp. 240–1 for these arguments.

17. From J. Adams to J. Sullivan, May 26, 1776; and J. Adams to R. H. Lee, November 15, 1775. Adams wrote a book reserving praise only for state systems with a bicameral legislature, strong executive, and three branches separated by checks and balances in an unsuccessful attempt to impose a single model of government on all the states. See J. Adams, *A Defence of the Constitutions of Government of the United States of America,* in *The Works of John Adams, Second President of the United States: With a Life of the Author, Notes and Illustrations, by his Grandson Charles Francis Adams,* Vol. 6. Boston: Little, Brown and Co., 1856 [1787].

18. J. A. Smith, *The Spirit of American Government: A Study of the Constitution: Its Origin, Influence and Relation to Democracy,* edited by C. Strout. Cambridge, MA: Belknap Press of Harvard University Press, 1965 [1907], pp. 20, 22. See also W. Adams, 2001, pp. 199–207, 267; J. T. Main, *The Anti-Federalists: Critics of the Constitution, 1781–1788.* New York: W. W. Norton & Company, 1961, pp. 17–19; W. Holton, *Unruly Americans and the Origins of the Constitution.* New York: Hill and Wang, 2007, pp. 168, 174–5; J. T. Main, 1973, pp. 170–1, 188–93, 209, 221; F. Lundberg, *Cracks in the Constitution.* Secaucus, NJ: Lyle Stuart, Inc., 1980, pp. 146–53.

19. W. Adams, 2001, p. 271; P. T. Conley and J. P. Kaminsky (eds.), *The Constitution and the States: The Role of the Original Thirteen in the Framing and Adoption of the Federal Constitution.* Wisconsin: Madison House, 1988, p. 52.

20. See T. Bouton, 2007, pp. 54–5, 194–5.

21. A. Hamilton, "Opinion as to the Constitutionality of the Bank of the United States," 1791.

22. C. Beard, 1986 [1913], p. 176.

23. A total of 59 senators representing third parties were selected by their state legislature, elected by state voters, or appointed by the governor to fill a vacancy. See United States Senate, "Senators Representing Third or Minor Parties," accessed June 8, 2022, www.senate.gov/senators/ SenatorsRepresentingThirdorMinorParties.htm.

24. Although L. Fisher has demonstrated occasions when the Senate's foreign policy priorities have diverged from the President's, it is still rare and non-existent during war time. See L. Fisher, *The Constitution between Friends*. New York: St. Martin's Press, 1978, pp. 192–213; and L. Fisher, *The Politics of Executive Privilege*. Durham, NC: Carolina Academic Press, 2004, p. 238.

25. Only the 21st amendment, repealing the 18th amendment which prohibited alcohol, was passed by a second method of ratification by state constitutional conventions. There are as many as four methods for amending the Constitution contained in Article V.

26. It goes without saying that Rome beat out the even more democratic Iceland, which in 1072 established its own hybrid system of local direct democracy and island-wide representative democracy.

27. In *Federalist #63*, Hamilton and Madison thought that unicameral legislatures were dangerous because the majority could make decisions without minority checks. John Adams argued that with a unicameral legislature "a people cannot be long free." J. Adams, *Thoughts on Government*, 1776, in R. J. Taylor et al. (eds.), *Papers of John Adams*. Cambridge, MA: Belknap Press of Harvard University Press, 1977, pp. 86–93.

28. The myth persists today, in no small part due to Madison's claim in *Federalist #43* that the equal votes in the Senate was a compromise between the Virginia and New Jersey Plans to protect the small states. This claim just doesn't hold up to his other pronouncements about the role of the Senate.

29. Jefferson called inequality of representation "the only republican heresy" in the Constitution. T. Jefferson to H. Tompkinson (Samuel Kercheval), "Proposals to Revise the Virginia Constitution: I, July 12, 1816," in P. Ford (ed.), *The Writings of Thomas Jefferson*, Vol. 10. New York and London: G. P. Putnam's Sons, 1892–9, p. 37. The equality in the Senate has evolved today into a less than subtle code for racism in which the demographic supermajority white small-population states make claims to resources they might otherwise lose to states with more diverse and larger metropolitan areas. These small-population states, while cur-

rently leaning more conservative in favor of "limited" government, which is again code for less spending in more racially diverse large population states, in fact receive disproportionately more than their share of federal tax revenue that they contribute in payments. Today the argument about small v. large states persists despite the reality that no state has a uniquely distinct set of interests that is tied strictly to either its geographic size or number of residents. For example, while we tend to think that small states are rural and large states are urban, Maryland is very urban and California is very rural. Even small rural states don't all have the same perspective on important policy issues. For example, much of small-population rural Vermont's agriculture is organic while similarly populated rural North Dakota is conventional. The size of a state doesn't matter but demographics and economics do. See J. Toobin, "Our Broken Constitution: Everyone Agrees that Government Isn't Working. Are the Founders to Blame?" *The New Yorker*, December 1, 2013, accessed June 8, 2022, https://www.newyorker.com/magazine/2013/12/09/our-broken-constitution.

30. S. Levinson, 2006, p. 58. See also R. Dahl, *How Democratic Is the American Constitution?*, 2nd edition. New Haven: Yale University Press, 2003, pp. 46–7.

31. G. Mason, June 26, 1787, Madison notes, in M. Farrand, *RFC*, Vol. 1, 1911, p. 428; G. Morris, July 2, 1787, in M. Farrand, *RFC*, Vol. 1, 1911, pp. 511–14; R. Sherman, Madison's Notes, June 26, 1787, in M. Farrand, *RFC*, Vol. 1, 1911, p. 423 and Yates' Notes, pp. 431–2.

32. Gouverneur Morris later supported six or eight years. See G. Morris, July 2, 1787, in M. Farrand, *RFC*, Vol. 1, 1911, p. 512. Jefferson had earlier wanted the Senate's members appointed by the House for nine-year terms. See T. Jefferson to E. Pendleton, August 26, 1776. Alexander Hamilton wanted it to be modeled after England's aristocratic House of Lords, "a most noble institution." A. Hamilton, Madison's Notes, June 18, 1787.

33. For another view on Madison's advocacy for the Senate with seven-year terms, see R. Yates, *Notes of the Secret Debates of the Federal Convention of 1787, Taken by the Late Hon Robert Yates, Chief Justice of the State of New York, and One of the Delegates from That State to the Said Convention*, Tuesday, June 12, 1787. Honolulu: University Press of the Pacific, 1839. Hamilton similarly saw the Senate as "a permanent barrier agst. every pernicious innovation" and "regulate the fluctuations of a popular assembly." See A. Hamilton, Madison's Notes, June 18, 1787; and A. Hamilton, Speech at the New York Ratifying Convention, June 24, 1788).

34. J. Madison, Constitutional Convention Debates, Term of the Senate, June 26, 1787. John Adams saw the Senate as "guardians of property against levellers for the purposes of plunder." J. Adams, 1856 [1787], p. 118. Gouverneur Morris thought the Senate would watch over and constrain the "dupes." G. Morris, in M. Farrand, *RFC*, Vol. 1, 1911, p. 514.

35. G. Morris, in M. Farrand, *RFC*, Vol. 1, 1911, p. 514. See also J. Madison, Vices of the Political System of the United States, April 1787. Madison makes the same point in numerous places. See J. Madison, June 6, 1787, in M. Farrand, *RFC*, Vol. 1, 1911, p. 136; J. Madison to T. Jefferson, October 24, 1787; *Federalist Paper #10*; J. Madison, May 31, 1787, in M. Farrand, *RFC*, Vol. 1, 1911, p. 50; J. Madison, Note to His Speech on the Right of Suffrage, August 7, 1789, in M. Farrand, *RFC*, Vol. 3, 1911, p. 454; and both Madison and Hamilton in *Federalist #63*. A. Hamilton makes a similar point in *Federalist #60*; and A. Hamilton to R. Livingston, April 25, 1785. See also W. Holton, "'Divide et Impera': 'Federalist 10' in a Wider Sphere," *The William and Mary Quarterly*, Vol. 62, No. 2, 2005, pp. 188–91.

36. "The Address and Reasons of Dissent of the Minority of the Convention of Pennsylvania to Their Constituents," in J. F. Manley and K. M. Dolbeare, *The Case Against the Constitution: From the Antifederalists to the Present*. Armonk, NY: M. E. Sharpe, Inc., 1987, p. 77. See also W. Adams, 2001, p. 65.

37. M. Klarman, *The Framers' Coup: The Making of the United States Constitution*. New York: Oxford University Press, 2016, p. 173.

38. G. Morris, July 5, 1787, in M. Farrand, *RFC*, Vol. 1, 1911, p. 533.

39. I.4 has long continued to leave the states a wide range of options to suppress the vote because there is no enumerated right to vote in the Constitution, only the 15th, 19th, 24th, and 26th amendments' prohibition on interfering with that right. This leaves it up to the states to continue to engage in voter suppression by excluding large numbers of working class voters who are disproportionately people of color, impeding the forming of viable third parties, and making it difficult to run for and hold office.

40. See also T. Bouton, 2007, p. 262.

41. Such a shortsighted and narrow focus on the Senate, as if removing it as a check would somehow "fix the Constitution," is illustrated in A. Jentleson's *Kill Switch: The Rise of the Modern Senate and the Crippling of American Democracy*. New York: Norton Liveright, 2021. Because Article V prohibits abolishing the Senate without consensus of the states, the problem lies in the Constitution not merely the Senate.

42. L. Cutler, "To Form a Government," in R. Goldwin and A. Kaufman (eds.), *Separation of Powers: Does It Still Work?* Washington and London: American Enterprise Institute for Public Policy Research, 1986, p. 2.

43. W. Holton, 2007, p. 211.

Chapter 5

1. In J. A. Ernst, *Money and Politics in America, 1755–1775: A Study in the Currency Act of 1764 and the Political Economy of Revolution.* Chapel Hill: University of North Carolina Press, 1973, p. 18.

2. A. Hamilton to J. Duane, September 3, 1780.

3. A. Hamilton, January 9, 1790. He also believed that "public debts are public benefits" and the "price of liberty." Madison later warned of the "perpetuity and progression of public debts and taxes" with each new loan. J. Madison, "Political Observations," April 20, 1795.

4. Self-sufficient farmers' fears that taxes would push them into landless poverty were not far off. See A. Singletary, *Massachusetts Gazette*, January 25, 1788. Hamilton recognized that taxes would push them into growing for commercial markets. A. Hamilton to ———, December–March, 1779–80. Farmers' refusal to grow commercial crops contributed to Hamilton's concerns about the lack of labor and high wages. The lack of debtor relief and the danger of farmers losing their lands for unpaid debts was one reason Framer Luther Martin opposed the Constitution. L. Martin, Genuine Information VIII, January 22, 1788. See also Chapter 7.

5. E. J. Ferguson, "Political Economy, Public Liberty, and the Formation of the Constitution," *The William and Mary Quarterly*, Vol. 40, No. 3, 1983, p. 405.

6. See M. M. Schweitzer, "State-Issued Currency and the Ratification of the U.S. Constitution," *The Journal of Economic History*, Vol. 49, No. 2, 1989, pp. 311–22.

7. E. J. Ferguson, July 1983, pp. 405.

8. J. T. Main, *The Anti-Federalists: Critics of the Constitution 1781–1788.* New York: W. W. Norton & Company, 1961, pp. 73–5.

9. Internal tariffs allowed states to raise tax revenue without imposing taxes on their own population to repay war debts. Tariffs and import bans were also used to raise the cost of goods produced in or imported into some states in order to provide a favorable market for goods from their own state. Virginia, for example, banned the importation of slaves into the state, and later supported the ban on imported slaves after 1808 in I.9.1 to force South Carolina and Georgia to buy its slaves.

10. See M. Jensen, *The New Nation: A History of the United States during the Confederation, 1781–1789.* New York: Vintage Press, 1959, pp. 339–45.

11. R. Einhorn, *American Taxation, American Slavery.* Chicago: University of Chicago Press, 2006, p. 198.

12. Ibid., p. 134.

13. Today, local, state, and federal governments have the parallel power to tax, although Congress retains exclusive authority to impose some kinds of taxes and the states are prohibited from using others.

14. The text was developed in a secret meeting on March 28 and included proposals for half, third, and quarter ratios, with Madison proposing three-fifths. Southern delegates argued for the lower ratio because slaves "had no interest in their labor" and "did as little as possible," a nod to the problems they faced with the refusal of work and apparent widespread resistance to slavery. See R. Einhorn, 2006, pp. 142–3.

15. For a detailed account, see R. Einhorn, pp. 118, 120–4, 164.

16. While the import tax is a flat *ad valorem* tax on all imports, the tariff is imposed selectively on specific imported items. See R. Einhorn, 2006, p. 149. The first income tax was imposed temporarily in 1861 during the Civil War.

17. D. Waldstreicher, *Slavery's Constitution: From Revolution to Ratification.* New York: Hill and Wang, 2009, p. 5.

18. R. Morris, Monday, August 5, 1782, *Journals of the Continental Congress, 1774–1789,* 34 Vols., published by the Library of Congress, 1904–1937, Vol. 22, January 1, 1782 to August 9, 1782, pp. 439–40.

19. J. Madison, Notes on Debates, January 28, 1783.

20. Morris unsuccessfully attempted to bully the states to issue these taxes to meet their requisition to Congress. See R. Morris, "To the Governors of North Carolina, South Carolina, and Georgia," in J. Sparks (ed.), *The Diplomatic Correspondence of the American Revolution,* Vol. 12. Boston: Nathan Hale and Gray & Bowen; New York: C. & C. H. Carvill; Washington, DC: P. Thompson, 2013.

21. J. Madison, Notes on Debates, January 28, 1783. For more on the Newburgh coup plot see E. Gerry to J. Adams, November 23, 1783; R. H. Kohn, "The Inside History of the Newburgh Conspiracy: America and the Coup d'Etat," *The William and Mary Quarterly,* Vol. 27, No. 2, 1970, pp. 187–220; R. Ovetz, "Opinion: America's First Attempted Coup also Tracks to Jan. 6," *Mercury News,* February 7, 2021.

22. R. Einhorn, 2006, p. 104.

23. R. Morris, *Journals of the Continental Congress, 1774–1789,* Monday, August 5, 1782, p. 441.

24. R. Morris to A. Hamilton, August 28, 1782, *The Revolutionary Diplomatic Correspondence of the United States,* Vol. 5, pp. 674–5. Morris

appointed Hamilton as Receiver of the Continental Taxes for the State of New York.

25. A. Hamilton to R. Morris, August 13, 1782.

26. See also W. Holton, "Did Democracy Cause the Recession that Led to the Constitution?" *The Journal of American History*, Vol. 92, No. 2, 2005, pp. 446, 448, 455; and W. Holton, *Unruly Americans and the Origins of the Constitution*. New York: Hill and Wang, 2007, p. 61.

27. Cited in W. Holton, 2005, pp. 464.

28. R. Morris to Appleton, April 16, 1782, in J. Sparks, (ed.), *The Revolutionary Diplomatic Correspondence of the United States*, Vol. 5. Boston: Nathan Hale and Gray & Bowen; New York: C. & C. H. Carvill; Washington, DC: P. Thompson, 1830, pp. 131–2. Hamilton would later make the same argument for his financial plan.

29. Ultimately the repayment of debt determined the placement of the capital in Washington, DC as the result of a deal between Madison, Hamilton, and Jefferson in the "room where it happens" portrayed in the musical *Hamilton*. The deal allowed Hamilton to assume the states' war debts at par. The play gets it right, though, that "it doesn't matter where you put the U.S. capital? | Cause we'll have the banks, we're in the same spot."

30. G. Nash, "Urban Wealth and Poverty in Pre-revolutionary America," *The Journal of Interdisciplinary History*, Vol. 6, No. 4, 1976, p. 548.

31. L. Soltow, "America's First Progressive Tax," *National Tax Journal*, Vol. 30, No. 1, 1977, p. 56.

32. T. Slaughter, *The Whiskey Rebellion: Frontier Epilogue to the American Revolution*. New York: Oxford University Press, 1986, pp. 96–7, 140, 160–1. Hamilton believed the tariff on imported goods was unacceptable because it weighed disproportionately on merchants and landowners. For the debate over the tariff, see A. Hamilton and J. Madison, *The Pacificus-Helvidius Debates of 1793–1794: Toward the Completion of the American Founding*, edited by M. Frisch. Indianapolis: Liberty Fund, 2007, Americanus (Hamilton) No. 2, p. 109.

33. Details about the rebellion are discussed further in Chapter 6.

34. L. Soltow, 1977, p. 53; and R. Einhorn, 2006, pp. 111, 196. The tax on slaves was based on assessments by the owners themselves.

35. C. Beard, *An Economic Interpretation of the Constitution of the United States*. New York: Free Press, 1986 [1913], p. 176.

36. R. Einhorn, 2006, p. 160.

37. Even today the only direct taxes on wealth are local taxes on land and residential and commercial property. No global tax on wealth has ever existed. See T. Piketty, *Capital in the Twenty-First Century*. Cambridge, MA: Belknap Press of Harvard University Press, 2014.

38. M. Klarman, *The Framers' Coup: The Making of the United States Constitution.* New York: Oxford University Press, 2016, p. 325.
39. J. Madison to G. Nicholas, May 17, 1788.
40. J. Madison to G. Nicholas, May 17, 1788. Several of the Framers supported the need for national taxes to protect national security, including Wilson. See J. Wilson, "Substance of an Address to a Meeting of the Citizens of Philadelphia, October Sixth," mdcclxxxvii, 1787, in P. L. Ford (ed.), *Pamphlets on the Constitution of the United States: Published During Its Discussion by the People, 1787–1788.* New York: Burt Franklin, 1888, p. 160.
41. The use of a public credit system to fund the military was attempted for hundreds of years, beginning with the Bank of England in the 1690s, the failed efforts to create a private bank of credit in 1714 in Massachusetts, and the sale of "war bonds" for specie and certificates beginning in 1756. As Ernst put it, "money as the 'sinews of war' was a familiar metaphor." War may have sparked the innovation of paper money but levelling later adopted it. J. Ernst, "Shays's Rebellion in Long Perspective: The Merchants and the 'Money Question'," in R. A. Gross (ed.), *In Debt to Shays: The Bicentennial of an Agrarian Rebellion.* Charlottesville: University Press of Virginia, 1993, pp. 60–1, 67; J. A. Ernst, 1973, pp. 21–2, 24, 26.
42. On this point, see E. Randolph, "Letter on the Federal Constitution," October 16, 1787, in P. L. Ford (ed.), 1888, p. 270.

Chapter 6

1. A. Smith, *An Inquiry into the Nature and Causes of the Wealth of Nations, Book V: On the Revenue of the Sovereign or Commonwealth*, chapter 1, On the Expenses of the Sovereign or Commonweal, Part II: On the Expense of Justice, 1776. J. Franklin Jameson made the same point, writing that "[n]othing is more necessary to the life of trade than a strong and firm government." See J. F. Jameson, *The American Revolution Considered as a Social Movement.* Boston: Beacon Press, 1925, p. 71.
2. On this point see P. Linebaugh and M. Rediker, *Many Headed Hydra: Sailors, Slaves, Commoners, and the Hidden History of the Revolutionary Atlantic.* Boston: Beacon Press, 2013.
3. Although the President is limited to two four-year terms, they have a maximum of ten years if they finish out another president's term (22.1).
4. F. Lundberg, *Cracks in the Constitution.* Secaucus, NJ: Lyle Stuart, Inc., 1980, p. 280.
5. The Senate struck one of the 17 amendments in Madison's proposed Bill of Rights that would have made the pickpocketing of powers by one branch of another unconstitutional. It read: "The powers delegated

by this Constitution are appropriated to the departments to which they are respectively distributed: so that the Legislative Department shall never exercise the powers vested in the Executive or Judicial, nor the Executive exercise the powers vested in the Legislative or Judicial, nor the Judicial exercise the powers vested in the Legislative or Executive Departments." *Constitution Daily*, "On this Day: James Madison Introduces the Bill of Rights," National Constitution Center, June 8, 2022, https://constitutioncenter.org/blog/five-items-congress-deleted-from-madisons-original-bill-of-rights.

6. A. Hamilton and J. Madison, *The Pacificus-Helvidius Debates of 1793– 1794: Toward the Completion of the American Founding*, edited by M. Frisch. Indianapolis: Liberty Fund, Pacificus (Hamilton) No. 1, 2007, p. 16.

7. R. Dahl, *How Democratic Is the American Constitution?*, 2nd edition. New Haven: Yale University Press, 2003, pp. 66–7.

8. E. Gerry, July 19, 1787, in M. Farrand, *FRC*, Vol. 2, 1911, p. 57. Similar reasoning was expressed by other Framers for an unelected Senate chosen by the state legislatures in staggered terms.

9. Statista, "Share of Electoral College and Popular Votes from each Winning Candidate, in all United States Presidential Elections from 1789 to 2020," accessed December 28, 2021, www.statista.com/ statistics/1034688/share-electoral-popular-votes-each-president-since-1789/.

10. J. Madison to T. Jefferson, February 28, 1801.

11. Thomas Paine thought the veto derived from conquest not constitution. T. Paine, "Constitutional Reform: To the Citizens of Pennsylvania on the Proposal for Calling a Convention," *The Complete Writings of Thomas Paine*, edited by P. Foner. New York: Citadel, 1945 [1805], p. 994.

12. See the debate on June 4, 1787, in M. Farrand, *FRC*, Vol. 1, 1911, p. 99.

13. There were only 433 vetoes by 1889 of which 29 were overridden, 15 over Andrew Johnson's veto alone. J. A. Smith, *The Spirit of American Government: A Study of the Constitution—Its Origin, Influence and Relation to Democracy*. Cambridge, MA: Belknap Press of Harvard University Press, 1965 [1907], p. 139; United States Senate, "Vetoes, 1789 to Present," accessed June 6, 2022, www.senate.gov/legislative/vetoes/ vetoCounts.htm.

14. J. Madison, July 25, 1787, Madison's Notes, in M. Farrand, *RFC*, Vol. 2, p. 110. According to John Adams, the veto was "an impregnable barrier" against the legislature. J. Adams, chapter 4, Opinions of Philos-

ophers, Dr. Franklin, *The Works of John Adams*, Vol. 4. New York: Little, Brown, and Company, 1851, p. 398.

15. J. A. Smith, 1965 [1907], pp. 140–1.

16. For the number of vetoes by president, see US House of Representatives, "Presidential Vetoes," accessed June 6, 2022, https://history.house.gov/Institution/Presidential-Vetoes/Presidential-Vetoes/.

17. Hamilton proposed the "administration by single men" in 1781. See A. Hamilton to R. Morris, April 30, 1781. This extraordinarily wide-ranging letter was likely written in part by Elizabeth Hamilton.

18. A. Hamilton to R. Morris, April 30, 1781, brackets in original. See also A. Hamilton to J. Duane, September 3, 1780; M. Jensen, *The New Nation: A History of the United States During the Confederation, 1781–1789*. New York: Vintage Press, 1959, pp. 50–1 and 54–5; and J. Ferguson, *The Power of the Purse: A History of American Public Finance, 1776–1790*. Chapel Hill: University of North Carolina Press, 1961, p. 116. Hamilton proposed that later Newburgh co-plotters General Alexander McDougall be appointed "secretary of Marine" and Robert Morris to head the "department of finance," which they later were.

19. M. Jensen, 1959, pp. 56–7 and 60. See also J. Ferguson, 1961, pp. 116–19, 173–4.

20. In M. Klarman, *The Framers' Coup: The Making of the United States Constitution*. New York: Oxford University Press, 2016, p. 48.

21. Morris hardly hid his efforts to merge his personal interests in global trade with the security interests of the Congress. He used government money to obtain goods which he sold to the government and used the government's credit to obtain credit, money, goods, and ships for his business. Morris frequently did for himself and business partners what he claimed he was unable to do for Congress, woefully undersupplying the army during the Revolution. When he received specie from requisitions and foreign loans on behalf of the government he would use it to pay his partners while issuing certificates based on his own line of credit to other creditors. This left a complex web of accounts with unpaid credit lines, bills past due, and personal losses passed on to the government's books. Morris was hardly alone in using his government authority to engage in self-dealing. Quartermaster Timothy Pickering estimated that war profiteering, such as by Morris and his partners, doubled the public debt. Three of the worst profiteers were Framer Thomas Mifflin, General Nathanael Greene, and Jeremiah Wadsworth; the last two combined handled about $200 million of spending in 1779–80 alone. Mifflin escaped a court martial and none were never held accountable. See J. Ferguson, "Business, Government, and Congressional Investigation in the Revolution," *The William and Mary*

Quarterly, Vol. 16, No. 3, 1959, pp. 294–7, 302, 308–15, 318; J. T. Main, *The Sovereign States, 1775–1783*. New York: New Viewpoints, 1973, pp. 262–3; M. Jensen, 1959, pp. 380–1.

22. Despite providing ample evidence to the contrary, Charles Rappleye repeats this myth in the subtitle of his biography of Morris. See C. Rappleye, *Robert Morris: Financier of the American Revolution*. New York: Simon & Schuster, 2010. After Morris had retired from Congress he took all of the records home for six months before returning them without making any complete accounting. Morris was investigated several times by Congress and Pennsylvania state committees although he avoided any tangible accountability at that time. See J. Ferguson, 1959, pp. 316–17.

23. Ibid., p. 318.

24. See Govtrack, Statistics and Historical Comparison, accessed December 28, 2021, www.govtrack.us/congress/bills/statistics.

25. L. Fisher, *The Politics of Executive Privilege*. Durham, NC: Carolina Academic Press, 2004.

26. Congress ceded its control of monetary power to coin money and pay the debt by passing the Federal Reserve Act 1913. The members of the Federal Reserve Board of Governors, which is appointed to long 14-year terms by the President, and the twelve regional banks which are appointed by the banks, cannot be removed and are exempt from audits or transparency laws. For this reason, historian Thomas Wilson called the Fed the "Supreme Court of Finance." T. Wilson, *The Power "To Coin" Money: The Exercise of Monetary Powers by the Congress*. Armonk, NY: M. E. Sharpe, 1992, p. 233.

27. L. Fisher, 1991, p. 113; see also Office of Information and Regulatory Affairs, www.whitehouse.gov/omb/information-regulatory-affairs/.

28. J. A. Smith, 1965 [1907], p. 318.

29. Among the earliest treaty bypasses were the 1845 annexation of Texas by a simple majority in both houses and Hawai'i in the same way in 1898. See L. Fisher, *The Constitution between Friends: Congress, the President, and the Law*. New York: St. Martin's Press, 1978, pp. 201–2, 204.

30. L. Fisher, 2004, p. 233.

31. L. Fisher, *Constitutional Conflicts between Congress and the President*, 3rd edition. Lawrence: University Press of Kansas, 1991, p. 106; L. Fisher, 1978, p. 128; and The American Presidency Project, www.presidency. ucsb.edu/statistics/data/executive-orders.

32. They were mostly used as ceremonial purposes, with only 75 issued between Presidents Monroe (1817–25) and Carter (1977–81). They increased dramatically in number beginning with President Reagan. President Bush II issued 161 in total, with 58 impacting about 1,100

distinct provisions of law. See also, Congressional Research Service, *Presidential Signing Statements: Constitutional and Institutional Implications,* January 4, 2012 (RL33667).

33. A. Hamilton to J. Duane, September 3, 1780.

34. G. Mason, Debate in the Virginia Convention, June 17, 1788, in M. Farrand, *FRC,* Vol. 3, 1911, pp. 326–7.

35. For example, in 2019 President Trump declared a national emergency on the US-Mexico border to reallocate money from the Defense Department to build his border wall which Congress has refused to fund in full. Trump wasn't the first to propose building a wall. After a string of defeats in the Indian war, officers Henry Lee and Frederick Steuben proposed building a 1,500 mile wall along the frontier to keep out native warriors. Although not limited to war, presidents have long had and commonly used these powers to rule unilaterally using fiat power.

36. L. Fisher, 1991, pp. 206–9; L. Fisher, *Congressional Access to National Security Information: Precedents from the Washington Administration.* Washington, DC: Law Library of Congress, 2009, 2009-002846.

37. B. Gellman and G. Miller, "Black Budget Summary Details U.S. Spy Network's Successes, Failures and Objectives," *Washington Post,* August 29, 2013, accessed June 6, 2022, https://www.washingtonpost.com/world/national-security/black-budget-summary-details-us-spy-networks-successes-failures-and-objectives/2013/08/29/7e57bb78-10ab-11e3-8cdd-bcdc09410972_story.html.

38. R. Kohn, *Eagle and Sword: The Beginnings of the Military Establishment in America.* New York: The Free Press, 1975, p. 111.

39. A. Hamilton, January 9, 1790.

40. A. Hamilton to G. Washington, August 5, 1794; G. Washington, to Carlisle, PA, Citizens, October 6, 1794; and G. Washington, "A Proclamation," August 7, 1794, September 25, 1794, and November 19, 1794, in J. D. Richardson, *Compilation of the Messages and Papers of the Presidents,* Section 1 (of 4) of Volume 1: George Washington, from Annals of Congress, Fourth Congress, second session, 2796, Annals of Congress, Third Congress, 1413, and Sixth Annual Address, United States, 2004.

41. Hamilton admitted as much in A. Hamilton to A. Church, October 23, 1794.

42. For more than two years Hamilton relied on informants to write frequent extensive letters and intelligence reports, some under the pen name "Tully," calling it an "insurrection" that threatened to "destroy" and "overthrow" the federal government, although it began and long remained a series of meetings and protests against the taxes to fund his

public credit plan. The September 7, 1791 Pittsburgh meeting denounced the plan as "an evil still greater, the constituting a capital of nearly eighty millions of dollars in the hands of a few persons who may influence those occasionally, in power, to evade the Constitution." This critique of elite power continued throughout the crisis and even spread to Maryland, South Carolina, and Kentucky. A. Hamilton to G. Washington, September 1, 1792; A. Hamilton to J. Jay, September 3, 1792; A. Hamilton to J. Jay, September 8, 1792; A. Hamilton to G. Washington, August 2, 1794; A. Hamilton to G. Washington, August 5, 1794; A. Hamilton, Tully I, August 23, 1794; Tully II, August 26, 1794; Tully III, August 28, 1794; Tully IV, September 2, 1794; A. Hamilton to J. Jay, November 1–4, 1794; and Carlisle Petition, August 14–29, 1794, Rawle Family Papers, I, 31, 132, Historical Society of Pennsylvania.

43. L. Fisher, 1978, p. 21.

44. L. Fisher, 1978, p. 261.

45. J. Locke, *The Second Treatise of Civil Government*, Section 141, edited by C. B. McPherson. Indianapolis and Cambridge: Hackett Publishing Company, 1980 [1690].

46. G. Washington, Farewell Address, *Philadelphia Daily American Advertiser*, September 19, 1796.

47. G. Washington, September 19, 1796. In this, he concurred with Ben Franklin's warning about "Despotic Government" in his September 17, 1787 speech to the convention.

48. A. Lincoln, letter to A. G. Hodges, esq., April 4, 1864. "The Privilege of the Writ of Habeas Corpus shall not be suspended, unless when in Cases of Rebellion or Invasion the public Safety may require it" found in I.9.2 has been little protection against presidents such as Woodrow Wilson, Franklin D. Roosevelt, George W. Bush, and Barak Obama who have revoked it anyway. See also A. Taylor, "The U.S. Keeps Killing Americans in Drone Strikes, Mostly by Accident," *The Washington Post*, April 23, 2015, accessed June 6, 2022, https://www.washingtonpost.com/news/worldviews/wp/2015/.

49. J. Madison, *Federalist #41*.

50. In *Federalist #25* Hamilton also asserted "how unequal parchment provisions are to a struggle with public necessity" because the rules "fettering the government with restrictions" can be ignored when necessity calls. In a cynical nod to the Anti-Federalist critique of Article II, he also warned that "military establishments ... would be apt to swell beyond their natural or proper size," becoming "engines for the abridgment or demolition of the national authority." Justice Jackson wrote in the 1949 case *Terminiello v. Chicago* that a majority would "convert the constitutional Bill of Rights into a suicide pact."

51. This was foreseen in the William Randolph Hearst-financed Depression-era film, *Gabriel Over the White House*, 1933, in which a populist president shuts down Congress and rules by fiat.
52. F. Lundberg, 1980, p. 13.

Chapter 7

1. J. Madison to W. Bradford, June 19, 1775.
2. In M. Klarman, *The Framers' Coup: The Making of the United States Constitution*. New York: Oxford University Press, 2016, p. 283; C. C. Pinckney, *The Documentary History of the Ratification of the Constitution*, Vol. 27. Madison: University of Wisconsin Foundation, January 17, 1788, p. 124. This was echoed by Massachusetts ratifying convention delegate Thomas Dawes. See T. Dawes, in Ibid., January 18, 1788, Vol. 6, p. 1245.
3. M. Merrill, "The Anticapitalist Origins of the United States," *Review*, Fernand Braudel Center, Vol. 13, No. 4, 1990, pp. 488, 491. See the Introduction for what is meant by "capitalist society."
4. G. Vidal, "The Second American Revolution," in J. Birnbaum and B. Ollman (eds.), *U.S. Constitution: 200 Hundred Years of Anti-Federalist, Abolitionist, Feminist, Muckraking, Progressive, and Especially Socialist Criticism*. New York: New York University Press, 1990, pp. 177–8; L. Fisher, *Constitutional Conflicts between Congress and the President*. New York: New York University Press, 1991, p. 253; F. Lundberg, *Cracks in the Constitution*. Secaucus, NJ: Lyle Stuart, Inc., 1980, p. 250.
5. This clause was also drawn from Jefferson's draft of the 1776 Virginia state constitution, Article 5 of the 1787 Northwest Ordinance.
6. James Madison originally proposed the text to Edmund Randolph. See J. Madison to E. Randolph, April 8, 1787. In his notes, James McHenry noted that Edmund Randolph offered this because the Articles "does not secure the harmony to the States. It cannot preserve the particular States against seditions within themselves or combinations against each other." See Virginia Plan, May 29, 1787, in M. Farrand, *RFC*, Vol. 1, pp. 20–3, 25. The language was debated again on July 18, 1787, see M. Farrand, *RFC*, Vol. 2, 1911, pp. 47–9.
7. George Mason opposed slavery because he feared laborers and slaves collaborating together. J. Madison Constitutional Convention Debates, August 22, 1787. Putting these powers in the Constitution federalized all of these threats. See W. Wiecek, *The Guarantee Clause of the U. S. Constitution*. Ithaca, NY: Cornell University Press, 1972, pp. 42, 51, 78.
8. Even an attempt to democratize a state constitution was repressed as a form of "domestic Violence." The 1841–2 Dorr Rebellion, in which insurgents passed their own new state constitution, held their own elec-

tions for a new state government, and attempted to govern, established a precedent for the federal government to overturn state constitutions under the guarantee clause. This paved the way for John C. Calhoun to claim a right to "nullify" majority rule as a natural extension of the guarantee clause. In an effort to protect slavery from economic democracy, Calhoun went so far as to reject the right of the majority to even *change* a state constitution because "the government of the uncontrolled numerical majority is but the absolute and despotic form of popular governments." See W. Wiecek, 1972, pp. 80–4, 86–110, on Calhoun see 135. See also R. Ovetz, 2019, pp. 57, 167, 227, 231, 233, 261, 317.

9. Law professor William Wiecek concluded that these powers were designed "to stop state legislatures from implementing reform programs … as another bulwark in the defense of property against expropriative radicalism." See W. Wiecek, 1972, pp. 5, 27–33.

10. In addition to British support for native peoples, Holton argues that the long history of slave rebellions in the state "helped steer Virginia into the American Revolution." After Lord Dunmore issued his 1775 emancipation proclamation granting freedom to runaway slaves who fought with his troops, the war in Virginia became as much one between slave owners and slaves and the landed elite and tenants or the landless, making it as much a struggle over home rule as who would rule at home. See W. Holton, *Forced Founders: Indians, Debtors, Slaves, and the Making of the American Revolution in Virginia.* Chapel Hill: Omohundro Institute and University of North Carolina Press, 1999, pp. 137–9, 158–9, 161, 163. For the concerns about the lack of an army, see R. Kohn, *Eagle and Sword: The Beginnings of the Military Establishment in America.* New York: The Free Press, 1975, pp. 74–7.

11. It was long assumed that such threats required that a state legislature be incapable of meeting to request assistance. This was overlooked in instances when the legislature could meet and did not make any request such as during the 1894 railroad strike in Illinois. Today, presidents are understood to have the power to "call out the National Guard" at any time despite being under the command of state governors. See also R. Ovetz, *When Workers Shot Back: Class Conflict from 1877 to 1921.* Chicago: Haymarket Press, 2019, pp. 57, 167, 227, 233, 261, 528.

12. Similar warnings came from Madison and fellow Framer Nathaniel Gorham. Madison warned that a weakness of republics was the "want of Guaranty to the States of their Constitutions & laws against internal violence." See J. Madison, "Vices of the Political System of the United States," April 1787. For the risk of spreading, see N. Gorham, July 18, 1787, in M. Farrand, *RFC,* Vol. 2, 1911, pp. 47–9. There were strong historical parallels with the Shays' Regulators, but not to Cromwell, as

Hamilton suggested in *Federalist #21*. A closer analogy would be to the Levelers and Diggers who rose against what they saw as Cromwell's betrayal of the Civil War. One group of rebels organized into a coalition to oppose Cromwell before they were betrayed, denouncing him for pursuing "private and selfish interest" and destroying "common rights" and "common wealth" through excise taxes, enclosures, and capital punishment for small economic crimes. See J. Donohue, "Unfree Labor, Imperialism, and Radical Republicanism in the Atlantic World, 1630–1661," *Labor: Studies in Working Class History of the Americas*, Vol. 1, 2004, pp. 47–8.

13. Hamilton later argued that the executive has unlimited discretion to exercise its war power. See A. Hamilton and J. Madison, Pacificus (Hamilton) No. 1, *The Pacificus-Helvidius Debates of 1793–1794: Toward the Completion of the American Founding*, edited by M. Frisch. Indianapolis: Liberty Fund, 1793–1794 [2007], p. 16.

14. Hamilton's argument that a funded debt was a source of capital drew on the ideas of David Hume, who believed that debt became capital for investment that increased the productivity of labor and grew profits. D. Hume, *Political Discourses*. Edinburgh: Printed by R. Fleming, for A. Kincaid and A. Donaldson, 1752, pp. 128–9, cited in A. Hamilton, July 1795. Although Madison opposed paper money and the first Bank of the United States, as President he signed the bill chartering the second bank and in doing so embraced paper money. See T. Wilson, *The Power "To Coin" Money: The Exercise of Monetary Powers by the Congress*. Armonk, NY: M. E. Sharpe, 1992, p. 8.

15. A. Hamilton, "Report Relative to a Provision for the Support of Public Credit," January 9, 1790; A. Hamilton, "Final Version of the Second Report on the Further Provision Necessary for Establishing Public Credit (Report on a National Bank)," December 13, 1790; A. Hamilton, "Final Version of the Report on the Subject of Manufactures," December 5, 1791; and A. Hamilton, July 1795. In this way, Hamilton identified the function of finance capital as the expansion of capital that Karl Marx would later develop. Hamilton devised the public credit system as it functions today in which government relied on borrowing to fund its operations. See A. Hamilton, "Opinion as to the Constitutionality of the Bank of the United States," 1791; S. Bologna, "Money and Crisis: Marx as Correspondent of the New York Daily Tribune, 1856–57," *Common Sense*, No. 14, 1993, pp. 63–89; and J. Ricciardi, "Marx on Financial Intermediation: Lessons from the French *Crédit Mobilier* in the *New York Daily Tribune*," *Science & Society*, Vol. 79, No. 4, 2015, pp. 497–526. Hamilton devised much of his public credit plan years

earlier in a 1781 letter to Robert Morris. A. Hamilton to R. Morris, April 30, 1781.

16. J. Rasmus, *Alexander Hamilton and the Origins of the Fed.* Lanham, MD: Lexington, 2019, pp. 25, 35, 42. Quoting Adam Smith that "neither the large wages … can bribe him rather to work for other people than for himself," Hamilton feared that cheap land would lead to a labor shortage and rising wages as workers became farmers. This is why he advocated for increasing immigration, using child labor, and introducing new technologies that would increase the productivity of labor and reduce wages and dependence on it. A. Hamilton, "Prospectus of the Society for Establishing Useful Manufactures," August 1791; A. Hamilton, "Final Version of the Report on the Subject of Manufactures," December 5, 1791; A. Smith, *An Inquiry Into the Nature and Causes of the Wealth of Nations*, Book I, chapter 1, Of the Causes of Improvement in the Productive Powers of Labour, and of the Order According to which its Produce is Naturally Distributed Among the Different Ranks of the People, and Book V, chapter 1, On the Revenue of the Sovereign or Commonwealth: On the Expenses of the Sovereign or Commonwealth, Part II: On the Expense of Justice, Book 1, chapter 1, cited in Hamilton, December 5, 1791; and A. Hamilton, "The Defence of the Funding System," July 1795. See also J. Wilson, "On the Improvement and Settlement of Lands in the United States," mid-1790s, in K. L. Hall and M. D. Hall (eds.), *Collected Works of James Wilson*, Vol. 1, collected by Maynard Garrison. Indianapolis: Liberty Fund, 2007 [1790], pp. 373–86. It didn't escape critics of Hamilton's public credit plan that it "shall drain the laborer of his hardearned pittance." Franklin, in (Philadelphia) *Independent Gazetteer*, August 30, 1794, quoted in A. Hamilton, Tully IV, September 2, 1794.

17. Watson Institute, International and Public Affairs Cost of War Project, Brown University, "U.S. Budgetary Costs of Post-9/11 Wars Through FY2022: $8 Trillion," September 2021, accessed June 6, 2022, https://watson.brown.edu/costsofwar/figures/2021/BudgetaryCosts.

18. R. Kohn, 1975, pp. 67–9. Hamilton made an explicit connection between the public credit system, government land holdings, and the need to fund the military. A. Hamilton, December 13, 1790. See also M. Merrill, 1990, p. 486. Many elites and army officers engaged in the Indian war owned large tracts and depended on suppressing native resistance and squatters in order to develop or sell it. See R. Kohn, 1975, pp. 54–62, 67, 96, 100.

19. T. Slaughter, *The Whiskey Rebellion: Frontier Epilogue to the American Revolution.* New York: Oxford University Press, 1986, p. 94.

20. While Washington pursued a scorched earth assault on the native confederation, he also attempted to divide and conquer the unified front by carving out treaty promises at Fort Stanwix.
21. G. Mason, Constitutional Convention Debates, June 6, 1787.
22. L. Fisher, *Constitutional Conflicts between Congress and the President*, 3rd edition. Lawrence: University Press of Kansas, 1991, p. 258.
23. Ibid., p. 261.
24. 1952 *Youngstown Sheet & Tube Company v. Sawyer*.
25. A. Hamilton and J. Madison, Helvidius (Madison) No. 4, 1793–1794 [2007], p. 87.
26. J. Madison, *Political Observations*, April 20, 1795. In his farewell speech, Washington also warned the branches not to encroach upon one another's power, because it "tends to consolidate the powers of all the departments in one, and thus to create, whatever the form of government, a real despotism." He dreaded that "usurpation" of constitutional powers "is the customary weapon by which free governments are destroyed." G. Washington, Farewell Address, *Philadelphia Daily American Advertiser*, September 19, 1796. John Adams also thought that war would dramatically increase the debt and "rouse up a many headed and many bellied Monster of an Army to tyrannize over Us … and accellerate the Advent of Monarchy and Aristocracy." J. Adams to T. Jefferson, May 11, 1794.
27. J. Madison, "Vices of the Political System of the United States," April 1787. Article VI prohibited any state from entering into a treaty without the consent of Congress.
28. Treaty of Paris (1783), The Definitive Treaty of Peace.
29. M. Klarman, 2016, p. 23.
30. R. Buel, "The Public Creditor Interest in Massachusetts Politics, 1780–8," in R. A. Gross (ed.), *In Debt to Shays: The Bicentennial of an Agrarian Rebellion*. Charlottesville: University Press of Virginia, 1993, p. 52; and S. Patterson, "The Federalist Reaction to Shays's Rebellion," in R. A. Gross (ed.), 1993, pp. 110–11, 114–15.
31. L. Hacker, *Triumph of American Capitalism: The Development of Forces In American History to the End of the Nineteenth Century.* New York: Simon & Schuster, 1947, p. 193.
32. Hamilton later reversed position, arguing that Congress has no role in treaty making at all. A. Hamilton and J. Madison, Pacificus (Hamilton) No. 1, 1793–1794 [2007], pp. 11, 14–16. See L. Fisher, "Judicial Errors that Magnify Presidential Power," *The Federal Lawyer*, January–February 2014, pp. 67–72. Fisher argues that the assumption of exclusive presidential authority for all foreign policy originates in several federal court misinterpretations of then Congressman John Marshall's

claim that the President was the "sole organ of the nation in its external relations, and its sole representative with foreign nations," while in practice viewing foreign policy as a shared power between Congress and the President. The damage has been done, however. The alarming danger of judicial deference to the executive in all areas of foreign policy and national security appears to be entirely based on faulty judicial reasoning.

33. L. Fisher, *The Constitution between Friends: Congress, the President, and the Law*. New York: St. Martin's Press, 1978, pp. 93, 218–19.
34. F. Lundberg, 1980, p. 258.
35. L. Fisher, 1978, pp. 204–8; L. Fisher, 1991, pp. 226–7, 236–7.

Chapter 8

1. It was borrowed directly from Article IV of the Articles of Confederation.
2. J. Madison to T. Jefferson, October 17, 1788.
3. In feudalism the serf was tied to the land of the lord, could not be sold, and had the right to work the land and a share of what they produced in exchange for their service and obedience.
4. Judicial review also helped spark the French Revolution, leading to its explicit ban in Articles 1 and 3 of chapter 5 of the 1791 constitution. See J. Ralston, "Study and Report for the American Federation of Labor Upon Judicial Control," Washington, 1919, in D. Ettrude, *The Power of Congress to Nullify Supreme Court Decisions*, Vol. 2. New York: H. W. Wilson, 1924, No. 8, pp. 53–4.
5. Paper money and tender laws were often subject to judicial review. On several occasions when colonial legislatures attempted to retire colonial debts and remove the paper from circulation, creditors managed to convince parliament and the Privy Council to block its use. H. Abraham, *The Judicial Process: An Introductory Analysis of the Courts of the United States, England, and France*, 6th edition. New York: Oxford University Press, 1993, p. 303; and F. Lundberg, "Court over Constitution," in J. Birnbaum and B. Ollman (eds.), *U.S. Constitution: 200 Hundred Years of Anti-Federalist, Abolitionist, Feminist, Muckraking, Progressive, and Especially Socialist Criticism*. New York: New York University Press, 1990, p. 196.
6. See T. Bouton, "A Road Closed: Rural Insurgency in Post-independence Pennsylvania," *The Journal of American History*, Vol. 87, No. 3, 2000, pp. 867–74.
7. T. Jefferson to J. Madison, December 16, 1786. Ironically, Jefferson was one of hundreds of Virginians who lost to foreign creditors in federal lawsuits. See W. Holton, *Unruly Americans and the Origins of the Con-*

stitution. New York: Hill and Wang, 2007, p. 187. George Mason also wrote that the British and Loyalists have "constantly accused us of engaging in the war to avoid the payment of our just debts; but every honest man has denied so injurious a charge with indignation." G. Mason to P. Henry, May 6, 1783.

8. T. Jefferson to J. Madison, December 16, 1786.

9. The two clauses that are sometimes evoked to justify such power are "The judicial Power shall extend to all Cases, in Law and Equity, arising under the Constitution, the Laws of the United States, and Treaties made" (III.2.1) and "the Judges in every State shall be bound thereby" (VI.2), which makes the federal courts supreme over all state courts.

10. C. Beard, "The Supreme Court: Usurper or Grantee?" *Political Science Quarterly*, Vol. 27, No. 1, March 1912, pp. 2–3; C. Hobson, "The Negative on State Laws: James Madison, the Constitution, and the Crisis of Republican Government," *The William and Mary Quarterly*, Vol. 36, No. 2, 1979, p. 228.

11. C. Beard, March 1912, pp. 4, 18–19, 21.

12. For example, Gouverneur Morris supported the need for judicial review because "encroachments of the popular branch of government ought to be guarded against." G. Morris, Wednesday, August 15, 1787, in M. Farrand, *RFC*, Vol. 2, 1911, p. 299. Morris later claimed that the Constitution "had vested in the judges a check ... to prevent an invasion of the Constitution by unconstitutional laws." G. Morris, First Speech on the Judiciary Establishment, Delivered in the Senate of the United States, January 8, 1802. Where exactly that existed in the Constitution he never said but Morris was in the position to know. Perhaps the most important member of the Committee of Style in the final days of the Convention, he conceded finessing the final language of the Constitution, particularly concerning the judiciary. G. Morris to T. Pickering, December 22, 1814.

13. Madison's position on this was evasive and often contradictory. At different times he supported a revisionary council including judges, advisory judicial review before a law is passed, that each department should be its own judge when it came to questions of constitutionality except in the case of state laws, and for the courts to have the power of judicial review. Once Madison lost the Congressional "negative" on state laws, he aggressively shifted his support to vetoes, or what he more commonly called an "absolute negative" by the courts. See also C. Beard, March 1912, pp. 8–10, 20; and F. Lundberg, 1990, pp. 197–8. Madison was a passionate advocate for judicial review, or what he and others preferred to call a "negative," which was not strictly thought of as judicial but could also belong to the other two branches. Madison pre-

ferred a Congressional veto of state laws that violated federal law and
the Constitution included in the Virginia Plan. He favored "a controul-
ing power at least is so, by which the general authority may be defended
against encroachments of the subordinate authorities," because "without
the [British] royal negative or some equivalent controul, the unity of
the system would be destroyed." J. Madison to T. Jefferson, October 24,
1787. See also J. Madison to G. Washington, April 16, 1787.

14. See also H. Abraham, 1993, p. 301; and M. Jensen, *The Making of the
American Constitution.* Huntington, NY: Robert E. Krieger Publishing
Company, 1964, p. 110. See also C. B. Ames, *The Law Student,* Vol. 1,
January 1924, reprinted from *Texico Star,* September 1923, in
D. Ettrude, 1924, p. 78.

15. J. Madison to T. Jefferson, October 24, 1787.

16. J. Madison to G. Washington, April 16, 1787, italics in the original. For
Madison, the importance of the judicial veto lay in its service as a
minority check by providing a form of "supremacy" inseparable from
judicial review. J. Madison to T. Jefferson, October 24, 1787. He
thought it an important impediment to "the aggressions of interested
majorities on the rights of minorities and of individuals." J. Madison to
G. Washington, April 16, 1787.

17. See, among others, O. Ellsworth, in the Connecticut Convention,
January 7, 1788.

18. J. Wilson, "Remarks of James Wilson in the Pennsylvania Convention
to Ratify the Constitution of the United States," December 7, 1787, in
Collected Works of James Wilson, Vol. 1. Indianapolis: Liberty Fund,
2007. Marshall similarly asked the Virginia ratifying convention to
consider of Congress and the states: "Can they make laws affecting the
mode of transferring property, or contracts, or claims, between citizens
of the same state? Can they go beyond the delegated powers? If they
were to make a law not warranted by any of the powers enumerated, it
would be considered by the judges as an infringement of the Constitution which they are to guard. They would not consider such a law as
coming under their jurisdiction. They would declare it void" (J.
Marshall, statement to the Virginia Ratifying Convention, June 20,
1788). In *Federalist #78,* Hamilton clumsily both confirmed and denied
that judicial review was in the Constitution. He called the judiciary
"beyond comparison the weakest of the three departments of power"
because it "has no influence over either the sword or the purse" and has
"neither FORCE nor Will" because the President was needed to enforce
its rulings. Paragraphs later he then wrote that "[n]o legislative act,
therefore, contrary to the Constitution, can be valid" because "[t]he
interpretation of the laws is the proper and peculiar province of the

courts." He then pivoted back, denying "a superiority of the judicial to the legislative power" before landing on judges as "faithful guardians of the constitution" who provide an "excellent barrier to the encroachments and oppressions of the representative body." In his Constitutional plan all laws contrary to the constitution would be ruled void. See A. Hamilton, June 18, 1787, in M. Farrand, *RFC*, Vol. 1, 1911, p. 293.

19. J. Madison to T. Jefferson, October 24, 1787. He repeated this elsewhere in *Federalist #44* as well as his June 8, 1789 speech introducing the Bill of Rights, in which the "independent tribunals of justice ... will be an impenetrable bulwark against every assumption of power in the legislative or executive."

20. Abraham says there were eight uses of judicial review by state courts prior to 1789 and another ten state courts used it between 1789 and 1803. See H. Abraham, 1993, p. 303. Lundberg confirms the number was eight, taking place in seven states. F. Lundberg, *Cracks in the Constitution*. Secaucus, NJ: Lyle Stuart, Inc., 1980, p. 210. For the states that prohibited and used judicial review, see J. A. Smith, *The Spirit of American Government: A Study of the Constitution—Its Origin, Influence and Relation to Democracy*, edited by C. Strout. Cambridge, MA: Belknap Press of Harvard University Press, 1965 [1907], pp. 86–9.

21. The case, originally brought under the 1789 Judiciary Act, was reargued in the circuit court, which concurred with the earlier decision. P. T. Conley, "The First Judicial Review of State Legislation: An Analysis of the Rhode Island Case of Champion and Dickason v. Casey (1792)," *Rhode Island Bar Journal*, Vol. 36, No. 1, 1987, pp. 5–8; W. Holton, 2007, pp. 269–70; S. R. Boyd, "The Contract Clause and the Evolution of American Federalism, 1789–1815," *The William and Mary Quarterly*, Vol. 44, No. 3, 1987, pp. 539–40; and J. W. Ely, "Origins and Development of the Contract Clause," *Vanderbilt Public Law Research Paper*, No. 05-36, November 1, 2005, pp. 219–20.

22. Other federal court cases in which state laws were ruled as unconstitutional infringements on the right of property include the 1795 *Vanhorne's Lessee v. Dorrance*, with Framer William Patterson writing for the circuit court majority, and the 1794 *Skinner v. May*, in which the circuit court overturned a Massachusetts law restricting the slave trade. P. T. Conley, 1987, p. 5.

23. Cited in J. A. Smith, 1965 [1907], p. 88, 93; C. Beard, March 1912, pp. 32–4; see also C. Beard, *The Supreme Court and the Constitution*. New York: Paisley Press, 1912, pp. 113–18.

24. H. Abraham, 1993, p. 303.

25. *Fletcher v. Peck*, 10 U.S. 87 (1810), p. 10.

26. J. A. Smith, 1965 [1907], pp. 111–12.

27. F. Lundberg, 1980, pp. 221, 237.

28. E. C. Smith and H. J. Spaeth, *The Constitution of the United States.* New York: HarperCollins, 1991, pp. 34, 42.

29. H. Abraham, 1993, p. 272. See the list of cases on pp. 273–9.

30. See R. L. Buell, *The Nation*, June 14, 1922, No. 114, pp. 714–16 in D. Ettrude, 1924, p. 32.

31. See J. Rosen, "Supreme Court Inc.," *The New York Times Magazine*, March 16, 2008, accessed June 7, 2022, www.nytimes.com/2008/03/16/magazine/16supreme-t.html.

32. In a related earlier 1784 case, Pennsylvania Supreme Court Judge George Bryan wrote that the charter establishing the University of Pennsylvania was not a contract case. See F. McDonald, *We the People: The Economic Origins of the Constitution.* Chicago: University of Chicago Press, 1958, p. 170. Charters are not merely an arcane legal device but the very tool used to colonize the continent. Rhode Island, for example, was one of the states founded as a chartered corporation, renaming itself in 1776 the Governor and Company of the English Colony of Rhode-Island and Providence Plantations. In fact, Hamilton long foresaw the existence of corporations as artificial persons. See A. Hamilton, Opinion as to the Constitutionality of the Bank of the United States, 1791.

33. Paine was then writing on commission from Robert Morris and his business partners. T. Paine, "Dissertations on Government; the Affairs of the Bank; and Paper Money," February 18, in M. D. Conway (ed.), *The Complete Writings of Thomas Paine.* New York and London: G. P. Putnam's Sons, 1906 [1786], Vols. 1 and 2, pp. 379–80.

34. The full opinion can be found at: www.law.cornell.edu/supremecourt/text/17/316, accessed June 7, 2022.

35. "Freedom of contract" inverted the same principle the Supreme Court had used to justify protecting former slaves from being forced into debt peonage following emancipation.

36. C. Beard, March 1912, pp. 29–30.

37. See Congressional Research Service, CRS Legal Sidebar Prepared for Members and Committees of Congress, "'Court Packing': Legislative Control over the Size of the Supreme Court," December 14, 2020, p. 2, accessed June 7, 2022, https://crsreports.congress.gov/product/pdf/LSB/LSB10562.

38. See also R. L. Buell, in D. Ettrude, 1924, pp. 35.

39. See case cited in F. Lundberg, 1980, p. 203.

40. However, the 16th amendment has been undermined by minority checks in Congress. The income tax was almost immediately gutted by the creation by Congress of a tax code that gave massive tax cuts to the

rich for donations to their own "charitable" foundations and non-profits, which continue today without limit. My forthcoming, co-authored book is about the role of non-profits as a product of elite power.

41. According to Lundberg, "Congress, in short, is explicitly empowered by the Constitution to regulate the Court, not vice versa. Yet the Court more often seems to regulate Congress." See F. Lundberg, 1980, pp. 202–3.

42. This prolific Anti-Federalist writer was never positively identified. Some historians suggest it was John Yates, a New York State Supreme Court Judge and Framer who left early with John Langton, denying Hamilton a quorum and preventing him from voting. Numerous absences and the refusal of three delegates to sign led the Framers to sign as individuals rather than states, which allowed Hamilton to sign the Constitution as the lone New York delegate.

43. Brutus, XI, January 31, 1788; and Brutus, Antifederalist, No. 81, "The Power of the Judiciary, Parts 1 to 3," February 7, 14, and 28, 1788, *The New-York Journal* and on Teaching American History. He also warned that "there is no power provided in the constitution, that can correct their errors, or control their adjudications. From this court there is no appeal." Brutus, *Antifederalist*, No. 80, "The Power of the Judiciary, Part 2," January 31, 1788, *The New-York Journal*.

44. J. A. Smith, 1965 [1907], pp. 65, 69.

45. For more on this strike, see R. Ovetz, *When Workers Shot Back: Class Conflict from 1877 to 1921*. Chicago: Haymarket Press, 2019, pp. 193–322.

46. *In re Debs et al.*, 158 U.S. 564, 15 S.Ct. 900, 39 L.Ed. 1092, No. 11, May 27, 1895. For more on the Debs case see R. Ovetz, 2019, pp. 255, 270–1.

Chapter 9

1. The language of the ERA is based on the biology of sex and silent on the question of gender.

2. Although the ERA fell short of the required 38-state ratification by the 1982 deadline, it is being challenged in the courts.

3. See L. Cutler, "To Form a Government," in R. Goldwin and A. Kaufman (eds.), *Separation of Powers: Does It Still Work?* Washington and London: American Enterprise Institute for Public Policy Research, 1986, p. 13.

4. Framer James Wilson used a clever maneuver to force through a bill in the Pennsylvania Assembly to establish a ratifying convention that didn't contain the date it was supposed to meet. See B. Konkle, *George Bryan and the Constitution of Pennsylvania, 1731–1791*. Philadelphia: W.

J. Campbell, 1922, pp. 306–7, 321; and Centinel XII, XIII, and XIV, H. Storing (ed.), *The Complete Anti-Federalist*, Vol. 2. Chicago: University of Chicago Press, 1981, pp. 189, 191, 194; S. Cornell, "Aristocracy Assailed: The Ideology of Backcountry Anti-Federalism," *The Journal of American History*, Vol. 76, No. 4, 1990, p. 1164; and J. B. McMaster, *The Political Depravity of the Founding Fathers: Studies in the History of the United States*. New York: Noonday Press, 1964, pp. 74–5.

5. Locke added that "after some interval of fruitless attempts, [revolutions] still brought us back again to our old legislative of king, lords and commons: and whatever provocations have made the crown be taken from some of our princes heads, they never carried the people so far as to place it in another line." J. Locke, *The Second Treatise of Civil Government*, edited by C. B. McPherson. Indianapolis and Cambridge: Hackett Publishing Company, 1980 [1690], p. 120, Section 223.

6. Article XIII required that "nor shall any alteration at any time hereafter be made in any of them; unless such alteration be agreed to in a congress of the united states, and be afterward confirmed by the legislatures of every state."

7. Hamilton had begun calling for a convention as early as 1780. See A. Hamilton to J. Duane, September 3, 1780.

8. S. Lynd, *Class Conflict, Slavery, and the United States Constitution*. Indianapolis: Bobbs-Merrill Company, Inc., 1967, p. 120.

9. J. Madison to T. Jefferson, December 4, 1786.

10. Proceedings of the Commissioners to Remedy Defects of the Federal Government, Annapolis in the State of Maryland, September 14, 1786, accessed June 7, 2022, http://academic.brooklyn.cuny.edu/history/dfg/amrv/annapoli.htm.

11. R. Feer, "Shays's Rebellion and the Constitution: A Study in Causation," *The New England Quarterly*, Vol. 42, No. 3, 1969, p. 393.

12. R. Yates, Notes of the Secret Debates of the Federal Convention of 1787, Taken by the Late Hon Robert Yates, Chief Justice of the State of New York, and One of the Delegates from that State to the Said Convention, May 30, 1787.

13. D. Lazare, "US Constitution: Hiding in Plain Sight," *Cosmonaut*, September 29, 2020.

14. J. Madison to T. Jefferson, October 24, 1787. This is indicated in the removal of the names of the states from the Preamble by the Committee of Style, which included Madison and four others. See E. Chemerinsky, *We the People: A Progressive Reading of the Constitution for the Twenty-First Century*. New York: Picador, 2018, p. 61.

15. J. Madison to G. Washington, April 16, 1787. Hamilton thought it necessary to overcome "the democratical jealousy of the people." A.

Hamilton, "Conjectures about the New Constitution," September 17–30, 1787. See also C. Beard, *The Supreme Court and the Constitution*. New York: Paisley Press, 1912, p. 75.

16. J. Wilson, August 30, 1787, in M. Farrand, Vol. 2, 1911, p. 469.

17. These originated in Jefferson's and Madison's 1798 Virginia and Kentucky Resolutions.

18. A. Jackson, President Jackson's Proclamation Regarding Nullification, December 10, 1832.

19. Sanford Levinson pointed out that this absence was because the Framers saw "the people ... as merely the objects, and not the active subjects, of governance." S. Levinson, *Our Undemocratic Constitution: Where the Constitution Goes Wrong (and How We the People Can Correct It)*. New York: Oxford University Press, 2006, p. 18.

20. J. Story, *Commentaries on the Constitution of the United States: With a Preliminary Review of the Constitutional History of the Colonies and States, before the Adoption of the Constitution, in Three Volumes*, Vol. 1. Boston: Hilliard, Gray and Company; Cambridge: Brown, Shattuck, and Col., 1833, p. 298.

21. W. A. Williams, *The Contours of American History*. Chicago: Quadrangle Books, 1961, p. 162.

22. There are even higher orders such as the popular writing of a constitution.

23. T. Jefferson to J. Madison, September 6, 1789, in *The Papers of Thomas Jefferson*, Vol. 15, March 27, 1789 to November 30, 1789. Princeton, NJ: Princeton University Press, 1958, pp. 392–8. See also T. Jefferson to H. Tompkinson (Samuel Kercheval), Proposals to Revise the Virginia Constitution: I, July 12, 1816, in P. Ford (ed.), *The Writings of Thomas Jefferson*, Vol. 10. New York and London: G. P. Putnam's Sons, 1904–5, p. 37. Justice Story asked, "where is the record of such assent in point of law or fact?" J. Story, 1833, p. 298.

24. The states were not much better at first. There was also no direct popular plebiscite on the first revolutionary state constitutions until 1780 in Massachusetts, although the vote was fraudulent. Fewer than half the states provided for a process to amend the constitution. W. P. Adams, *The First American Constitutions: Republican Ideology and the Making of the State Constitutions in the Revolutionary Era*. Chapel Hill: University of North Carolina Press, 1980, pp. 64, 97, 141.

25. The number has increased from 14 since 2006. See National Conference of State Legislatures, "Initiative and Referendum: States," n.d., accessed June 7, 2022, www.ncsl.org/research/elections-and-campaigns/chart-of-the-initiative-states.aspx; S. Levinson, 2006, p. 12.

26. See F. Lundberg, *Cracks in the Constitution.* Secaucus, NJ: Lyle Stuart, Inc., 1980, p. 102.

27. M. Klarman, 2016, p. 618.

28. Klarman makes this same point. See Ibid.

29. This was enshrined in I.4.1, which allows the states to establish the rules for voting by so that "The Times, Places and Manner of holding Elections for Senators and Representatives, shall be prescribed in each State by the Legislature thereof."

30. T. Bouton, *Taming Democracy: "The People," the Founders, and the Troubled Ending of the American Revolution.* New York: Oxford University Press, 2007, pp. 57, 183; Pennsylvania Ratifying Convention, "The Address and Reasons of Dissent of the Minority of the Convention of Pennsylvania to Their Constituents," in J. F. Manley and K. M. Dolbeare (eds.), *The Case against the Constitution: From the Antifederalists to the Present.* Armonk, NY: M. E. Sharpe, Inc., 1987 [1787], p. 75.

31. O. G. Libby, "The Geographical Distribution of the Vote of the Thirteen States on the Federal Constitution, 1787–8," *Bulletin of the University of Wisconsin Economics,* Vol. 1, No. 1. Madison: University of Wisconsin, 1894, pp. 1–116.

32. The total population was then about three million. C. Beard, *An Economic Interpretation of the Constitution of the United States.* New York: Free Press, 1986 [1913], p. 250. See also F. Lundberg, 1980, p. 18. For the state ratifying convention vote totals see O. G. Libby, 1894, pp. 1–116. Historian Jackson Turner Main gives a higher estimate of 60 percent voting for Anti-Federalist delegates to the state ratifying conventions. J. T. Main, *The Anti-Federalists: Critics of the Constitution 1781–1788.* New York: W. W. Norton & Company, 1961, p. 286. Anti-Federalists were strongest further inland where self-sufficient farming dominated, while Federalists were stronger closer to the coasts where commercial trade predominated. C. Clark and N. Hewitt, *Who Built America? Working People and the Nation's History to 1877,* Vol. 1. New York: Bedford/St. Martin's Press, 2007, p. 241.

33. For the sequence of votes, see F. Lundberg, 1980, pp. 167–73. Rhode Island finally relented after being threatened with invasion, punitive tariffs, forcible collection of its war debts, and secession by Providence and several towns. One of the leaders of the federalist party, William Ellery, was later rewarded by President Washington with a patronage position as customs collector for the district of Newport for helping engineer the final ratification. See P. T. Conley and J. P. Kaminsky (eds.), *The Constitution and the States: The Role of the Original Thirteen in the Framing and Adoption of the Federal Constitution.* Wisconsin: Madison House, 1988, pp. 274–89. There was concern about ratifica-

tion by Georgia. It didn't send any delegates to Annapolis and initially voted in 1787 not to send any delegates to the Convention, only deciding to do so shortly before it began. Georgia eventually ratified by an unanimous vote, primarily because it expected the Constitution to allow for an army to fight its war against several native tribes, including the Creek nation, and weaken the Spanish who backed them. W. Holton, *Unruly Americans and the Origins of the Constitution*. New York: Hill and Wang, 2007, pp. 244–6, 269.

34. C. Beard, 1986 [1913], pp. 54–6.

35. For the flaws in Herbert Storing's 1981 *The Complete Anti-Federalist*, see J. P. Kaminski, "Antifederalism and the Perils of Homogenized History: A Review Essay," *Rhode Island History*, Vol. 42, 1983, p. 35; and J. Hutson, "The Incomplete Antifederalist, Reviewed Work(s): The Complete Anti-Federalist by Herbert J. Storing," *Reviews in American History*, Vol. 11, No. 2, 1983, pp. 204–5. Today it is impossible to purchase a new print copy of *The Complete Anti-Federalist* because the University of Chicago Press no longer offers it. Despite their continued relevance to the many problems with our constitutional system, there is no complete collection available to the public. Only a few of the Anti-Federalist documents are online, in contrast to the numerous sources of the complete Federalist Papers both online and in print. Considering how many duplicate and redundant historical studies of the constitutional era and its charismatic icons exist, this silencing of the Anti-Federalists is a form of ideological censorship by scholars in this field.

36. It is estimated that about three-quarters of the elite were Federalists. Brown provides an excellent analysis of the class composition of the Anti-Federalist and Federalists on the issue of ratification. See Roger H. Brown, *Redeeming the Republic: Federalists, Taxation, and the Origins of the Constitution*. Baltimore: Johns Hopkins University Press, 1993, pp. 201–3, 208–17. See also J. T. Main, "The Antifederalists: Critics of the Constitution," in J. F. Manley and K. M. Dolbeare (eds.), 1987, p. 70.

37. See J. W. Ely, "Origins and Development of the Contract Clause," *Vanderbilt Public Law Research Paper*, No. 05-36, November 1, 2005, p. 212.

38. J. T. Main, "Charles A. Beard and the Constitution: A Critical Review of Forrest McDonald's *We the People*," *The William and Mary Quarterly*, Vol. 17, No. 1, 1960, pp. 94–5; and J. T. Main, *The Anti-Federalists: Critics of the Constitution, 1781–1788*. New York: W. W. Norton & Company, 1961, p. 177; J. T. Main, "The Antifederalists," in Birnbaum, J. and B. Ollman (eds.), *U.S. Constitution: 200 Hundred Years of*

Anti-Federalist, Abolitionist, Feminist, Muckraking, Progressive, and Especially Socialist Criticism. New York: New York University Press, 1990, pp. 69–70. To illustrate another class divide, most Anti-Federalists served in the militias during the Revolution while Federalists were more likely to be veterans of the Continental Army. Nearly half of Washington's cabinet were of the latter. An estimated third of the Framers served in the Continental Army. See R. Kohn, *Eagle and Sword: The Beginnings of the Military Establishment in America.* New York: The Free Press, 1975, pp. 13, 77, 308.

39. C. Beard, 1986 [1913], p. 252.
40. National Archives Foundation, Amendments to the U.S. Constitution, accessed June 7, 2022, www.archivesfoundation.org/amendments-u-s-constitution/.
41. Dr. James Hutchinson, writing as "An Old Whig," insightfully recognized that considering the difficulty of reaching the vote thresholds for amendments, "the conditions upon which an alteration can take place, are such as in all probability will never exist. The consequence will be that, when the constitution is once established, it never can be altered or amended without some violent convulsion or civil war." Dr. James Hutchinson, An Old Whig I, October 12, 1787.
42. J. A. Smith, *The Spirit of American Government: A Study of the Constitution—Its Origin, Influence and Relation to Democracy*, edited by C. Strout. Cambridge, MA: Belknap Press of Harvard University Press, 1907, pp. 44, 47.
43. D. DeSilver, "Proposed Amendments to the U.S. Constitution Seldom Go Anywhere," Pew Research Center, April 12, 2018.
44. Center for the Study of the American Constitution, Department of History, Attempts to Revise The Articles of Confederation, n.d., accessed June 7, 2022, https://csac.history.wisc.edu/document-collections/confederation-period/attempts-to-revise/.
45. W. E. B. DuBois, *Black Reconstruction in America.* New York: The Free Press, 1935.
46. D. Lazare, *The Frozen Republic: How the Constitution Is Paralyzing Democracy.* New York: Harcourt Brace & Company, 1996, p. 157. The National Archives lists three such amendments during the twentieth century at Amending America: Proposed Amendments to the United States Constitution, 1787 to 2014, accessed June 7, 2022, www.archives.gov/open/dataset-amendments.html#how.
47. S. Levinson, 2006, pp. 20, 22, 96, italics in original.
48. M. Klarman, *The Framers' Coup: The Making of the United States Constitution.* New York: Oxford University Press, 2016, p. 624.

Chapter 10

1. R. Cooper, "The Case against the American Constitution," *The Week*, February 1, 2017, accessed June 8, 2022, https://theweek.com/articles/677164/case-against-american-constitution.

2. Peter Linebaugh notes how "[t]he twin absurdities, property in land (real estate) and property in persons (slavery) became the economic and social foundation of civilization." P. Linebaugh, "A Foul Field Full of Foolish Fascist White Folk," unpublished essay, February 14, 2021.

3. J. Toobin, "Our Broken Constitution: Everyone Agrees that Government Isn't Working. Are the Founders to Blame?" *The New Yorker*, December 9, 2013, accessed June 8, 2022, https://www.newyorker.com/magazine/2013/12/09/our-broken-constitution.

4. D. Lazare, "US Constitution: Hiding in Plain Sight," *Cosmonaut*, September 29, 2020, accessed June 8, 2022, https://cosmonautmag.com/2020/09/us-constitution-hiding-in-plain-sight/.

5. See Constitute, n.d., www.constituteproject.org/constitutions?lang=en.

6. On participating budgeting, see S. Leindecker and M. Fox, *Beyond Elections: Redefining Democracy in the Americas*, DVD. Oakland: PM Press/Estreito Meios Productions, 2008. On the Athenian Assembly, see C. L. R. James, "Every Cook Can Govern: A Study of Democracy in Ancient Greece, Its Meaning for Today," *Correspondence*, Vol. 2, No. 12, 1956.

7. J. Freeman, "The Tyranny of Structurelessness," *The Second Wave*, 1972, accessed June 8, 2022, www.jofreeman.com/joreen/tyranny.htm.

8. While Zinn's classic book *A Peoples' History of the United States* inspired me to study the Constitution more deeply, his people power theory of change accepts part of the pluralist premise that the Constitution makes change possible if only enough people get organized to shift power. Ironically, Robert Dahl, the founder of pluralism, rejected his own theory at the end of his life when he realized that the Constitution was fundamentally undemocratic and a barrier to change. H. Zinn, "Some Truths Are Not Self-evident," in J. Birnbaum and B. Ollman (eds.), *U.S. Constitution: 200 Hundred Years of Anti-Federalist, Abolitionist, Feminist, Muckraking, Progressive, and Especially Socialist Criticism.* New York: New York University Press, 1990, p. 261; R. Dahl, *How Democratic Is the American Constitution?*, 2nd edition. New Haven: Yale University Press, 2003.

9. See S. Levinson, *Our Undemocratic Constitution: Where the Constitution Goes Wrong (and How We the People Can Correct It).* New York: Oxford University Press, 2006, p. 35.

10. M. Bookchin, "Libertarian Municipalism," in J. Biehl (ed.), *The Bookchin Reader.* Black Rose Press, 1999, pp. 172–96; D. Bookchin, "Libertarian Municipalism: A Politics of Direct Democracy," in D.

Bookchin and B. Taylor (eds.), *The Next Revolution: Popular Assemblies and the Problem of Direct Democracy.* London: Verso, 2015, pp. 77–86.

11. D. Bookchin, 2015, pp. 82 and 84.

12. Such an approach could use a workers' inquiry into the organization of work to devise new tactics, strategies, and objectives for moving past capitalism. See R. Ovetz, *Workers' Inquiry and Global Class Struggle: Tactics, Strategies, Objectives.* London: Pluto Press, 2020.

13. Bookchin's libertarian municipalism foresaw the need for policy to be made by local assemblies, separate from the administration of its decisions by the confederation of assemblies. However, this risks evolving into a new system of checks and balances based on the division of labor between those making and administering decisions. This danger can possibly be pre-empted with short terms of service, compensation for delegates such as release from community obligations, local delegates who rotate on and off assemblies and councils, instant recall, instantaneous transparency, and widespread engagement made possible by real-time communication. D. Bookchin, 2015, p. 81.

14. R. Zibechi, *Dispersing Power: Social Movements as Anti-state Forces.* Chico: AK Press, 2010, pp. 11–31. See also P. Linebaugh, G. Caffentzis, R. Linebaugh, and D. Coughlin, *Midnight Notes Goes to School: Report from the Zapatista Escuelita.* New York: Autonomedia, 2014.

15. C. L. R. James, *The Future in the Present: Selected Writings.* London: Allison and Busby, 1977.

16. The New Deal and other social democratic expansions of the state didn't invent social welfare, they coopted it and integrated the management of this "social reproductive labor" into government as a service to the capitalist economy. Today, the term mutual aid continues to be used by self-organized groups and government agencies alike, such as when fire departments put out calls for "mutual aid" from other departments around the state, the country, and the rest of the world. For an analysis of the role of reproductive labor (or what is today commonly called care work) to capitalism, see M. Dalla Costa and S. James, *The Power of Women and the Subversion of the Community.* Bristol: Falling Wall Press, 1971.

Index

Marshall, John, 136, 217
Martin v. Hunter's Lessee, 139
Mason, George, 111, 123, 213, 218
Mifflin, Thomas, 209
militia, 16, 24, 48, 50–1, 64, 67, 74,
   112–13, 119–22, 129, 144, 193,
   227
Militia Act, 112
minority checks, 3, 20, 22, 30–1, 34–5,
   57, 59, 72–3, 84, 96, 104, 109, 128,
   151, 154, 160, 164–5, 178, 183,
   201, 222
Missouri Compromise, 62
mob, 8, 13, 18, 22, 131
Monroe, James, 70
Montesquieu, 20, 34
Morris, Gouverneur, 10, 19, 22, 48,
   55, 68, 70–1, 81–3, 102, 148, 178,
   202, 219
   see also Committee on Style, and
   Committee of Eleven on Postponed
   Matters
Morris, Robert, 19, 23, 45, 47, 65–6,
   70, 91, 96, 105, 182, 198, 209, 215,
   222
   see also Superintendent of Finance,
   and Morris's tax plan
Morris's tax plan, 191–2
   see also Robert Morris
Mount Vernon Compact, 147

National Emergencies Act, 123
National Guard, 110, 119, 124
*National Labor Relations Board v. Jones
   & Laughlin Steel Corporation*, 141
negative, 4, 34, 104, 136, 175, 219
   see also veto
New Deal, 58, 79, 230
New Jersey Plan, 201
North Atlantic Treaty, 125
Northup, Solomon, 62

oligarchy, 1

Pacificus-Helvidius newspaper debates,
   123
Paine, Thomas, 140, 182, 208

paper money, 24, 30, 38, 45, 47, 50–2,
   55–6, 65, 67, 71, 87–9, 136, 147,
   153, 179, 180, 191–2, 207, 215, 218
people out of doors, 10, 13, 17–18,
   20, 24, 39, 42–3, 46, 50, 52, 54–5,
   64–5, 76, 102, 106, 129, 131
person, 27, 62, 95
Pickering, Timothy, 209
Pinckney, Charles Cotesworth, 27, 63,
   117
plutocracy, 1
poll tax, 87, 89, 91
*Pollock v. Farmers' Loan and Trust
   Company*, 94
Preamble, 14, 22, 24, 41, 44, 224
privileges and immunities, 37, 69, 129,
   140
protect life and property, 118

Randolph, Edmund, 30–1, 57, 147,
   153, 192, 213
Regulator Rebellion, 46, 56, 64–5, 86,
   134
   see also Shays' Rebellion
replevin laws and orders, 57, 70, 124,
   131–3
representative democracy, 1, 2, 8, 12,
   14, 44, 99, 167–8, 201
republic, 1–2, 14, 18, 38, 73, 98
   see also democratic republic
requisition, 65, 87–8, 94, 196, 205
Revenue Act, 93
Roe v. Wade, 17
Roosevelt, Franklin D., 79, 111, 212
Rutledge, John, 27, 91

*A. L. A. Schechter Poultry Corporation v.
   United States*, 141
Schuyler, Philip, 147
Dred Scott v. Sanford, 62, 138
Secret Committee of Trade, 105
separation of powers, 2, 4, 20, 35,
   99–100
settler colonialism, 42, 60, 77, 96, 116,
   122–3
Shays' Rebellion, 30, 42, 48, 50, 64,
   87, 132, 187
   see also Regulator Rebellion